Praise for Race in the Global Era

"Clarence Lusane's crisp and lucid essays are always ahead of the curve. He powerfully demonstrates the limits of nation-bound thinking and provides fresh insights into the politics of racism in the age of multinational capital. *Race in the Global Era* not only deserves the widest possible readership, but it ought to be translated into at least fifty languages."

—Robin D.G. Kelley, author of *Yo' Mama's DisFunktional!: Fighting the Culture Wars in Urban America*

"There has been much commentary about the border less future, but little of it has the depth, clarity, and alacrity of Lusane's Race in the Global Era. Lusane takes conventional analysis and pushes its limits, using both his tools as a scholar and his passion as an activist to inform his arguments."

—Julianne Malveaux, author of *Sex, Lies, and Stereotypes: Perspectives of a Mad Economist*

"Clarence Lusane is one of America's most thoughtful and critical thinkers on issues of race, class, and power."

—Manning Marable, author of *Black Liberation in Conservative America*

"At a time when many black leaders and intellectuals are focusing narrowly on the plight of the black male, Clarence Lusane is to be commended for his sensitivity to the broader issue of gender, and the political concerns and contributions of black feminists."

—Barbara Ransby, activist and historian, Univ. of Illinois

CLARENCE LUSANE is an author, activist, scholar, lecturer, and free-lance journalist in Washington, D.C. For more than 25 years, he has been active in national black politics, U.S. foreign policy, and on domestic policy issues. Lusane has traveled to and lectured in Haiti, Panama, South Korea, East Germany, Zimbabwe, Cuba, Mexico, Jamaica, and England. Lusane also writes numerous articles for the *Black Scholar*, *Crossroads,* and *Z Magazine.*

RACE IN THE GLOBAL ERA

African Americans at the Millennium

CLARENCE LUSANE

Foreword by Julianne Malveaux

SOUTH END PRESS, Boston, MA

Library of Congress Cataloging-in-Publication Data
Race in the Global Era: African Americans at the Millennium/ by
Clarence Lusane.
p. cm.
Includes bibliographical references and index.
ISBN 0-89608-573-2 (paper).—ISBN 0-89608-574-0 (cloth)
    1. United States—Race relations. 2. Racism—Political as-
pects—United States. 3. Afro-Americans—Politics and government.
4. Afro-Americans—Social conditions—1975– 5. Afro-Americans in
mass media. I. Title.
    E185.615.l93 1997
    305.896'073—dc21   97-31302
                                                              CIP

South End Press, 116 Saint Botolph Street, Boston, MA 02115
    02 01 00 99 98 97   1 2 3 4 5 6 7

Contents

Acknowledgments

I wish I could blame all my friends for my mistakes and misjudgments in this book and take credit for any insights, but alas the reverse is closer to the truth. No book emerges solely from the mind of one individual and, therefore, credit must always be given to the wide array of friends, acquaintances, associates, enemies, strangers, family, and "others" who contribute in countless ways to what eventually ends up on a bookshelf.

This list is, of course, desperately incomplete. Among the fabulous and brilliant people, *inter alia*, whose intellectual and political fingerprints are on this present work are Nikol G. Alexander, Karen Bass, Jean Carey Bond, Chris Booker, Sylvia Castillo, James Early, Amir el-Islam, Charles Green, Zahra Hamarani, Daryl Harris, Mark Harrison, Geoffrey Jacques, Keith Jennings, Charles Jones, Peniel Joseph, Robin D.G. Kelley, Melvin Lewis, Manning Marable, Rowena Martineau, Cheryl Mayia, Leith Mullings, Ridan Nytagodien, Basil Patterson, Barbara Ransby, Nathalie Richardson, Selina Roberts, Jocelyn Sargent, Karin Stanford, James Steele, Curtis Stokes, and Makani Themba. Through conversations, resources, and other means, they helped to stimulate and massage my thoughts on the many issues discussed in this book.

Over the last few years, I have had the great pleasure and honor to be associated with a number of African American research institutions that have provided me with immense material and non-material support including the Du Bois Bunche Center for Public Policy (Medgar Evers College), Institute for Research in African American Studies (Columbia University), Center for Drug Abuse Research (Howard University), and Ralph J. Bunche International Affairs Center (Howard University).

I also want to thank the Howard University faculty and students, who worked on the Million Man March survey including Lorenzo Morris, Joseph P. McCormick and Maurice Carney among others.

My thanks and appreciation to *The Progressive* magazine's Black Voices Media Project, and *Covert Action Quarterly* magazine who have generously published my work over the years and in which some of these essays have appeared in other forms.

Dionne Brooks, my editor, and South End Press have, as usual, been absolutely indispensable and disciplined in pushing this project forward.

Foreword

By Julianne Malveaux

Ever since President William Jefferson Clinton, biting at his lower lip, eyes misting over, suggested a race dialogue, there has been much race entertainment in the policy arena. Should the U.S. Congress apologize for slavery? An apology without remediation is an empty genuflection for our nation's terribly flawed past. Should O.J. Simpson's creditors be able to cash in and melt down his Heisman trophy? Whether we care or not, the O.J. question will get as much media attention as the more substantive one about slavery.

Myriad things get thrown into the mix of our race talk, whether it is analysis or entertainment. Talk of Ebonics may be covert talk about assimilation versus cultural integrity. Talk of welfare reform may be the real talk about family values. Whose families do we value, after all, those of corporate executives on the federal dole or those of mothers with two or more children who are trying to go back to school? How affirmative is our action? California's Proposition 209 passed, but millions of Californians, especially in cities like San Francisco and Los Angeles, say they prefer diversity to the narrow white occasion that 209 will produce. Is it an affirmative action to hanker for a segregated past? Or is it certainty that whenever there is economic insecurity whites will prevail? Is there something politically incorrect, even unpalatable, about these questions? Do they make you squirm? Unless we are uneasy, race talk becomes the talk of shadows and mirrors, of skewed stereotypes and misplaced emotion.

Where does race talk fit in a global future? Is it inevitable that national economies meld into an international market? The relationships that various populations have with a global economy has yet to be determined. There has been much commentary about the borderless future, but little of it has the depth, clarity, and alacrity of Clarence Lusane's *Race in the Global Era*. Lusane takes conventional analysis and pushes its limits, using both his tools as a scholar and his passion as an activist to inform his arguments. He weaves race talk, race entertainment, and race analysis into a sociopolitical framework that is all the more compelling for its unwillingness to cleave to popular clichés. This is race talk that is unexpectedly exciting, challenging, and uncharted. Lusane is all the more provocative because he looks at a set of issues through a kaleidoscope that has race, but not only race, as a critical lens. Unlike many of his peers, Lusane tackles class, gender, and nationalism as other factors in the determinants of an African American future in a global society.

Both frontally and subtly, Lusane addresses the role that the media plays in exporting a certain interpretation of "blackness" as an identifiable feature of U.S. culture. Why do people in Japan, Thailand, and Italy know Michael Jackson, Michael Jordan, and O.J. Simpson? Does the fact that these celebrities are all males say anything about the conclusions an international community might reach about African Americans? Does the fact that these men are tied with golden handcuffs to corporations that magnify their images raise any contradiction for those millions of minimum and sub-minimum wage workers who mortgage their futures to buy jeans, sneakers, and anything else that can be connected to a smiling, affable, African American face? Indeed, the face need not smile. Even the snarling postures of gangsta rappers are exportable for international entertainment. The "cool pose" of young black men whose poignant, painful poetry speaks to a chilling urban reality is repackaged as beat-driven boogie rhythm, angry, assaultive, misogynistic lyrics notwithstanding.

There is acceptance for the smiling black spokesperson, but less for the competitive business executive, and even less for those African Americans critical of the status quo. Lusane expertly captures the mixed acceptance of African American images, and the ways that all Americans interpret their space in a global society.

The ranks of race commentators are bloated with drive-by assessment and add-water-and-stir cogitation. Lusane distinguishes himself, though, with pointed, penetrating explorations, distinctive observations, and a comprehensive review of the state of race in a global era. Whether he is writing about the Million Man March, gangsta rap, the CIA-Contra drug connection, Ebonics, or the links between capitalism, race, and violence, Lusane's thinking is fresh and enlightened. This voice is rich, layered, and has a resonance that is powerful, incisive, and caring, unlike any other on the national scene. *Race in the Global Era* takes us past conventional 20th-century analysis and provides us with a prism through which we can view the challenges that African Americans, and the nation, face in the new millennium.

Julianne Malveaux
Washington, DC
September 1997

To all the children in my life

Introduction

As the countdown to the next millennium nears, we find ourselves in amazing times. Products and capabilities, such as cellular phones, video conferencing, and the Internet, that were barely imagined only a few years ago, if at all, have become part of our daily lives. The demise of the Cold War has given way to a new, uncharted political period latent with great opportunities and immense dangers. Virtually every point on the globe is instantly accessible from nearly every other point. Social, economic, cultural, and geographical barriers have fallen as new technologies bridge heretofore alienated relationships and connect groups from every corner of the earth. For the first time in history, as writer William Greider notes, "One World" is more than a metaphor.

As the year 2000 draws near, the entire globe waits in anticipation of a new century with the hope that the destruction and social devastation of the old will be addressed and eradicated. Even as that hope burns bright, regional and intranational conflicts abound, amassing waves of small wars and civil strife that are unrestrained even when international intervention occurs.

As the changes brought by new technologies and expanding global ties occur more rapidly than we can often comprehend, social relations are also being reconfigured. Race, gender, and class issues intersect and remold each other, constantly creating new relations that challenge all previous notions. Across the globe, the tension between racial groups appears to be growing. In post-Communist Europe, old enemies come together in NATO even as new civil strife brought by the rise of fascist and racist groups ripples through both the East and West. In England, police brutality and harassment and the rise of racially charged murders have marked the 1990s. Some British writers have joined the new eugenics movement and published so-called scholarly works that "scientifically" explain the inferiority of blacks and other people of color. In France, as elsewhere in the West, racial antagonism manifests itself in attacks on immigrants from Africa, Asia, and the Middle East. The Pasqua laws, passed in the early 1990s, gave French police extensive powers to stop, question, and detain those they perceived to be potential undocumented aliens. In post-Apartheid South Africa, black leadership struggles to bring justice and equality to a rigid system of economic division that has carried over from the Apartheid days. In post-dictatorship Latin America, new democracies are searching for ways of inclusion for all sectors of society even as a resurgent black consciousness movement grows in the region. From Uruguay and Brazil to Argentina and Peru, Afro-Latinos are organizing and mobilizing. In all these circumstances, race relations intersect with class, nationality, gender, ethnic, and religious issues, creating a complex arrangement of pressures and sources of conflicts.

In the United States, race relations and how they are conceived are in turmoil. A range of incidents in the 1990s alone have brought the deteriorating state of U.S. race relations to the public consciousness with the force of a lightening bolt. From the public responses to the O.J. Simpson trials, the Million Man March, black church burnings, street uprisings in Los Angeles, gangsta rap, and accusations such as Susan Smith's and others against the ghosts of black men to the public policy initiatives of Republicans and Democrats to race-tinged, citizen-driven ballot initiatives to the regular and regulated day-to-day racial disparities that exist, these are the worst of times.

The perception gap between people of color and whites—colored people are from Venus, white people are from Mars—regarding the significance of race expands as interpretations of the events and circumstances discussed above by academics, journalists, and politicians make concessions to a racial paradigm that leaves little room for an honest appraisal of the social dynamics of race in a postindustrial, capitalist society. Ideological conservatives blame liberals, cultural predispositions, and genetic makeup. Liberals, many of whom hold the same assumptions as conservatives, simply retreat and through their silence sanction the assaults, embrace the consequences, and render ideological differences between the two irrelevant.

It is one theme of this book that a change in how whites think about race, in general, and African Americans, in particular, from the early post-civil rights period to the present has occurred. This change has taken place on a global scale from South Africa to Brazil to England. It can be called, in a term used by political scientists, a mass "paradigm shift" on the issue of race—that is, a fundamental overthrow of the way race has been conceived since the heyday of the civil rights and Black Power eras. In the second half of the 20th century, the elimination of state-sanctioned legal racial segregation led to the spread of the ideology of color blindness, which is the central theme underpinning the myth of racial democracy.

A combination of factors have contributed to these shifts, including permanent transformation in the economic life of millions of whites, the rise of conservative political and religious demagogues, a pervasive media propagation of race that denies the existence of racism, and the influence of an intelligentsia—under the cover of "objective" and "nonpartisan" research—that unabashedly promotes racist theories, public policies, and stereotypes. Most critically, change has been driven by global political, economic, and cultural forces that generally are unacknowledged and unexplored. It has become impossible to understand contemporary race relations within a simple narrow national framework.

A State of Urgency

For our purposes, the most important discussion is the debate within the black community regarding the nature and causes of the crisis facing African Americans, and pathways toward solutions. From across the black political spectrum, there seems to be agreement that much of what can be called black life is in a desperate state. The essays in this book explore manifestations of contemporary racial politics or, more precisely, ways in which race crisscrosses and unites the span of society.

Race is only one of many prisms through which to analyze the political and social life of African Americans, and not necessarily always the most determinate one. In the United States (and elsewhere), it is a critical prism and one in which there has been insufficient interrogation of its contemporary dynamics. While issues of race are a daily source of news and entertainment, race is generally divorced from the more radioactive concern of racism, which is randomly lumped with other forms of discrimination and oppression. Racism is reduced to a relic of the past that only occasionally bursts onto the nation's conscious in the form of Klansman David Duke, rogue cop Mark Fuhrman, or, in a creative and distorted theoretical twist, through the newly created vehicle of the African-American racist.

Interrogation of the dominate U.S. racial paradigm is critical because it is exported to the rest of the world. An interactive dynamic exists at the nation-state level, where national leaders from England, Germany, France, and even South Africa have consulted with U.S. government and nongovernment leaders on how to handle racial issues. A similar interaction has occurred between community-based organizations in the United States and abroad. The interaction has been primarily in one direction. While the world has given rapt attention to the O.J. Simpson trials, the Million Man March, and the stories regarding CIA involvement in cocaine smuggling, few in the United States have given equal attention to issues of race in other nations.

Candid analyses of race and racism are urgently needed as the nation and world go through profound and unprecedented transformations. These changes are not necessarily racial or ethnic, but because they encounter societies as they are currently constructed, race and ethnicity filters their impact.

The Black Paradoxical Moment

Black America meets these changes at a crucial, if not decisive, moment in its history. Without question, there is a spirit of resistance that exists in the black community, even in the face of generally overwhelming and unrelenting odds. Yet there are few honest observers who would characterize the overall picture facing African Americans in this era as rosy and hopeful. Much of the consternation in the black community can be seen in these frustrating paradoxes:

- While black women have made great strides in countless fields— even as they continue to carry the disproportionate, multiple burdens and responsibilities of childrearing, homemaking, and socialization—they have become the demons of choice for New Democrat liberals, old-line conservatives, and prominent black nationalists.

- While the political growth of black elected officials has been remarkable—from less than 300 in 1965 to over 8,500 in 1995—African Americans have perhaps less public policy influence than at any point in the last four decades.

- While African Americans have achieved substantial positioning and influence at the very highest echelons of the Democratic Party—to the point where the party of old-time segregationists such as Lester Maddox and George Wallace selected the late Ron Brown, an African American, as chairperson—the Democratic Party under Bill Clinton has become more and more reactionary with each political season.

- While the black community has experienced the largest growth of a black middle class in U.S. history—estimated to be 40 percent by some analysts—the even larger growth of the black poor has proceeded unabated.

- While black intellectuals have achieved more popularity, have more resources at their disposal—and more access to the media than they have ever had—and due to white benefactors, funders, and supporters, they are also wealthier than ever—they exhibit a profound inability to produce socially and politically useful and accessible works.

- While black men are unrivaled in appreciation for their entertainment and athletic abilities—to the point where Michael Jackson and Michael Jordan are paid millions unrelated to their best-known skills to merely associate their name and likeness with a wide variety of commodities—the generalized view of black men as predatory, criminal, and in need of containment reflects itself in public policies whose impact (if not purpose) is to fill the jails and prisons of the nation in unprecedented numbers.

- While black unemployment figures rise—accompanied by the unprecedented social phenomena of tens of thousands of African Americans in their twenties and thirties never having had a full-time job—the demand for the elimination of affirmative action and other programs that economically benefit African Americans grows shriller.

- While progressive multinational, multiracial, multigender coalitions have historically been the vehicle of progress for black America—from the NAACP to the Mississippi Freedom Democratic Party, from Martin Luther King's "Coalition of Conscience" to the Children's Defense Fund and the National Rainbow Coalition—the rise of a conservative neonationalist movement in the black community, most dramatically manifested in the Million Man March, has defined much of mass black politics in the 1990s.

- While we live in an age where nearly unlimited information is available almost instantaneously—via the Internet, CD-ROMs, and dozens of 24-hour news programs—misinformation about black life, from perceptions about the actual number of African Americans in the United States to stereotypical views of blacks in terms of intelligence, welfare, and crime, is at an all-time high.

These paradoxes of black life give rise to some important strategic questions. Why has the growth in black elected and appointed officials not resulted in greater public policy favors for the African-American community? Why does it appear that the black wealthy have abandoned the black poor? Why have popular black academic intellectuals with so many resources produced so little of use to the black community and had so little impact? Why does traditional black leadership continue to give unquestioned loyalty and support to the Democratic Party even though the party has abandoned all pretense to a program of progressive racial inclusion? While it is wrong to indict all black leaders, intellectuals, elected officials, and other sectors of black life, many African Americans most in need feel a complete abandonment by the black elite despite the committed efforts of some.

Racism and the Rise of White Conservatism

Racism, whether unvarnished or polished, continues to be a central theme in U.S. social, economic, political, and cultural life. It was absolutely central to the assumption of conservative power in recent years, albeit with a new urgency and intensity. As the gross disproportionalities that African Americans suffer in health, criminal justice, education, and other areas became even more pronounced, implicit and often explicit code-wording strategies successfully launched many of the Republicans into power. Under the conservative leadership of Newt Gingrich, Rush Limbaugh, Bob Dole, Pat Buchanan, and Ralph Reed, these strategies have become open, naked assaults unconstrained by political or moral considerations on communities of color. Already, in the Gingrich era, Republicans brazenly call for female chain gangs and defend slavery. Although some of these extremists have been repudiated by conservative spokespersons, years ago they would not have had even the veneer of legitimacy. "States rights," once a rallying cry for opposition by civil rights leaders and liberals, has become the political objective of the 1990s by both parties, with little vocal or active challenge by Democratic black leadership.

Yet, it is on similar terrain that Clinton and the Democratic Leadership Council (DLC) came to power. Formed as a political counterweight to Jesse Jackson's progressive wing of the Democratic Party, Clinton and the DLC (which actually included a number of black members, such as Mike Espy and Bill Gray) adopted a strategy to win back white voters who had defected to the Republican Party in the 1970s and 1980s. This was in lieu of going after the millions of unregistered and unmobilized black, Latino, and even white voters who could have possibly been won to a liberal or even progressive program. In the end, the distinction (and the desire for distinction) between Ronald Reagan's Republicans and Clinton's Democrats disappears.

The "turning back," as scholar Stephen Steinberg frames it, in race policies and politics is not occurring at some random historic moment. The retreat is shaped by and, in turn, is shaping the redefined context in which the United States finds itself at the end of what has been called the "American century." Increased direct corporate authority and influence on public policy and policymakers, political parties, and governmental institutions are eroding even the symbols of democracy. With little real input into the decisions that determine the economic and social state of the nation, massive white frustration and disillusionment takes the form of blaming the traditional scapegoats: African Americans, Latinos, Asians, gays and lesbians, and the poor. This unwarranted blaming is encouraged and reinforced by the media, politicians, religious leaders, and intellectuals in hundreds of ways on a daily basis.

In the face of attacks and disintegration, as a significant degree of chaos reigns in national black politics, the liberal integrationist paradigm as a guide for black political agency has effectively come to an end. That is, the belief in the permanence of the welfare state and the lasting benevolence of the Democratic Party are shattered illusions embraced only as last ditch acts of desperation. Other modes of black politics are faring no better. Black nationalism has never disappeared as a resource in the black community and, at various historical points has dominated black politics. In this era, nationalism is driven by several factors, including the sanctioning and validation of institutional racism by conservative policymakers; racism manifested in every arena of popular culture; the devastating impact of globalized economies on white workers and their racialized response; and just low-down, unashamed personal racism. Yet contemporary black nationalism demonstrates little capacity to theorize or intervene practically on the complexities of modern black life as it is affected by public policy, global politics, and gender issues. Black conservatives, perhaps even more rabidly than during the Reagan era, continue to be Trojan horses of white supremacy. Their solutions, encapsulated in warped constructions of "self-help" and "color blindness," amount to little more than genocide. Finally, radicalism has been marginalized and remains on the periphery of debate within the black community. Efforts at regroupment have begun, but the road back to becoming a significant influence in black politics appears to be a long one with many potholes.

Strategy Crisis

Despite the differences among black political activists, and with the exception of black conservatives, there is one reoccurring theme on which they unite: the Black Leadership Unity Fallacy (BLUF). Perhaps the most consistent strategic theme has been the notion that liberation, whatever the path, would require black leadership to be united. The repeated failure of attempts at black leadership unity has been attributed to the defects of individuals, attacks by the state and racists, and organizational ineptitude. While all of these have been important factors, at base is the flawed notion that black interests can be aggregated across class, gender, and ideological fault lines. This fallacy has led energies and resources to be spent on efforts that were doomed from the beginning and unable to address the pressing concerns of the most needy and desperate sectors of the black community. Rejection of the BLUF does not imply that consolidation of as broad a base as possible around particular campaigns and issues should not occur. Instead rejection signals a more sober and careful construction of coalitions in the black community built not just on race, but on a panorama of concerns and an ideological clarity on goals, objectives, and methods.

In the period ahead, the BLUF must be replaced with a strategy that constructs platforms and outlets for the silenced voices of black America. Black leadership in all forms, at best, continues to speak on behalf of the black dispossessed rather than with or behind them. The black poor, much ballyhooed in black leadership circles, must have expressive vehicles themselves that articulate and struggle for their interests, unfiltered by considerations external to their interests. The resources, skills, and experiences possessed by other sectors of the black community must be brought to bear on building these institutions and organs of mobilization and organization. As long as black politics is representational rather than organically driven, the crisis of the black poor will deepen, the alienation of the black middle class will continue, and the possibility of abatement of racism will remain illusive.

These essays interrogate black life at the end of an era. They also confront the pivotal and challenging questions facing African Americans as a new century dawns. An uneasiness pervades the black community as we search for answers and even the right questions to raise as a sense of collapse grows. Some seek conservative solutions in a call for a new morality, black self-help, and patriarchy. Others cry for economic development and an accommodation with capitalism. Still others demand more political power in the form of additional elected officials, more registered voters, and more seats at the table of the Democratic or Republican Parties. While all of these demands bear scrutiny and assessment, for the most part, they are besides the point. More fundamental is the recognition of a new historic juncture that completely reconfigures not only questions of race, but of every social, political, economic, and cultural issue facing the nation and, indeed, the international community.

It is not just that the new millennium is upon us. As a practical matter, the transition to the 21st century is mainly symbolic. Those who don't have jobs on December 31, 1999 won't have a job one day later on January 1, 2000. What is significant is that the chronological dawn of the new century coincides with an historic global transformation that now requires different modes of conceptualizing, socializing, and working. It also means the creation of new organizational forms and structures appropriate to the new period. All these concerns mean thinking and acting on old issues in new ways as well as identifying emerging ones. It is of paramount importance to recognize that 21st-century issues cannot be resolved with 20th-century paradigms. In the essays that follow, there are several themes:

Race matters and rules are in transition in profound and fundamental ways. It is insufficient to simply think of race in black-and-white terms. Race in the United States must be placed in a multilayered context in which issues of citizenship, class, gender, culture, and race are mixed into a pool of multiple Asian communities, multiple Latino communities, and significantly, multiple black communities.

There is a need to go beyond the political forms (i.e., political parties) of the 20th century. These forms, Left and Right, besides being undemocratic, are linear, static, and ill-equipped for the rapid adjustments and nuances that will characterize political participation in the future. Building and rebuilding coalitions and virtual political agency have already begun to supplant people's notion about political change.

Think globally, act locally and globally. In effect, the option to act locally has been disappearing rapidly over the last two decades. Now, every purchase is a global act and every business transaction is a step into the international community. Leisure activities are Internetted and hot-linked. Joining the local, national, regional, and global—what has been termed "globalization"—must be the beginning of political activism.

Institutions and economic and political systems critically determine the quality of and opportunities in people's lives. These essays reject all theories that blame African Americans, other people of color, women, and the poor for the multiple crises engulfing their communities. The thesis of personal responsibility is a fig leaf in social science that masks conservative reductionism regarding the role of the state and capital in shaping the life of society and the lives of citizens.

Finally, black intellectual life is also in transition. Contemporary black intellectualism, in general, suffers from a lack of purpose and is profoundly disconnected from the struggles and issues of the black community. The commodification of intellectual life has not escaped African Americans in academia and, indeed, is the inspiration of intellectual work in many cases. This situation is a break from historical patterns where black intellectuals were more involved in the daily concerns of black America. However, a new generation of black theorists have emerged today whose contributions are already challenging conventions and old-school black politics. This new generation, it should be noted, is significantly influenced by theoretically advanced critiques offered by black women thinkers on a broad array of issues, from postmodernism to feminism to social policy to black politics.

The issues addressed in these essays have sparked widespread concern and discourse among the elite and the masses of black people. This nexus is critical since it allows popular debates at a variety of levels. An examination of these issues allows us to overcome elite dismissals of popular issues, while at the same time, operating at a level of interrogation that is more substantive than generally pursued.

Chapter One examines at the impact of contemporary capitalist globalization on communities of color. It connects the current economic crisis of the black community with transformations both at national and global scales. Chapter Two reviews the contradictions between conservative attacks on welfare and welfare recipients and their support for corporate welfare. It analyzes how the collapse of the welfare state, through racializing and gendering the debate, becomes a vehicle for ideological assaults and capital accumulation. Chapter Three investigates racially charged issues, such as retreats on immigration and the elimination of affirmative action, that have occurred in recent years in California. These issues are markers for how the national debate and political struggles over them will take shape. Chapter Four looks at the controversy over Ebonics. It examines the ways the issue intersects with concerns around class, gender, and ideology, and the role of language struggles in this era of globalization. Chapter Five discusses the O.J. Simpson trials and phenomena. This case was a critical watershed in race and gender politics in the United States. Its global meanings and ramifications are also examined. Chapter Six interrogates the life, death, and meaning of the late rapper, Tupac Shakur. The chapter locates Shakur's life in the context of the issues facing black youth, cultural workers, and social theorists. Chapter Seven analyzes the ways in which the media projects the black image on a global scale. Blackness, particularly blackness as codified in the United States, has global signification that has increased dramatically in this period.

Chapter Eight examines the CIA-Contra-cocaine controversy. It argues that these links must be framed by global economic and political policies as well as the media's role in defending state and capital initiatives. Chapter Nine looks at the dominant paradigms on race that have evolved in the United States in the post-civil rights era. Chapter Ten analyzes the racial politics of the New South and contends that while important changes have occurred regarding southern racial politics, the ideology of a new South serves to hide ways in which racial hierarchy is reproduced and must be challenged. Chapter Eleven looks at the political significance and role of Nation of Islam leader, Minister Louis Farrakhan. The thesis is that, in many ways, Farrakhan embodies the long historical trend of blending black nationalism with conservatism. Farrakhan's militant rhetoric and targeting of genuine racial concerns obviates a more deep-seated conservatism that supports patriarchy, minimized state intervention, moralism, and capitalism. Chapter Twelve begins by analyzing the meaning of the Million Man March and what lies beyond it. The march is critiqued for its gender and political significance for black politics. The chapter next argues that African Americans must become part of the struggle, indeed, play a leading role, for a global civil society.

Globalization's Impact on Race Relations

"Our loyalties must transcend our race, our tribe, our class and our nation; and this means we must develop a world perspective."[1] —Martin Luther King, Jr.

Swoosh! That's the sound of a Michael Jordan basket as he defends his position as perhaps the greatest NBA player ever. It is also the symbol copyrighted by Nike that appears ubiquitously on its basketball shoes (including the Air Jordan line), caps, T-shirts, and other products. Jordan, the NBA, and Nike are global symbols that embody intersecting race, economic, and cultural discourses that define the current era. For many people around the world, the commodified image of Jordan is one of their few entreés into black America. Jordan represents more than just a media-constructed, popular-culture icon; he also manifests the connection between new global labor relations, global cultural production and promotion, and race. Nike pays Jordan about $20 million annually to promote their basketball shoes, which is more than the collective salaries of the Nike workers in the factories in Indonesia that produce the shoes.[2] The shoes, which cost Nike $5.60 a pair to produce, are sold in the United States for as much as $150 disproportionately to inner-city black youth who have (literally) bought into a commercialized notion of black authenticity that captures neither their reality nor their likely destiny.[3]

Meanwhile, Nike's Indonesian workers, overwhelmingly women, struggle for basic benefits and health care, and against sexual and physical abuse, low pay, and wages under $2.50 per day in a nation where the living wage begins at $4.25 a day.[4] Nike, Jordan, and other transnational athletic products, corporations, and black NBA superstars all deny culpability in this exploitation. Nike subcontracts its labor production thereby disallowing direct complicity in the exploitative working conditions that are endemic in such labor. Jordan and other NBA celebrities simply claim that their only involvement is the endorsement, making it clear where their alliances lie in the enduring struggle between capital and labor.

The NBA's own racial house is out of order. While African Americans constitute 80 percent of the league's players, they are virtually invisible in the management and ownership areas.[5] Yet, it was the star capabilities and marketing of certain black players in the 1980s and 1990s—including the "Dream Teams" that participated in the Olympics—furthering the cultural force of U.S. basketball, that brought the NBA from financial abyss and rebuilt it into a national and international economic powerhouse. As this sliver of globalization demonstrates, a complicated nexus of race, gender, economics, culture, and politics is defining the issues of our times. The new world disorder necessitates a critical rethinking by black leaders, scholars, and activists as we confront the new millennium.

This chapter focuses on the impact of globalization on the economic and social life of African Americans. I argue that there is an unbreakable interdependence between the local and domestic issues facing the U.S. black community and their intersection with international economic and social concerns. My thesis is that it has become impossible to discuss the advancement of the black community without theorizing about the location and relevance of African Americans in the global sphere, and that a progressive social and political program must weld together local, national, and international strategies that account for the new historic moment in which we find ourselves.

Racial Negotiation in the Globalization Era

> "We have to look at discrimination not simply as a deviation from law in the U.S.A.; rather we must see it as part of a larger, international norm, and as consistent with a worldwide corporate culture that transcends national boundaries."[6] —Patricia J. Williams

The age of globalization is upon us. Here at the edge of the millennium, we live in a period and time when the world has shrunk considerably, and where economic and technological reach has brought together desperate nations, peoples, and cultures. The industrial age, to a great degree, has passed, and the digital-information era is shaping and defining all that we do and how we think.

Researcher Jerry Mander argues that "Economic globalization involves arguably the most fundamental redesign and centralization of the planet's political and economic arrangements since the Industrial Revolution."[7] Scholar Anthony Giddens defines globalization as "the intensification of worldwide social relations which link distant localities in such a way that local happenings are shaped by events occurring many miles away and vice versa."[8] Economist Robert Burnett writes that globalization refers to "the organization of production, distribution, and consumption of cultural goods on a world-scale market."[9] Where these various definitions of globalization find unity is in the view that economic, social, political, and cultural life is being reordered before our very eyes. This new stage of capitalism—postindustrial, post-Cold War, transitional, information, and high-technology-driven—and the new-found power of global corporations can be summed by economist Lester Thurow, "For the first time in human history, anything can be made anywhere and sold everywhere."[10]

The new capacities of global capitalism to produce and distribute virtually any commodity on a global scale has profoundly transformed the relation between labor and capital. Under these circumstances, labor's ability to bargain in its interests—that is, for increased wages, better benefits, greater safety guidelines, and more job protection—is severely undermined. For black workers, the impact of this transformation is compounded by racially discriminatory labor markets; lack of access to skills training; the disappearance of low-skill, mid-to-high-wage jobs; political peripherization in public policy and the major parties; and an ideological backlash that seeks to reverse the gains made by African Americans in the civil rights and Black Power periods.

In response to these developments, a large number of scholarly and popular studies have been written that are critical of the impact of globalization on labor, politics, the environment, and local cultures. This includes *Global Dreams*; *The Case Against Globalization*; *Jihad vs. McWorld*; *Lean and Mean*; *One World, Ready or Not*; *When Corporations Rule the World*; and *The Work of Nations*.[11] These works and others provide an outstanding critique of the social and human harm being wrought by an unchecked globalization process where there is little national or international authority. They highlight the necessity of a global response from below that can retard the debilitating impact of globalization from above. Although much attention has been paid to the importance of globalization on gender, class, cultural, and environmental issues, there is little discussion of the significance of these transformations on race relations. Economist Jeremy Rifkin's *The End of Work* is an exception. He dedicates an entire chapter to the historic impact of new technologies on African-American labor. For the black labor force, this is an old tale with a postindustrial twist. As Rifkin notes, "The story of automation's effect on African Americans is one of the least known yet most salient episodes in the social history of the twentieth century. The experience of the black community needs to be properly analyzed, for it provides a much needed historical backdrop for understanding the likely impact that re-engineering and the new automation technologies are going to have on the lives of working people around the world."[12] He demonstrates how technological changes in the past have had devastating economic consequences for black workers. Mechanization and technological innovations, among other factors, ended the sharecropping system, displacing millions of black farm laborers in the 1940s and 1950s. In 1949, only 6 percent of cotton harvesting was mechanical. By 1964, only 15 years later, that number had jumped to 78 percent and, by 1972, it was 100 percent.[13] Rifkin's insights echo that of analyst Sidney Wilhelm.

More than a quarter of a century ago, Wilhelm predicted that African Americans were being made obsolete as workers by new technologies. With keen insight, he wrote, "With the onset of automation, the Negro moves out of his historical state of oppression into one of uselessness. Increasingly, he is not so much economically exploited as he is irrelevant....[W]hite America, by a more perfect application of mechanization and a vigorous reliance upon automation, disposes of the Negro; consequently, the Negro transforms from an exploited labor force into an outcast."[14] Wilhelm also predicted the long-term costs of these changes. He writes, "An underestimation of the technological revolution can only lead to an underestimation of the concomitant racial revolution from exploitation to uselessness; to misjudge the present as but a continuation of industrialization rather than the dawn of a new technological era, assures an inability to anticipate the vastly different system of race relations awaiting the displaced Negro."[15] In making the link between race, automation, and the new international economic configurations, Rifkin and Wilhelm's observations are the exception among globalization scholars.

Beyond the economic ramifications, globalization and the new technologies are restructuring race relations, both domestically and internationally, in a wide variety of areas. All together, global race relations are being changed even as the consciousness of that transformation lags behind. In practical terms, however, these changes are already manifested in the daily lives of people. Three critical ways in which globalization is affecting race relations are:

- It undermines progressive economic integration of marginalized racial groups as it destroys jobs, fosters competition, depresses wages, cuts worker's benefits, and limits opportunities;

- It gives rise to new race-conscious political and social movements that attempt to resist racialized social assaults, policies of containment and imprisonment, and the elimination of the welfare state and;

- It has a negative cultural impact as manufactured racist and negative images of racial and ethnic groups are projected to the world, which has little or no alternative framework for assessing the lives and cultures of these communities.

Race, Work, and the Global Economy

The changing world economy is fundamentally remapping the way the world works and black workers are carrying a significant portion of the load. Access to jobs, already disproportionately tenuous for black workers, has become even more constricted in the current era. As scholar Holly Sklar notes, "While some workers have jobs with no future, others have futures with no jobs."[16] Responding to the jobs development crisis, President Clinton stated, "All the advanced nations are having difficulty creating new jobs, even when their economies are growing....We have to figure out how to unlock the doors for people who are left behind in this new global economy."[17] Chair of the Council of Economic Advisers Laura D'Andrea Tyson spoke similarly, "Globalization has depressed the wage growth of low-wage workers. It's been a reason for the increasing wage gap between high-wage and low-wage workers."[18] Despite this acknowledgment of the difficulties wrought by the new global economy, neither Clinton nor his administration nor Congress have adequately addressed the concerns of U.S. workers, but have instead, consistently acted in the interests of the transnational corporate elite.

In this era, job competition takes place on a global scale. Governments around the world, including the United States, have made it clear that they no longer have full employment as a goal. U.S. workers are not only competing with their next door neighbor for that potential new job, but with 700 million people around the world who are unemployed and beholden to the vicissitudes of capital.[19] As the International Forum on Globalization notes, "As many as one-third of U.S. workers are swimming in a global labor pool."[20] At any given moment, millions of U.S. workers are held hostage to the threat of replacement workers from lands thousands of miles away.

The International Labor Organization (ILO) reports that there are over 34 million people under/unemployed in the industrialized Organization for Economic Cooperation and Development (OECD) nations. In 1996, in Germany, France, Italy, and Sweden, unemployment was up 11.3 percent. In the United States and Great Britain, while unemployment stabilized or diminished , income disparities grew sharply.

In Latin America and the Caribbean, unemployment rose, particularly in urban areas. According to the ILO, the only developing nations that have seen significant growth in the last 20 years outside of Asia have been Chile, Jordan, and Mauritis. Depressingly, not a single African country has seen economic growth in the last two decades. ILO also reports that millions have shifted to laboring in informal sectors of the economy, including the illegal realm.[21]

Authors Richard Barnet and John Cavanagh note that the global economy can be divided into a pyramid of seven groups of nations. At the very top are about 24 nations located in North America, Western Europe, Japan, Australia, New Zealand, and South Africa. These economies generate about four-fifths of the world's economic activity. They are followed by the eight countries—Brazil, Mexico, Argentina, South Korea, Taiwan, Singapore, Hong Kong, and

India—who do large-scale manufacturing. A third group—including China, Thailand, Indonesia, and Malaysia—has reached the stage of limited industrialization. Developing rapidly with large inflows of Western capital, the former communist nations of Eastern Europe constitute a fourth group. More or less on economic par with the countries of Eastern Europe, the oil-producing countries of the Middle East make up a fifth block of economic power. The sixth group is composed of the poor nations in Asia, Latin America, and Africa whose prospects for development are dim making them vulnerable to exploitative investment and economic dependence. At the very bottom are the poorest of the poor nations, virtually all located in Africa with the notable exception of Haiti.[22]

Across the globe, economic woes and the social havoc that they generate have been racialized. In the United Kingdom, more than a million manufacturing jobs were lost between 1966 and 1976, and in Germany, "new technologies enabled manufacturers to eliminate more than 500,000 jobs in a single 12-month period between early 1992 and 1993."[23] Many of these jobs throughout Europe were held by black workers. Official employment and economic data from the United States, Canada, and England document that black unemployment is at least twice that of white unemployment. In Canada, a study by the Commission on Systemic Racism in the Ontario criminal justice system found that over an eight-year period black imprisonment grew 204 percent, while the white incarceration increase was 23 percent. The study also found that whites charged with drug crimes are released at twice the rate of blacks.[24]

The perception that globalization is having a racial impact has led to organized resistance at the regional and state levels. In Europe, efforts have unfolded that unite racial justice concerns with the economic issues facing the region. In 1990, the Standing Conference on Racial Equality in Europe (SCORE) was formed to address the economic, social, and racial impact of a unified Europe on blacks and other ethnic minorities. SCORE has chapters in all of the major European capitals and carefully monitors and assesses the European Union (EU) process. In 1994, they issued their "Black Manifesto for Europe." Among the demands of the manifesto were:

- Amend the Treaty of Rome to outlaw discrimination by race

- Adopt as a European Union Directive "The Starting Line," which promotes racial equality in law;
- Allow free movement for all EU residents, whether citizens or not;
- Ban incitement to racial harassment and eradicate racial violence;
- Create an anti-racist and anti-sexist immigration policy that is open to democratic scrutiny, in conjunction with the black, migrant, and minority communities who are most affected;
- Grant independent legal status to black, migrant, and minority women and promote the mainstreaming of their concerns in all areas of European work; and
- Give asylum seekers easy access to the EU and proper legal representation; they should not be detained, nor returned to countries where they could be in danger.

SCORE also outlined what it considers to be a racial bill of rights. It demanded that all black, migrant, and minority residents of the EU should have the right to vote in all elections; equal rights to housing; equal rights to education, including their own language, history and culture; equal rights to health and social services; and the right to family reunion.

In France, progressive groups are organizing against racial discrimination and economic attacks on workers. On May 1, 1997, May Day, thousands of workers marched in Paris to protest racism and unemployment. Organized by the French Communist Party *(PCF)* and the Socialist Party *(PS)*, the rally called for the creation of 700,000 youth jobs, reduction of work hours to 35 with full pay, and elimination of the racist anti-immigration Pasqua-Debre' laws. It was the first time in 14 years that *PCF* and *PS* had held joint actions. The crowd was estimated to be between 23,000 and 60,000, the largest in years. There were also provincial support marches in Marseilles, Toulouse, and Bordeaux. The French government, under former-President Jacques Chirac, made cuts in social programs and wanted to make more in pensions, unemployment insurance, and health care benefits. Unemployment in France is around 13 percent, one of the highest in all of Europe. Further evisceration of the French welfare state would be calamitous because 25 percent of the nation's workers are employed by the state.[25]

In Latin America, blacks in the region have come together under the auspices of the Organization of Africans in the Americas (OAA) and the Mundo Afro organization to counter the negative impact of the globalized economy. In December 1994, at their first symposium on racism and xenophobia in the region, OAA identified some common problems faced by blacks, including lack of access to political, financial, and educational institutions; human rights abuses; hunger; crime; murders of black people, black street children in particular, by death squads; and forced sterilization of women. According to Marta Moreno Vega, director of New York's Caribbean Cultural Center, who attended the meeting, "The most important thing to come out of the [1994 Mundo Afro] conference was an affirmation of the African presence in Latin America, which is often ignored throughout the globe. And the fact that organizations have developed and are continuing to develop, that are looking at the African experience as the center for political, economic, and social movement."[26]

Economic State of Black America

"Historically, discrimination was a powerful force in regimenting a disproportionate number of blacks to the secondary sector. Today, this segmentation continues even though more overt forms of racism have subsided".[27] —Thomas D. Boston.

In the 1980s, the loss of millions of manufacturing jobs due to plant closings, runaway shops, and the imposition of new technologies was central to the diminished fortunes of the working class in the United States and to increased national poverty. Between 1983–1988, 9.7 million U.S. workers lost jobs through plant closings and layoffs.[28] Companies that symbolized America's global corporate dominance in the past joined the exodus. General Electric, the company that hired superpatriot Ronald Reagan as its spokesperson, cut 25,000 domestic jobs while adding 30,000 foreign positions. RCA cut 14,000 domestic jobs while adding 19,000 globally.[29] It is estimated that in the United States during the 1970s, between 32 and 38 million jobs disappeared.[30] As Rachel Kamel notes, "Manufacturing employment in the U.S. fell by 1.4 million between 1978 and 1990 and the numbers out of work are increasing despite economic recovery."[31]

Deindustrialization had an injurious economic impact on black workers, who worked in large numbers in the factories of Detroit, St. Louis, Chicago, Pittsburgh, and other industrial cities. Driven by the desire for higher profits, close proximity to natural resources, access to local markets, and most critically, cheap labor, large-and medium-sized corporations fled North America and Europe as rapidly as they could. In 1950, one-third of all U.S. jobs were in manufacturing. By the mid-1980s, only 20 percent were employed in manufacturing, and by 1990 that had dropped off to 10-14 percent; it is projected that by 2005, the number will drop to between 2.5 and 5 percent.[32] Studies also show that blacks are paid less for the same positions.

The loss of manufacturing jobs have contributed to black job displacement. Those jobs have been replaced by low-wage work that generally offers fewer benefits and more exploitative working conditions, that is, no labor unions or collective bargaining. These often subminimal wage jobs include positions in areas such as retail sales, food service, janitorial, housekeeping, and low-level health delivery, jobs disproportionately held by African Americans. Between 1980–1987, half of all new jobs went to temporary and part-time workers.[33]

Black workers, already suffering from an unemployment rate that has historically been at least twice that of whites, are especially hard hit in this new era. In the 1970s, for example, "up to half of the huge employment declines for less-educated blacks might be explained by industrial shifts away from manufacturing toward other sectors."[34] This trend continued into the 1980s and 1990s. As the *Wall Street Journal* noted, referencing a General Accounting Office (GAO) report, African Americans suffered the worst in the recession of the early 1990s. According to the *Journal*, "Black wage earners made up nearly one-third of the 180,000 manufacturing jobs lost in 1990 and 1991," which translated into about 60,000 jobs lost at companies such as ITT, Bank of America, Sears, Coca Cola, Safeway, Campbell's Soup, Walt Disney, and General Electric.[35] Even more remarkable was the conclusion that "Blacks were the only racial group to suffer a net job loss during the 1990-91 economic downturn."[36] The GAO noted, "The high African American displacement rate was partially due to the impact of the recession on industries and occupations in which African Americans were disproportionately represented; however, differences still persisted after accounting for industrial and occupational affiliations, education levels, and worker age."[37]

Downsizing is happening at large firms as well as small ones because both are able to take advantage of the productivity that comes from employing the new technologies that make everything from telecommunications to transportation more efficient, faster, and profitable. Companies are now able to decrease their workforce while increasing their profit margin. In the past, increased productivity was qualitatively tied to a combination of new technologies and an expanded workforce. For the present and the foreseeable future, that is no longer the case. *The Nation* magazine reports that "the Fortune 500 firms shed 4.4 million jobs between 1980 and 1993, but during this same period, their sales increased 1.4 times, assets increased 2.3 times, and CEO compensation increased 6.1 times."[38] With these results, there is little incentive for companies to do anything but continue to downsize where possible. In 1995 alone, U.S. companies cut about 600,000 workers.[39]

In the 1990s, profits have grown for the top corporations. In 1992, profits jumped 19 percent, in 1993, they rose 20 percent, and in 1994, they shot up an amazing 40 percent.[40] In the United States, the richest 1 percent own as much as the bottom 95 percent.[41] They also own 46 percent of all corporate stock; while the richest 10 percent own 90 percent.[42] "Between 1980 and 1992, the nation's 500 biggest corporations more than doubled their assets from $1.18 to $2.68 trillion. In 12 years, the number of jobs at America's 500 largest corporations fell from 15.9 to 11.5 million."[43]

Between 1967-87, in many cities where African Americans comprise a significant proportion of the population, job losses in manufacturing have been severe. In Philadelphia, a 64 percent loss resulted in the disappearance of 160,000 jobs. In Chicago, it was 60 percent (326,000 jobs), in New York, 58 percent (520,000 jobs), and in Detroit, 51 percent (108,000 jobs).[44] African Americans in the South were also hurt by manufacturing downsizing. As economist Lester Henry observed, "Plant closings in the 1970s...were heaviest in the Northeast and in the old South, the two areas of the country where

African Americans are most populous."[45] The erosion of black middle- and blue-collar classes, due to job loss has exacerbated the economic crisis facing the black poor in these cities as localities struggle to compensate for the tax revenues that disappeared with jobs, middle-class flight, and declining federal and state financial support.

Even though there have been spots of reindustrialization, there is speculation that racial discrimination is also playing a role in this new era of fluid global investments. While evidence is scarce, the placement of new plants, and therefore jobs, outside of easy accessibility by inner-city residents can be seen as having a racial impact given the disproportionate inner-city residency of the black community. Even if premeditation is not present, the consequences of these site decisions exacerbate the job search crisis growing among the black poor. Political scientist Robert Smith writes, "A study of the location decisions of Japanese firms in the United States and of American auto companies found a fairly consistent pattern of location in rural and suburban areas about thirty miles from the nearest concentration of blacks, a distance that is thought to be about the limit of worker commuter time."[46] Henry notes, "The pattern of firms, both foreign and domestic, when choosing sites for opening new plants, has been away from predominantly nonwhite areas...The Japanese and other German firms have also show a similar preference for plant location in suburban and sunbelt areas where few nonwhites reside.[47]

One of the consequences of globalization is a severe reduction in the size of organized labor as a result of less manufacturing work. Union membership in the United Auto Workers fell during the 1980s by close to 500,000 workers—one-third of its peak total.[48] Steel unions were also especially hard hit by the loss of jobs in their fields. From 1974 to 1988, almost half of all jobs in the steel industry disappeared—a fall from 480,000 to 260,000.[49] Overall, labor union membership went from about 35 percent of all nonagricultural workers in 1960 to about 17 percent at present. If government employees are excluded, the number falls to about 13.4 percent.[50] Labor militancy has also declined in recent years. For example, strikes involving 1,000 workers or more averaged about 300 in the 1960s; in 1991, there were only 40.[51] Labor has lost control over job cuts, wage decreases, and work rules, and in some instances, has given back benefits won in the past. The give-backs are part of the necessary tactical moves by labor to hold on to jobs that are rapidly leaving the country. Labor's major weapon, the strike, has become impotent as capital is no longer held hostage to production shutdowns.

In the public sector as well, black job cuts have been disproportionate. According to the *San Jose Mercury News*, when the federal government downsized in 1992, it fired blacks at more than twice the rate of whites. An editorial noted, "Blacks who were 17 percent of the executive branch workforce in 1992, were 39 percent of those dismissed. Whites made up 72 percent of the workforce and only 48 percent of those fired."[52] The *Mercury News* stated, "It's not that they have less education, experience, or seniority. The difference has nothing to do with job performance....Blacks are fired more often because of their skin color....Rank didn't help. Black senior managers went out the door as often as black clerks. It gets worse. The deck is stacked against fired minority workers with legitimate grounds for reinstatement, the study shows. They win only one in every 100 appeals."[53] A General Accounting Office study found that blacks, more than whites or Latinos, "experience the longest spells of unemployment among displaced workers who eventually found jobs and showed the largest loss in wages in their new jobs."[54]

Other factors affecting black job loss are recent international trade agreements. In 1993, President Clinton forced through Congress the North American Free Trade Agreement (NAFTA), which had begun as a policy objective of the Bush administration. Although he did not explicitly say so, Clinton believed that NAFTA would provide economic progress and development gains for all thereby benefiting African Americans and other minorities. His "rising tide will lift all boats" view was a means of attacking racial divisions. This perspective mitigated against explicit race-oriented social programs in favor of general economic ones.

While not guaranteeing that even its economic components will work, this view completely fails to address racial discrimination in its broad political and social forms. The argument is also reductive in that it narrows racism down to economic disparities rather than a system of relationships of power that are not only economic, but social, political, and cultural. While economist Martin Carnoy contends that

Clinton's class approach to race may garner some economic benefits for African Americans that are more substantial than what occurred under Presidents Reagan and Bush, it

> ...does not solve the problems of wage discrimination and the lack of decent-paying jobs and upward mobility for those same people. It does not overcome the disintegration of the inner-city, or reduce the job discrimination and financial and educational difficulties faced by young blacks getting college educations. It falls far short of even a moderately aggressive use of federal agencies to reduce discrimination by enforcing civil rights legislation and of the kind of ideological reconstruction needed to push the electorate toward resolving racial inequality. It still consciously avoids putting the race issue explicitly on the table through either a return to solid enforcement of civil rights legislation or a thorough discussion of what must be done to begin to rebuild family and community in inner-cities. Hence, it not only avoids dealing with solutions to racial inequality, but runs the risk of failing even to address that (class) part of racial inequality associated with the disproportionate number of working blacks in lower-income groups."[55]

Many civil rights leaders, economists, and labor leaders testified before Congress that NAFTA would be most injurious to African Americans. Working-class African Americans engaged in fields of work, such as manufacturing, are most likely to be adversely affected. This perspective was shared by Thea Lee, an economist at the Economic Policy Institute. In her 1993 testimony before Congress, she stated that "African Americans, Hispanics, and Asian Americans hold a disproportionate share of the production jobs likely to be displaced by NAFTA."[56]

William Lucy, president of the Coalition of Black Trade Unionists (CBTU), argued a similar point. He wrote, "Black workers are more likely to be employed in those industries which will experience large job losses to Mexico including automobiles and trucks, apparel, household glassware, ceramics, major household appliances, and electronics....High-wage manufacturing jobs remain the only practical path of upward mobility for millions of black workers who do not have college degrees."[57] CBTU was one of the few black interest groups to take an early position against NAFTA, dating back to at least the 102nd Congress.

A statement issued by the Congressional Black Caucus captured a number of their arguments. It stated, in part:

Our trade deficit with Mexico has already grown in many industries. Estimates of probable job losses due to NAFTA have reached as high as one million. State and local governments will lose tax revenues from businesses who relocate and individuals who become jobless. In those regions that suffer the most intense job losses, the corresponding loss of tax revenues will be substantial. NAFTA will have a negative impact on the generation of revenues in this country precisely at a time when entitlement benefits and services are under great peril. Also, an examination of the average hourly wages for production workers in those industries already affected reveals that the jobs being lost are high-wage, not only low-wage manufacturing jobs. Those who lose jobs because of import competition do not climb up the job ladder, but fall back to lower wages or fall off the job ladder into unemployment. There is little to support the claim of NAFTA proponents that free trade will create higher wage jobs for U.S. workers because Mexican workers will take jobs at the lower end of the skills ladder while American workers will move up to better paying jobs.

There has not been sufficient progress made with Mexico related to environmental protection. NAFTA must preserve the rights of states and the federal government to set high individual standards for the environment, conservation, health and safety. NAFTA does not provide a secure, dedicated source of funding for border clean-up, environmental infrastructure, conservation initiatives, protection of communities and worker health. The treaty does not prevent the flight of industries which seek to take advantage of lax environmental, health and safety standards in other countries. Further, there are not sufficient opportunities for public participation in trade and environmental disputes and in investment and trade decisions affecting individual communities.

...The Minority Business Community has never been fully consulted or considered on NAFTA. There are no current proposals to provide technical, financial marketing or educational assistance to small business in general, or to minority business in particular, interested in trade with or investment in Mexico. Remedies must be carefully explored and should accompany the NAFTA.

Preferential treatment for Mexico—especially in areas of sugar, citrus and apparel—could result in significant diversion of trade from the Caribbean. Such a diversion would stall economic growth, and dislocate productive activity in both the United States and the Caribbean. If NAFTA takes effect in January, U.S./Caribbean commerce could erode by next spring. Using the textile industry as an example, NAFTA calls for a progressive reduction of tariffs on Mexican textiles and apparel over the next decade.[58]

Some analysts have argued that African Americans and the working population in general should prepare for the 21st century by reeducating themselves in the areas of high technology and computer science.[59] Projections of job creation in the early years of the 21st century, however, demonstrate that most will come in areas of low-pay, low-skill work. In the 1996–1997 edition of the Department of Labor's *The Occupational Outlook Handbook,* 20 occupations are expected to grow over the next 10 years. The top 10 occupations and their projected growth are cashiers (562,000 jobs), janitors and cleaners (559,000), retail salespersons (532,000), waiters and waitresses (479,000), registered nurses (473,000), general managers and top executives (466,000), system analysts (445,000), home health aides (428,000), security guards (415,000), and nursing aides, orderlies, and attendants (387,000).[60] Other jobs in the top 20 included truck drivers, secretaries, childcare workers, and maintenance repairers.[61] With the notable exceptions of general managers/top executives and system analysts, and perhaps registered nurses, most of the new jobs will be at or near minimum wage, keeping a large segment of even full-time workers under the poverty line. These are also categories that disproportionately hire women at very low pay and with few benefits.

These projections are grim news for the African-American community. Even if African Americans can prepare themselves for the jobs that are going to be created, it will be difficult to build families and communities on the wages that will be available. For African-American men, in particular, the traditional entry-level laboring positions that for generations allowed them to still earn a living wage with low level education have vanished like the smoke from the long-gone, not-to-return factories.

Neither should the illusion that black businesses will solve the black employment crisis be fostered. In 1993, the *Black Enterprise* top 100 industrial and automotive companies collectively employed only 45,628 blacks.[62] While this is a 22 percent increase over the previous year, it accounts for only 1 percent of the current black labor force. And, like other capitalist businesses, those black businesses with the potential to grow are capital intensive (media and technology) rather than labor intensive (manufacturing). Black businesses, however, are not located in the capital-intensive expansive area of the economy. As economist Margaret Simms states, "Most minority-owned businesses are not well represented in the kinds of industries where international trade possibilities are strong."[63]

In 1992, based on the latest U.S. Census Bureau data available, out of a total 17 million U.S. businesses, there were roughly 620,000 black businesses, with receipts of $32.2 billion.[64] These businesses averaged receipts of $52,000 per year with black women averaging $31,000 compared to the average of black men of $69,000.[65] Significantly, 56 percent of the businesses earned less than $10,000 per year. Perhaps, the most salient statistic regarding the black employment possibilities is the fact that 94 percent of black businesses were sole proprietorships![66] In other words, only 6 percent of black businesses hired anyone at all, whether that employee was black or not. In virtually every black community, nonblacks own the majority of businesses. In Washington, D.C., although blacks are 65 percent of the population, they own less than 10 percent of the city's businesses. In Los Angeles, according to the last census, one of every 10 Koreans own their business; for blacks it's one out of every 67.[67]

For the black community, especially its youth, the racial disparities in the economy are mirrored in other areas, such as education. Marian Wright Edelman, president of the Children's Defense Fund, sadly points out that "A black high school graduate is nearly one and a half times more likely to be unemployed than a white high school dropout, and a black college graduate is more likely to be unemployed than a white high school graduate with no college."[68] Edelman also gives some sobering statistics on the opportunity differences between white and black children:

- 78 percent of white children live with both parents compared to 39 percent of black children;
- 63 percent of white children live with parents who own their home vs. 28 percent of black children;
- 23 percent of white children have a father that works full-time and a mother that is at home full-time contrasted to a mere 8 percent of black children;
- 30 percent of white children have a parent that has completed college, only 13 percent of black children;
- 71 percent of white children are covered by health insurance compared to only 44 percent of black children;
- 16 percent of white children compared to 41 percent of black children are poor;
- 19 percent of white children live in central cities vs. 41 percent black children.[69]

While the white infant mortality is 7 per 1,000, the figure of 16 per 1,000 for African-American children is more than double the white rate, which approaches that of many developing nations. For whites, the low birth rate is 6 percent; for African Americans, it is 13 percent.[70] The future for children in the United States, in general, is so grim that the country was given a rebuke by the United Nations. A UNICEF report noted, "the living conditions of poor American children are far worse than those of poor children in most other industrial countries....Only four other countries—Australia, Canada, Ireland and Israel—have child poverty rates of more than 10 percent."[71] According to the report, without government help, the poverty rate in the United States and France would be 25 percent, but with the difference in their individual welfare systems, France has reduced child poverty to 6.5 percent while the United States has only reduced it to 21 percent.[72]

Jobs, Race, and Globalization

On January 11, 1944, in an address to Congress, President Franklin D. Roosevelt called for a "Second Bill of Rights under which a new basis of security and prosperity can be established for all—regardless of station, race, or creed."[73] Attempting to speak not only the immediate crisis of war and work in which the nation was immersed, he also set forth an inclusive vision for the country:

> The right to a useful and remunerative job in the industries or shops or farms or mines of the nation; the right to earn enough to provide adequate food and clothing and recreation; the right of every farmer to raise and sell his products at a return which will give him and his family a decent living; the right of every businessman, large and small, to trade in an atmosphere of freedom from unfair competition and domination by monopolies at home and abroad; the right of every family to a decent home; the right to adequate medical care and the opportunity to achieve and enjoy good health; the right to adequate protection from the economic fears of old age, sickness, accident, and unemployment; the right to a good education.[74]

Representative Ron Dellums (D–CA) has fashioned and updated Roosevelt's bill of rights into H.R. 1050, "A Living Wage, Jobs For All Act." As Dellums writes, "The bill is particularly significant at this time in that more and more of our people feel that they are slipping rapidly into an increasingly limited job market, a condition of seemingly permanent low wages, and the loss of real prospects for improvement in their economic condition. As more companies merge, downsize, reduce, layoff, and dismiss their workers, it is clear that opportunities to work for adequate wages are shrinking. Increasingly, it seems that the private sector views its responsibility as only making a profit for the top investors and to provide opulent benefits for its chief executives."[75]

The purpose of the bill is captured in its full title, "To establish democratic overall planning for such living wage job opportunities as will help fulfill basic human rights and responsibilities, facilitate conversion from unneeded military programs to civilian activities that meet basic human needs, and strengthen democracy by reducing poverty, inequality, violence and the concentration of economic power." H.R. 1050 calls on the president to "implement the economic and social obligations of the Federal Government under the Employment Act of 1946, the Full Employment and Balanced Growth Act of 1978, the Charter of the United Nations, the Charter of the Organization of American States, the Universal Declaration of Human Rights, and the International Covenant on Civil and Political Rights."[76]

Dellums is specifically trying to address the job and employment crisis that has been ignored by other policymakers and the White House. He writes, "H.R. 1050 acknowledges the increasing reality of growing unemployment and takes the responsibility of creating jobs in sectors which need work to be done; in building housing, educating our young, protecting and cleaning up the environment, providing childcare, healthcare, expanding public transportation, and in other areas of need. It is unrealistic to expect that corporations, which are only market-oriented, will take the responsibility for a healthy, national economy. Only we, the people, through our common action, can accomplish this. We need to realize the power of our joint action and take responsibility for our future. This bill is a step in that direction."[77]

For the black community, Dellums' bill and his effort to popularize the struggle for genuine full employment is critical. While specific race-remedy programs, such as affirmative action and minority set-asides, are important to maintain a broad view is necessary that locates black job issues within the framework of global labor changes. The battle for a guaranteed living wage is being fought in nation after nation as adjustments to a period in which fewer jobs will be available for more workers than ever. In Canada, Denmark, Japan, the Netherlands, and other countries, various forms of state welfare programs to cushion the cost of downsizing have been won by the struggles of labor organizers, community activists, and progressive elected officials.[78] In the United States, African Americans in solidarity with other sectors of society have to rebuild and reenergize a movement that seeks as its goal nothing short of a redistribution of economic and political power downward that provides development, prosperity, and fairness.

2

If I Were a Rich Man: Race, Gender, and Poverty

"The plantation and the ghetto were created by those who had power both to confine those who had no power and to perpetuate their powerlessness. The problem of transforming the ghetto is, therefore, a problem of power."[1]—Martin Luther King, Jr.

Largesse for the poor from the modern welfare state has never been an act of generosity and charity, but in fact, has always been a response to the political mobilization and organization of the poor and their allies. The real issue confronting the poor has been about power. To the degree that the poor has been demobilized and out of contention for power, as in the current period, retraction has occurred. The modern welfare state—its stability and even existence—is a consequence of the enduring political power struggle between capital and the state, on the one hand, and labor and its most marginalized sectors, on the other.

The modern welfare state is also a gendered one. Efforts to curtail state commitment to the poor are often waged on the ideological grounds of patriarchy, where it is argued that the traditional family, ostensibly the stabilizing core of both modernity and postindustrial society, is threatened by welfare policies. Male power, actualized through institutional and systemic economic and political power relations, has been undermined by the empowerment brought by women liberating themselves from the traditional family structure by their incorporation into the economic base of society and their role in the political and ideological struggles in the superstructure. A diminished or dismissed welfare state reasserts male privilege.

The political and ideological questions surrounding poverty and gender intersect with those of race, quilting together a popular yet benefactors of the welfare state. This framework sees those black, poor, and female sectors of society as social pariahs and the most undeserving of even the meager wages of welfare that they receive. Within the black community, this framework serves to demonize black women, reify the family and traditional family roles, and (re)center black men. This agenda then finds a confluence of support from white reactionaries, black conservatives, neoliberals, and some prominent black nationalists.

In fundamental ways, this construct is being played out on a global scale. The welfare state, which has been a central feature of post-War War I advanced capitalist nations, is being eroded away. From France and Canada to Australia and England, social spending on the poor and the lower rungs of the working class has come under attack even as the needs of the poor have increased dramatically in these societies.

Thus, the battle over welfare in the United States merges with ongoing global issues and concerns. The thesis of this chapter is that the elimination of welfare for the poor in the United States is viewed by policymakers as a necessary concession to capital in the postindustrial era to create a more acceptable atmosphere for investment and capitalist economic development. In the United States, the ideological component of this task is the requisite racializing and gendering of the debate both in the larger public discourse as well as within the African-American community. The debate in the black community over welfare reform explicates the ideological tensions of this period between those who, either explicitly or covertly, adhere to a reworked and sometimes Afrocentrized version of the cultural pathology thesis, and those who target economic and political powerlessness as the root causes of poverty. The policy, political, and strategic implications of the two views are diametrically opposed. The former leads to advocacy for the elimination of welfare programs while the latter demands a strengthening and expansion of the state's responsibility to the poor. While the former targets the poor as the unit of change, the latter targets political mobilization of the poor as a necessary strategy leading to institutional and systemic transformation.

Modern U.S. Welfare State Emerges

The United States was one of the last industrialized nations to institute welfare programs aimed at the poor and disadvantaged. In Germany, sickness insurance was instituted in 1883 and health insurance in 1880. In the United Kingdom, sickness insurance came in 1911 and health insurance in 1948. In both nations, insurance was not income or age determined. In the 1930s, the Great Depression created a dual crisis of stability and legitimacy, and forced a state response to the spontaneous social movements, many of them infused with socialist and communist yearnings, that threatened the entire social construct of liberal democracy. Social movements led by workers, blacks, farmers, and others forced concessions that withstood the crises of the period and lasted until the most recent times.[2]

In the 1950s and 1960s, the civil rights and Black Power movements won even more gains from a state that again sought and could afford social pacification. It is critical to note, however, that it was not only the movement from below that sparked these changes, but also movement from above. Changes in the nature of the postwar capitalist economy, most profoundly the expansion of U.S. capital on a global scale and the necessity of an expanded labor force that would include African Americans, women, and others, meant that a "progressive" wing of corporate elites saw the value in supporting an end to racial segregation. Social integration facilitated economic integration, which was good for business.

Finally, the welfare state was enhanced by the emergence of a black, political, managerial class that found itself engaged in policy debates and, increasingly, policy decisions. The administrative and managerial seizure of the cities, left behind by a fleeing white middle class, created a tension in the political system that mitigated a full-blown retrenchment and social take-back by conservative and reactionary forces, at least until Reaganism.

Just as Thatcherism in England would attack the gains of the English working class, so too would Reaganism, with plentiful support from congressional Democrats, erode the decades-old victories won by the U.S. working class, including African Americans. The prism through which Reaganist salvos would travel was initially into areas that could be easily racialized and genderized. Essential to this effort was winning the public ideological fray over how welfare was defined and viewed.

Redefining the Welfare Discourse

A critical struggle in the welfare discourse is the need to change the terms of the debate and popularized definitions of welfare. For most, welfare is reduced to government transfer programs that are aimed at the inner-city poor, who are disproportionately women of color. There is a twofold problem with this conception of welfare. First, it obscures the class power that lies behind state decisions regarding the distribution of wealth in the United States. A reductive casting of welfare only acknowledges and designates government aid to the poor as "real" welfare, thereby disaggregating billions of dollars in transfers that are given to corporations, veterans, farmers, the elderly, and other sectors of society. Second, a reductive definition of welfare serves the ideological mission of codifying and popularizing racist and sexist assumptions about the poor and poverty that are not only in variance with the facts, but construct bigoted social theories on which social policy is built.

Welfare, in its broadest sense, should more appropriately be seen as the normal operation of the modern capitalist economy that requires both economic transfers to help maintain social peace and ideological loyalty. Economic transfers further the interests of the economic elite. The emergence of the welfare state in 1935 was not as much a surrender to the social movements that rapacious capitalism inspired, but an adjustment in the functioning of the modern industrial nation state.

Political scientist Mack Jones argues similarly when he writes, "The concept of the welfare state comprises all of the interventionist practices of governments,...which involve transferring publicly generated resources to private individuals and groups and the pattern of beliefs and social relationship emanating therefrom. This definition subsumes not only those transfer payment programs earmarked for the poor and referred to pejoratively as 'welfare,' but the whole array of payment programs including those targeted to other non-poor population groups...ranging from price stabilization programs of the agricultural department, export subsidy and trade adjustment programs of the commerce department to the development programs of HUD."[3]

The retreat from welfare for the poor reflects the balance of power in the contestation between the needy and the political and economic elites. Even in this disengagement, capital's true agenda is exposed. While policymakers decry the welfare system as hopelessly bloated, anti-work ethic, and counter to free enterprise, major corporations are lining up to seize the economic opportunities available as welfare devolution to the states occurs. Researcher Adam Fifield documents, for example, how Lockheed Martin Corporation in Los Angeles has secured a four-year, $50 million contract to manage major parts of child support in California, including tracking down fathers, holding hearings, and even administering blood tests.[4] Lockheed, according to Fifield, has contracts to perform some aspect of welfare services in 45 states. In 1997, in Texas, a bidding war took place between Lockheed, Anderson Consulting, and EDS—H. Ross Perot's computer company—for a $2 billion contract to integrate Medicaid, Food Stamps, and welfare services into one computer system.[5] Policymakers claim that the objectives of privatization are reduced welfare rolls, integrated services, recipients being put to work, and a downsized public sector. They fail to add that poverty is unalleviated, very few recipients find permanent full-time work, and an inefficacy expressed in "a pattern of incompetence, cost overruns, and broken promises" is created.[6]

What is Welfare for the Poor?

The nation's welfare system for the poor is not just one program, but actually a number of federal and state programs that constitute what is popularly known as "welfare." At the federal level, this includes Supplemental Security Income (6 million), Food Stamps (20–25 million), Medicare (36 million), Medicaid (25 million), and perhaps the best-known and most debated, the former Aid to Families with Dependent Children or AFDC (14 million), now restructured as Temporary Assistance to Needy Families (TANF) since 1996.[7] Prior to the most recent reforms, states worked with the federal government to administer the various programs. While there were federal guidelines that had to be followed, states had a great deal of flexibility in some areas of administration and were able to apply for exemptions to the rules to experiment with different approaches to welfare.

AFDC was first created by the Social Security Act of 1935 as part of the New Deal legislation initiated during the Depression by the Franklin D. Roosevelt administration. In addition to what was then called Aid to Dependent Children, the act established social security and unemployment insurance. AFDC, along with Food Stamps and other federal welfare programs, were entitlements, which meant that the federal government guaranteed states that funds would be available to meet their needs no matter how those needs might grow—for example, in periods of economic recession.

A family had to meet certain income tests to be eligible for AFDC. States established need standards indexed to the poverty line and state-measured calculations of basic income needs. While a family's gross income could not exceed 185 percent of the state's need standard for the relevant family size, a family's net income had to be below the state's payment standard, which in 35 states was lower than the needs standard.[8] In 1994, the median cash transfer for welfare recipients for a single, nonworking mother of two was $366 in cash and $295 in Food Stamps.[9] This came to about 69 percent of the poverty line, which, in 1993, was $14,764 for a family of four. AFDC was unavailable to single people who had no dependent children.[10] The program was dominated by single women with children, who made up about 90 percent of all recipients.[11] AFDC families, due to their low-income status, also qualified for Medicaid, the federal health insurance program for the nation's poor.

There was also a work component attached to AFDC in the form of the Job Opportunities and Basic Skills Training (JOBS) program. Once their youngest child reached the age of three, the parent had to participate up to 20 hours per week; when that child reached six, up to 40 hours per week.[12] States were technically responsible for child care, transportation, and other work-related costs. In 1992, most states were providing JOBS slots for only about 20 percent of their eligible population.[13]

In the debates concerning welfare, many myths have been perpetuated regarding recipients. These include the views that most welfare recipients are single teenage mothers; that welfare families are vastly larger than the average family in the nation; that most people stay on welfare for many years, if not a lifetime; that most welfare recipients are urban African-American women; that welfare to the poor is bankrupting the nation; that welfare recipients live well off their benefits; that welfare recipients do not want to work; and that welfare creates a culture of dependency. All of these views, carefully crafted fables that do not hold up to scrutiny, facilitate the attacks on welfare and its recipients.

Those who benefit the most from AFDC and other welfare programs are children. In 1992, the welfare caseload consisted of 9.2 million children and 4.4 million adults (virtually all of them mothers).[14] Indeed, most of the beneficiaries are young children. About half the children on welfare are under six years old and one-quarter of them are under three.[15] These children are being raised by a mother who is 25 years old or older, and either divorced or separated.[16] The mother is generally unemployed and has, at most, a high school education.[17]

Studies also demonstrate that welfare families are about the same size as the average family not on welfare in the United States. In 72.7 percent of AFDC families, there were two or fewer children.[18] In fact, the average AFDC family size has decreased from 4 to 2.9 persons since 1969.[19] Despite the calls for a "family cap," which would make ineligible for assistance any new child(ren) born into a family already receiving assistance, at least 10 major studies have demonstrated that there is no direct effect on childbearing and getting on welfare.[20] In other words, there is no conclusive evidence that women are having more children to get or increase their welfare benefits.

Some studies have shown a correlation between nonmarital births and welfare among some women, but not in the way that many would believe given the racialized manner in which welfare is discussed and presented. According to these studies, white women appear to be more likely to have children out-of-wedlock if they live in states where welfare benefits are higher. On the other hand, out-of-wedlock births by black and Latino women are not significantly correlated with higher welfare benefits.[21]

From the propaganda war against welfare, it would be easy to conclude that welfare recipients choose to stay on welfare endlessly.

But, welfare is not a way of life for most of its recipients. The majority leave the system permanently within four years; only 15 percent of recipients stayed on welfare continuously for five years or longer.[22] Studies showed that:

- 50 percent of recipients exit AFDC in the first year of welfare;
- 75 percent of recipients exit AFDC in the first two years of welfare;
- 40 percent of women who exit welfare through earned income remain poor;
- 42 percent of women return to welfare within two years of leaving it; and
- 75 percent of those reentering welfare exit again, and 50 percent of those do so within 12 months of return.[23]

Racially, whites constitute a substantial proportion of welfare recipients since poverty is fairly widespread. In the mid-1990s, African Americans and whites have both constituted somewhere between 38 and 39 percent with some going back and forth. Latinos were about 16 percent, and other groups about 7 percent, of those receiving AFDC.[24] This translated into 5.3 million whites, 5.5 million African Americans, and 2.2 million Latinos receiving AFDC assistance.

Unlike corporate wealthfare (discussed later), welfare for the poor accounts for a very tiny share of the federal budget.[25] In 1993, for example, AFDC costs were $22 billion, less than 1 percent of the entire federal budget. The states' share of the welfare costs was only about 2 percent of states' budgets.[26] Even when Food Stamps and other welfare programs are included, welfare still constituted less than 3 percent of the budget. In addition, administrative costs for AFDC, around $3 billion annually, have remained fairly constant between 1970 and 1993, and as a percentage of overall AFDC costs, have dropped from 19 percent in 1970 to 13 percent in 1993.[27] In 1993, adding in state costs, AFDC cost $22.3 billion, which accounted for about 0.35 percent of the nation's gross domestic product.[28] These numbers remained consistent throughout the mid-1990s.

Welfare benefits under AFDC were so low that even combined with Food Stamps families fell far below the poverty line. States with higher costs of living tended to pay more; New York, for instance, paid a maximum of $577 per month, a maximum of $6,924 a year. In other states—Mississippi for example—the maximum cash benefit was as low as $120 per month. On average, national annual cash benefits paid totaled about $4,392, only 36 percent of the federal poverty line of $12,320 for a family of three.[29]

The Politics of Welfare Reform

"The AFDC program could use reform, but not in the ways the new reformists suggest. Provide the very poor with access to health care, so they don't have to leave low-paying jobs that don't provide it when their children get sick. Allow recipients to go to school while receiving aid, so they can learn skills that better suit them to the labor market."[30] —Julianne Malveaux

Although President Reagan was famous for his false "Welfare Queen" statement, welfare was not a central issue in either his 1980 or 1984 campaigns nor in the presidential campaign of 1988 between George Bush and Michael Dukakis. The current battle over welfare reform can be traced to President Clinton's 1992 campaign pledge to "end welfare as we know it." In their book *Putting People First,* candidates Clinton and Al Gore wrote, "It's time to honor and reward people who work hard and play by the rules. That means ending welfare as we know it—not by punishing the poor or preaching to them, but by empowering Americans to take care of their children and improve their lives. No one who works full-time and has children at home should be poor anymore. No one who can work should be able to stay on welfare forever."[31]

Clinton propose that federal rules be changed so that able-bodied welfare recipients be required to go to work rather than have the option of not participating.[32] Once in office, Clinton made good on his promise to attempt to reform the welfare system. He established a Working Group on Welfare Reform and continued to raise the issue during his first year in office. Unfortunately for Clinton, the debate would move quickly beyond his office and become one of the most hotly contested issues of modern times. Clinton's Working Group proposed the unsuccessful "Work and Responsibility Act of 1994."

The bill's major provision was to create a two-year time limit on unrestricted cash assistance that would, in effect, restrict most AFDC recipients to a lifetime maximum of 24 months in the program. While this was similar to proposals being advocated by some conservatives, the Clinton administration included numerous exemptions, such as for mothers with disabilities, mothers caring for disabled children, and mothers of infants. Other provisions of Clinton's plan included the creation of a new program known as WORK, different from and in addition to JOBS. WORK would provide subsidized employment opportunities for recipients who were no longer eligible for cash assistance. One important change being proposed was that recipients would be forced to participate in the JOBS program after their child turned one, rather than three as in the current rules. The administration also called for tougher guidelines and penalties regarding collection of support payments from reluctant and absentee fathers.

While the Clinton plan was not as draconian as many conservative proposals, a number of sources criticized it harshly, particularly the WORK provision of the legislation. Critics from the Left charged that the plan seriously underestimated the economic picture that recipients would face and that its funding request was much too low to meet even its own minimum job creation objectives. The Congressional Black Caucus Foundation (CBCF) wrote that welfare recipients need marketable skills, and "will also need the creation of public sector positions, in which they can provide necessary and constructive services to society, in the event they are unable to find a position through traditional means in the private sector."[33] The bottom line, declared the CBCF, was that welfare reform must include "considerable job creation, meaningful job training, and more money."[34]

The Clinton plan died and several other proposals, such as Rep. Robert Matsui's (D–CA) "Family Self-Sufficiency Act of 1994" and Sen. Lauch Faircloth's (R–NC) "Welfare Reform Act of 1994," were introduced. By far, however, the bill that set the tone and tenor of the debate was the Republican's "Personal Responsibility Act of 1995," which grew out of the GOP's "Contract with America." The bill did not merely reform welfare, it destroyed the very principles that guided federal policy toward the poor for six decades.

On August 22, 1996, Clinton signed the Republican welfare bill that ended AFDC and created TANF. Although outrage among liberals and progressives was loud and steadfast, Clinton made an election-year decision that said he would rather throw perhaps more than a million children into deeper poverty than risk losing to Republican candidate Bob Dole on the grounds that he was soft on welfare and had broken one of his most noted 1992 campaign promises.

Draconian and oppressive in several ways, the bill got rid of a 60-year guarantee of commitment to the nation's poor, whether they are children, the elderly, or the disabled.. Welfare is no longer an entitlement from the federal government to the states to provide funding based on need. States now receive fixed block grants that once exhausted, despite the need, will not be replenished. Recipients are also restricted to a lifetime limit of 60 months of receiving TANF. States are also obligated to force a large percentage of recipients into workfare programs under the threat of losing funding. There are many more aspects of the new legislation that punish recipients, deny assistance to legal immigrants, and penalize teenage mothers, among other things. As Clinton sheepishly pledged to "fix" certain aspects of the legislation, he remained loudly quiet as another battle concerning welfare unfolded.

Expanding Wealthfare as We Know It

Corporate welfare—what some have appropriately called "wealthfare"—was virtually untouched by Congress and the White House in their frenzy to cut the "undeserving" poor from the government dole. Perhaps one of the biggest myths perpetrated regarding the U.S. economy is that it is a private system that operates with no assistance from the government. In fact, government handouts to corporations constitute a major source of operating capital for the business community. The Washington, D.C. watchdog group, Essential Information, states, "Federal government estimates on corporate welfare spending for 1994 total $104.3 billion, while spending for social welfare programs on the poor is estimated at only $75.1 billion."[35]

The hypocrisy of railing against welfare for the poor while sanctioning welfare for the rich has drawn even sectors usually supportive of congressional initiatives. The *Washington Post* noted, "The current vogue of welfare reform in Washington is curiously narrow. After all, 'ending welfare as we know it' means cutting off, not only the proverbial unwed mothers, but also those indolent corporations that have grown fat feeding at the public trough.... This year, taxpayers will spend $51 billion in direct subsidies to business and lose another $53.3 billion in tax breaks for corporations, according to the Office of Management and Budget and the Joint Committee on Taxation. Those who want welfare recipients to work as a condition of public assistance should expand their efforts to cover corporations dependent on federal largesse."[36] Getting more specific, the *Washington Post* went on to say, "The most costly form of corporate welfare in 1994 will be subsidies for agribusiness, costing an estimated $29.2 billion. By contrast, the federal government will spend $25 billion on food stamps and $15 billion for Aid to Families With Dependent Children (AFDC), two of the programs most criticized by conservatives in the welfare reform debate. Ignoring the cost of corporate entitlements distorts the welfare debate and leaves most Americans with the false impression that poor people, rather than corporations or middle and upper income individuals, are straining the national budget."[37]

There are numerous additional examples that can be cited. Researchers Mark Zepezauer and Arthur Naiman list dozens of examples of welfare payments through government subsidies to various industries, including nuclear, aviation, mining, agricultural, and timber industries. They estimate that it costs taxpayers at least $448 billion a year in handouts to corporations and wealthy individuals compared to about $130 billion in welfare payments to the poor.[38] Further, they note that their figure for wealthfare leaves off numerous other payments, including state and local tax breaks for corporations.

The egregiousness of corporate welfare benefits has been so great that a coalition of conservatives, liberals, and progressives have joined together to attack the problem—albeit for different and often conflicting reasons. While the Left has argued against the hypocritical cruelty of cutting aid to the poor while throwing billions of dollars at the already rich, the Right, consistent with the slash-and-burn ideology of conservatism, wants to cut taxes and reduce the deficit. The Stop Corporate Welfare coalition, formed in August 1996, includes Republican tax terrorist Rep. John Kasich, chair of the House Budget

Committee and Americans for Tax Reform on the Right; the Cato Institute and the Progressive Policy Institute in the middle; and the Corporate Wealthfare Project, U.S. Public Interest Research Group, and Friends of the Earth. Out of the 12 wealthfare cuts that the coalition could find agreement on, it had victory on one: stopping legislation that would have doubled congressional funding for the Overseas Private Investment Corporation.[39]

In the 105th Congress, the Congressional Progressive Caucus (CPC) proposed H.R. 2534, "The Corporate Responsibility Act." The bill would make $800 billion in cuts in corporate welfare by getting rid of: funds to advertise and promote weapons ($500 million), depreciation ($32 billion), funds to 14 of the largest computer chip companies ($300 million), subsidies to millionaire farmers/ranchers ($40 million), use of federally owned lands by mineral companies ($200 million), advertisements for fast foods internationally ($110 million), and brand-name recognition promotion ($3.6 million). Overall, the CPC targeted 18 programs to be cut.[40]

The duplicity of attacking welfare payments to the poor while turning a blind eye to gifts to the rich raises critical issues regarding priorities and the political symbols used in shaping the welfare debate.[41] The issue of real need is obscured by a narrowing of the discourses about social policy for the poor. As Essential Information argues, "The problem is that corporate welfare has created a culture of dependency that has encouraged certain industries to live off the taxpayers. Year after year, these companies receive subsidies or handouts from the federal government and never learn to fend for themselves. And, unlike the vast majority of poor people who receive public assistance, most corporate welfare recipients are not particularly needy."[42]

Debate within the Black Community

To a significant degree, the debate in the black community has not focused on corporate welfare, the unjust nature of so-called welfare reform, or Clinton's betrayal of the black vote. Instead, much of the discussion has echoed the conservative jeremiads that welfare for the poor creates a culture of dependency. While black conservatives have been silent on the immorality of corporate welfare, they have been unrelenting in their attacks on welfare recipients and liberal black leaders who they view as welfare enablers. They promote a distorted perspective of the ideology of self-help and cultural pathology.

Black conservatives blame poverty and the issues that arise from being poor, such as family breakup, on welfare. Joseph Conti and Brad Stetson, both of the right-wing research group, the David Institute, state, "[W]elfarism contributes to family dissolution and ultimately hurts the people involved....Welfare programs and policies are a classic case of the iatrogenic nature of activist government policy: intending to help, it hurts."[43]

Arguments by black conservatives also tend toward patriarchy and recentering the role of men in the family. Brian Jones, president of the conservative Center for a New Black Leadership, writes, "To the extent that the incentives of the welfare system marginalize or even obviate the role of men as breadwinners and essential components of viable family units, it must be substantially reformed. As long as public policy undermines the economic rationale for marriage, communities will be powerless to confront very real impediments to socioeconomic mobility."[44]

Like their white counterparts, the black conservatives blame welfare for the economic condition of blacks. Black conservative Terry Lovelace notes, "[T]he current welfare state has helped destroy many black families by taking wage-earning fathers out of homes and replacing them with a monthly government check. Black Americans, though just 12 percent of the population, currently make up more than one-third of the entire welfare system in the United States."[45]

The conservative spin on welfare is often in sync with the views of some black nationalists. The plea for a ethos of self-help, long a common bond between black conservatives and black nationalists, means that welfare is seen as anathema to African-American self-determination. Minister Louis Farrakhan, leader of the black nationalist religious group, the Nation of Islam, while careful not to cast aspersions on the poor themselves, stated, "Welfare if you turn it around means farewell. It means bye to the spirit of self-determination. It means so long to the spirit that God gives to every human being and the duty that God gives to every human being to do something for self. It makes you a slave. Welfare, farewell."[46]

Not surprisingly, much of the defense of the rights and dignity of welfare recipients comes from black women scholars and activists. They identify not only the material harm and suffering brought by welfare reform, but also critique the ideological uses of welfare in promoting a white and male supremacist worldview. Scholar Wahneema Lubiano argues, "Read the newspapers, watch television, or simply listen to people talk: among other things, welfare queens are held responsible for the crack trade and crack babies. And they combine that with moral degeneracy within their families....She is [depicted as] the agent of destruction, the creator of the pathological, black, urban, poor family from which all ills flow; a monster creating crack dealers, addicts, muggers, and rapists—men who become those things because of being immersed in her culture of poverty....[Significantly, however,] the attacks on [welfare queens are] exercises of state power by means of invoking racist and sexist stereotypes passing themselves off as social-science-supported policy...."[47]

The particularizing of the attack on black women is not accidental. Black women become the supreme representation of the undeserving underclass in popular culture and imagery, thus doubling the predisposed prejudices that are readily available for the conservative project of eliminating the welfare state. According to historians Barbara Ransby and Tracye Matthews, "Regular attacks on our black women in the media, most often disguised as an attack on the admittedly inadequate welfare system, portray them as lazy, unfit mothers, members of a morally bankrupt underclass, who should be punished for their inability to sustain a middle-class family lifestyle on a sub-poverty income."[48]

Their words are again echoed by Lubiano, who writes, "The most immediately recognizable figure, the welfare queen, is omnipresent in the media—even when (and perhaps especially when) she is not explicitly named. Given a couple of centuries (and, in the corporate and/or mainstream press, an especially intense couple of decades) of seeing and hearing the behaviors and economic position of poor African Americans laid at the door of their 'problematic' family structure and/or culture, given the various ways in which every large urban newspaper and most small-town newspapers remind us of the 'blight' (political, social, and economic) of the cities, and given the ubiquity of political and community figures whose commentary focuses on attributing the 'decline of the nation' to the urban poor and the inappropriateness or inadequacy (take your pick) of state intervention against those problems, the welfare queen is omnipresent in discussions about 'America's' present or future even when unnamed."[49]

As perhaps the nation's most vocal advocates for poor children, the Children's Defense Fund (CDF) has produced numerous reports, fact sheets, briefing books, and other materials pointing out the harms that are likely to be a result of recent welfare reforms. As the CDF wrote in one strategy paper, these reforms "represent a fundamental shift in our nation's commitment to children. The federal government no longer will be the protector of last resort for hungry, disabled, poor, abused, and neglected boys and girls. It will pass the buck to 50 states with over 40 billion fewer dollars. And states are making no promises about how children will be protected."[50]

The Children's Defense Fund has also offered a number of conditions that they argue must be met if real welfare reform, beyond that passed by Clinton and Congress, and more importantly, the effort to end poverty are to be successful. This includes providing employment opportunities, childcare, education and training, job retention, health coverage, child support, family integrity, and work incentives. CDF calls for "substantial new investments" to achieve genuine reform and states that "If we merely impose a rigid new set of requirements on families receiving AFDC without providing more effective assistance to overcome their barriers to employment, we only add to the plight of our nation's poorest and most vulnerable children."[51]

The Joint Center for Political and Economic Studies (JCPES), a leading Washington, D.C.-based African-American think tank, has also weighed in on the debate. Similar to other liberal critiques, JCPES does not defend the welfare system, they note, "The welfare system is broken. Poor people who have to rely on Aid to Families with Dependent Children (AFDC), the program that provides cash assistance to families, know this better than anyone else. The current system does not reward initiative or hard work, and it discourages the formation and stability of two-parent families."[52] JCPES was deeply critical of the changes brought by the Clinton-signed bill. In their proposed agenda for reform, JCPES states that there are some important principles on which reform must be built:

- We must eliminate rules that make it difficult for two-parent families to receive help;

- Federal child support enforcement is the only effective way of ensuring that noncustodial parents who can pay support do so;

- Pro-work reform means encouraging all forms of work, including part-time work;

- Reforms must improve a parent's ability to support children by improving his or her skills and job prospects; and

- Finally, pro-work reforms must include job placement and job creation strategies.

In the aftermath of the 1994 Republican victories in Congress, the CBCF formed a working group of liberal and progressive lobby organizations to respond to the GOP's Contract with America. Among the groups and individuals involved were the Center on Budget and Policy Priorities, the Joint Center for Political and Economic Studies, the Institute for Policy Studies, the Democratic National Committee, congressional staffers, and other political activists. The CBCF's Working Group for a New Agenda for New Times (WGNANT) criticized the Republican Personal Responsibility Act and offered a number of suggestions for what would constitute meaningful welfare reform. Those proposals acknowledged the need to change the system as it existed, but offered to protect those most in need.[53]

The demands raised by the CDF, JCPES, CBCF, and other black groups generally went unheard. In the welfare reform that passed and was signed into law, few of the concerns about maintaining a cushion for the nation's poor were addressed. While lack of consensus was one factor, the overriding reason the black community was screwed was an unwarranted faith in the generosity and virtue of President Clinton rather than an effort to mobilize and organize the poor.[54]

Organizations Fighting Back

Discourses about welfare for the poor by conservatives, liberals, the major media, and academics tend to disregard the self-organization and resistance to marginalization by the poor themselves. This web of social science theorizing facilitates the erasure of the poor from the policy and political debates that have shaped welfare and welfare reform. While some progressive scholars—such as Frances Fox Piven, Richard Cloward, James Jennings, Mimi Abramovitz, Julianne Malveaux, Sanford F. Schram, to name a few—have noted the critical role that a mobilized poor has played in shaping welfare policies, in general, those movements have been whitewashed away, with important political consequences. As historian Robin D. G. Kelley notes, "The end result has been a failure to take into account opposition and human agency on the part of the poor. In particular, most social scientist overlook the role(s) of ideology and consciousness, the formation of oppositional movements among the inner-city poor, various forms of individual and collective resistance."[55] Scholar Marcia Bok sounds a similar concern when she writes that favorable policies for the poor will only come about as a result of "grassroots and mass movements in the United States."[56]

At the national level as well as the local, groups have organized to articulate and struggle for the rights and interests of the poor, involving the poor themselves in membership and leadership roles. The National Welfare Rights Union (a merger of the former National Welfare Rights Organization and several other groups) has perhaps been the most consistent and longest-fighting network of the poor across the nation. Also organizing on the national level are the Children's Defense Fund and Jobs With Peace. Significantly, all of these organizations are led by black women, although men are involved in a wide variety of roles.

Most activism regarding welfare rights, however, logically occurs at the local and state levels. Too often ignored as sites of contestation, the battles that are fought in these venues are much closer to the daily tribulations and struggles that welfare recipients experience. In *Under Attack, Fighting Back,* Mimi Abramovitz identifies a wide array of fight-back groups that have emerged in the 1990s to combat the punitive and ineffective welfare reforms coming from local and state officials as well as from the White House and Capitol Hill.[57] Among groups that she highlights are the Coalition for Basic Human Needs (Boston, MA), Parents for Justice (NH), Welfare Warriors (Milwaukee, WI), Welfare Warriors (Long Island, NY), Empower (Rochester, NY), the Reform Organization of Welfare (St. Louis, MO), Women for Economic Security (Chicago, IL), Women's Union (VT), Arise (Springfield, MA), Justice, Economic Development and Independence for Women (Salt Lake City, UT), and the Women's Economic Agenda (Oakland, CA).[58]

These groups and many more demonstrate the self-actualizing character of the poor and give lie to the popular notion that welfare recipients passively surrender to the assaults launched against them by policymakers. The material demands by these groups and poor individuals themselves for jobs, a living wage, educational opportunities, decent housing and fair rents, and accessible and adequate health care accompany the equally important demands for respect, dignity, and honor.

3

California Scheming

If there is any state in the nation that can be called global, it is California. It is the most racially and ethnically diverse state and is projected to become the first whose population is a majority of color. It is the home of the nation's technological revolution, sparking the global computer links that have transformed labor, pleasure, and social relations. These circumstances provided the political leadership of the state with the opportunity to guide the nation and perhaps the international community in addressing diversity concerns in this age of transition. Yet conservative elected leaders, the major political parties, and even academics have played anything but a progressive role on a number of critical race and ethnic issues.

In the 1990s, California became the font of racial conflict in the United States. From the Rodney King saga to the gestation of gangsta rap to the agonies of the O.J. Simpson adventure to legal fights over immigration to attacks on affirmative action to the struggle over Ebonics, the state has become the epicenter of the grand battle between those who would turn back the clock on racial progress and those who seek innovative and constructive ways to move forward. Therefore, it is useful and perhaps necessary to examine the meanings, myths, and movements concerning how California has waged struggles around immigration, affirmative action, and unequal education. These issues were codified in the campaigns over the passage of Proposition 187 in 1994, and Proposition 209 in 1996, and in response to the position taken by the Oakland Unified School District Board of Education regarding the role of black English vernacular (termed Ebonics) in the education process. All three of these issues generated elite and grassroots movements on the Right and the Left; forced responses from national political leaders, civil rights leaders, members of Congress, and the White House; and captured the attention of the world community.

These issues reflect the economic and political tensions and anxieties that increasingly define this age of transition. The shrunk and shrinking economy of the state—itself a consequence of defense cuts in a post-Cold War, post-Soviet world, and the subsequent loss of manufacturing jobs—shapes the mass response to the growth in immigration to California, the implementation of affirmative action, and the level of funding committed to public education. The fear of more job loss by whites to African Americans and Latinos, has helped to feed a racial backlash that has been exploited by conservatives across the state. From the conservative media to right-wing elected officials, whites are disingenuously told that affirmative action gives jobs to unqualified people of color and women; that Latinos and Asians are illegally entering the state, also taking jobs and state welfare resources; and that the poor, mainly people of color, are living luxuriously on the government dole at taxpayer's expense. While these issues have fed a resurgent, though weakened conservative crusade, they have also launched new multiracial mass movements and coalitions across the breadth and length of the state whose agendas now extend beyond the narrow issues that initially brought them together.

The growth of these movements is of high importance to the progressive movement as a whole since they indicate the resilience of people to resist even in situations where the balance of power is unfavorable. Although both propositions passed and the battleground shifted to the courts, and the controversy over Ebonics was diffused, the issues do not die and their political significance remains. More important, the issues consolidated several cores of activists who have vowed to continue to fight the conservative Right on a whole range of issues. These movements cannot be romanticized, however. They embodied the difficulties inherent in building coalitions with organizations that have conflicting interests and urgencies. Part of the problem is the tendency to reproduce organizational and political forms that reflect old styles of outreach, mass education, and political stances. Protest is a critical though limited form of struggle and is most effective in conjunction with other more sustaining strategies. Coalition forms, in some instances, are not conducive to the multiplicity of methods necessary to engage in contemporary struggles.

The issues raised in California remain at the center of the national political discourse on the nature and direction of race relations in the United States as the 20th century comes to a close. All indications are that, on the issue of race, the 20th century will end in ways very similar to the manner in which the 19th century ended: legitimation of proponents of eugenics; ideological and political campaigns against immigrants; creation of racist paramilitary groups; incessant attacks on the voting rights of African Americans; and growing economic inequality.

These concerns take on a global meaning. First, the issue of immigration necessarily raises international relationships and dynamics. The political and economic causes of immigration have often been obscured in the heat over the impact of immigration. Second, other nations and movements often look to the United States for guidance on resolving many of the racial and ethnic conflicts that they themselves are experiencing. The issues of immigration, affirmative action, and conflicting languages in education have been on the agenda of activists, administrators, and political leaders in England, France, South Africa, Nicaragua, and many other nations that have had to address the integration of marginalized communities into the broader society. Third, the downturns in the California economy are driven by changes in the global economy, the transformed role of the United States in the post-Cold War period, and by investment decisions made by transnational corporations over which state residents and leaders have little or no control.

Race, Class, and Politics in Contemporary California

California is the largest state in the nation. It has a population of nearly 30 million comprised of 58 percent whites, 25 percent Latinos, 10 percent Asians, and 7 percent African Americans. During the Reagan years, the state was one of the most prosperous in the nation due to the financial bonanza its large defense industry received as federal military spending exploded. As defense cuts went into effect in the late 1980s and 1990s, however, the economy took a sharp downturn.

In the new economic order, California has taken hard hits. A devastating recession, runaway shops, and downsizing in the military led to over 800,000 jobs leaving California between July 1, 1991 and July 30, 1992.[1] The end of the Cold War in the late 1980s reconfigured the global military role of the United States. Demands for cuts began to have an impact; some bases were closed, and the war industry was downsized significantly.

No longer the defense industry state, California has become the containment state. The state is building prisons at an alarming rate as it shifts its budget from schools and social programs to prison construction and criminal justice. The San Francisco-based Center on Juvenile and Criminal Justice's report, "From Class Rooms to Cell Blocks: The Effects of Prison Building on Higher Education and African American Enrollment," documents that in 1980–1981, 9.2 percent of California's general fund went to higher education and only 2.3 percent to corrections, but in 1996–97, corrections received 9.4 percent while higher education got only 8.7 percent. As the title of the study indicates, this shift has been particularly harmful to the prospects and opportunities facing African Americans in the state. In 1996, according to the report, California had twice as many African Americans in its prisons (45,000) as in its four-year public universities.[2] Broken down by gender, the study reports that between 1980 and 1995, the number of black men in prison increased more than 500 percent—from 8,139 to 41,434—while the number of black men in public higher education rose only 30 percent, from 8,066 to 10,479. By 2001, the ratio could be 7 to 1 if current trends continue.

The report, critical of the state's political leaders, especially the policies of Republican Governor Pete Wilson, states, "Since 1980, California has made policy and fiscal decisions that increasingly favor locking people up rather than providing them with higher education."[3] The study recommends a freeze on funding for prison construction, placing a cap on the state's prison population, creating more alternatives for nonviolent offenders, passing bond measures to renovate and expand the University of California (UC) and Cal State systems, and instituting aggressive efforts to promote minority enrollment in the state's universities. Finally, the report also notes that tuition increases at UC have far outpaced the growth in median household incomes. This has created a greater hardship on black families because while UC fees consume 35 percent of whites' median household earnings, they consume 57.5 percent of blacks'. Needless to say, Wilson and other officials in his administration have rejected the report.

California residents are going to jail and prison at such a fast rate that thousands are being let out due to overcrowding. It was reported in December 1996 that, for the first six months of that year, "an average 27,500 prisoners per month were released from jails due to overcrowding."[4] The situation is likely to worsen as unemployment increases, because more and more people will be forced to spend time in jail for minor crimes rather than pay even the small fines that they can no longer afford.

It is within this context that the backlash against the perceived advances of African Americans and Latinos have come under attack. Unwilling to focus their resentment on the policymakers and corporate executives in power, the poor, people of color, and women are scapegoated by those who fear further economic insecurity.

Saving "Our State" from Whom and for What

In California, "187" is the criminal justice code for murder. It is a popular term among gangbangers, gangsta rappers, and as it turns out, even state officials. In 1994, Californians voted in favor of Proposition 187, a ballot initiative that proposed cutting funding for public education and social services, including health care, to "illegal" immigrants and their children. The proposal was part of the national assault on immigration by the nation's conservative movement. Implementation of the law was projected to cost $10 billion in the first year.

The proposition was known by the name "Save Our State" (SOS), which raises questions as to what is being saved, who it is being saved for, who it is being saved from, and who is the "our"? For some, the message was an SOS for those who feared an imminent takeover of the state by so-called hordes of Spanish-speaking aliens streaming across the southern border. The 187 debate and immigration, in general, has never been about Canadians or Russians or Sweds coming to take "our" jobs. It was and remains tied to racial conceptions and notions. What is being saved are mythical views of job mobility and opportunities that were, and remain, controlled by financial elites and not poor immigrants.

The contemporary rising controversies over immigration are directly tied to the economic transformations wrought by globalization. In Latin America, Mexico in particular, labor is on the move as international corporations move in and remap the economies of the region. Linked with local financial elites, transnational corporations from Asia, Europe, Canada, and the United States have located operations in the region to take advantage of low wages, limited labor regulations, and governments willing to repress their own workforces.

Only four years after the contentious passage in 1993 of NAFTA, workers in Canada, the United States, and especially Mexico felt the deleterious effects of that legislation. According to the Washington, DC-based watchdog group, Public Citizen, 1,850,000 jobs have been lost in Mexico since NAFTA passed.[5] The percentage of Mexicans considered "extremely poor" grew from 31 percent in 1993 to 50 percent in 1996. The number of pesos to the dollar during this same period went from 3.1 to 1 to 7.88 to 1. While *Public Citizen* magazine noted that Mexico ranks fifth in the number of billionaires per country, 40 million of its 92 million citizens live on less than $5 a day.[6] The surprise is not how many Mexicans attempt to illegally come to the United States each year, but how many do not.

Although large numbers of illegal immigrants come to the United States annually—between 225,000 and 300,000, according to official statistics from the U.S. Census Bureau and the Immigration and Naturalization Service (INS)—these numbers are concentrated in a relatively few states.[7] About 40 percent go to California, 15 percent to New York, 11 percent to Florida, and 10 percent to Texas, states research by the Urban Institute. Illinois, New Jersey, and Arizona account for another 10 percent, while the rest are scattered in insignificant numbers around the country.[8]

Wilson's goals in defending Proposition 187 were completely political and had little to do with addressing the real impact of immigration on the state. Scholar Alejandro Ramos aptly demonstrated how Wilson and his charlatan economic advisers used bogus and faulty statistics to make a case for immigration reform. As Ramos noted, "the governor cites only those studies which conclude that immigrants receive more from the system than what they contribute overall."[9] For example, in estimating the number of undocumented aliens in the state, Wilson used the U.S. Census Bureau's higher unofficial estimate of 1.7 million rather than the more accurate INS estimate of 1.4 million.[10] The state also used studies that underestimated the amount of taxes collected from immigrants, off as much as 30 percent, and overestimated costs incurred by immigrants, according to Ramos. Wilson ignored at least 24 studies that conclude that immigrants are not economic burdens, including ones from the U.S. Department of Labor, U.S. Department of Justice, National Bureau of Economic Research, and the Urban Institute.

According to Proposition 187, schools must verify that every student in the school has legal status. In California, this would require interrogating about 10 million students on an ongoing basis. What this would mean is that students who look or sound "foreign" to a teacher might be subject to harassment on that criteria alone. For example, there are nearly 100,000 Puerto Ricans in the state. Puerto Ricans are U.S. citizens whose legal status is no different than that of any other U.S. citizen. Yet they become immediately suspect simply because they speak Spanish and are brown.[11]

The bill was coauthored by former Sacramento lobbyist Alan Nelson and former Western Regional Chief of the INS Harold Ezell. Nelson was a lobbyist for the Federation for American Immigration Reform (FAIR), one of the key groups fighting for the passage of SOS and pushing repressive immigration reform around the nation. FAIR calls for sealing the U.S. (southern) border. During the campaign, FAIR was exposed as having received more than $600,000, since 1988, from the ultra-conservative Pioneer Fund.[12] The latter is a group that has also sponsored research by various scientists, including the late William B. Shockley, who contended that blacks are inherently intellectually inferior to whites. In the Pioneer Fund's original charter, it called for "reproduction of individuals descended predominantly from white persons who settled in the original 13 states or from related stock." In 1985, in a move so hypocritical as to be laughable, the word "white" was removed.

Black leaders across the state, from Rep. Maxine Waters and then-Speaker of the Assembly Willie Brown to Rep. Ron Dellums and Los Angeles Police Department Chief Willie L. Williams, vehemently opposed the initiative. At the grassroots level, hundreds of black groups across the state spoke out against 187. Marches and demonstrations, some numbering as large as 70,000, and statewide coalitions were organized to defeat 187.

The battle over SOS inspired an historic turnout of Latino voters in the state of California. In 1990, 844,000 Latinos voted; in 1994, more than 1.1 million voted, an increase of 34 percent. Motivated and mobilized in opposition to SOS, 47.5 percent of eligible Latinos turned out to the polls.

Despite the heated opposition, Proposition 187 was approved by a wide margin of voters, 59 to 41 percent.[13] Although whites were the only racial/ethnic group to vote in majority supporting the initiative, it received strong support from every racial and ethnic group except Latinos. Whites supported 187 by a margin of 63 to 37 percent, while it was rejected by blacks (47 to 53 percent), Asians (47 to 53 percent), and Latinos (23 to 77 percent). The strength of black support for 187, as *Oakland Tribune* columnist Brenda Payton noted, was based on a growing economic insecurity that blames Latinos for taking (menial) jobs that were once held by African Americans.[14]

Within days of the vote, the bill was challenged in court and an injunction was imposed on its implementation. Jan Adams, writing in *Racefile,* summed up the Proposition 187 battle. Adams argued that 187 "so perfectly appealed to the racial anxieties of voting Californians that it is impossible to imagine an electoral strategy that could have defeated it."[15]

Proposition 209: Affirmative Reaction

"A society that has something special against the Negro for hundreds of years must now do something special for the Negro."[16] —Martin Luther King, Jr.

Two years after the passage of Proposition 187, voters in the state passed Proposition 209, known as the California Civil Rights Initiative (CCRI). Just as conservatives have done on other issues, their dishonest use of the term "civil rights" obscured that, in fact, the ballot initiative had the very opposite intent. CCRI's goal was simple: the complete elimination of state affirmative action programs in all applications. Affirmative action has served as a necessary though limited remedy to ongoing racial and gender inequities in U.S. society. The proposition prohibits any state government agency from implementing affirmative action programs, ends all minority or women set-aside programs, and ends all minority- or women-designated scholarships.

The attacks on affirmative action have escalated in this era. Pressures flowing from a more insecure global and national employment environment have fed the racially constructed myth that whites, especially white males, are losing jobs and educational opportunities due to government-ordered affirmative action programs that benefit women, African Americans, and Latinos.

The first blow in the campaign to rid the state of responsibility for affirmative action occurred on July 20, 1996 when the UC Board of Regents voted to end affirmative action in the UC system in admissions, faculty hiring, and business contracts. Protests by students, national civil rights leaders such as Jesse Jackson, and other supporters were to no avail, despite data demonstrating that a decline in black and Latino entrance into the system would occur. In February 1997, UC officials reported that, in fact, applications from African Americans and Latinos had declined. This decline occurred while the UC system was receiving a record number of applications (46,682) from California's high school seniors for the school year beginning in fall 1997 and as the number of black and Latino seniors in California also grew. At the same time, applications from out of state rose by 28.4 percent. Although the affirmative action decision would not take effect until the 1998 school year, some UC officials and others felt that a message had been sent to black and Latino students that they simply were not wanted.[17]

Leading the battle to end affirmative action in the UC system, and later the CCRI campaign, was Board of Regents member Ward Connerly, who is African American. Connerly, who achieved financial and career success through his years of friendship with Wilson, was used by a Republican and conservative cause that desperately needed a black face to be at the forefront of the attack on affirmative action. Like other black conservatives mainly sponsored by white conservatives, Connerly relished his puppet role in what used to be called the "Head Negro in Charge."

He mouthed the usual conservative babble about how African Americans "have become addicted" to government aid and affirmative action. He stated with no qualification, "I sense this yearning among white people just to really become color blind. They want black people to assimilate. And black people are fighting it with every fiber of their being."[18]

Connerly led the opposition to affirmative action on UC campuses, except when it came to himself and his friends. His company benefited through its designation as a minority-owned firm and, on at least one occasion, he intervened affirmatively on behalf of a community college student he knew with a mediocre 2.6 grade point average who was seeking admission to the state's premier public campus, UC Berkeley. Connerly pressed another regent to help that unqualified applicant get in, while thousands of better applicants were rejected.

Connerly's wishful notions about whites' sense of yearning has no basis. The fact that he and other affirmative action opponents deny is that broad race and gender inequities continue to exist. White males, who are 33 percent of the population, are:

- 88 percent of all tenured professors;
- 85 percent of partners in law firms;
- 95 percent of *Fortune 500* CEOs;
- 97 percent of school superintendents; and
- 99 percent of professional athletic team owners

What was the truth about affirmative action in California? Affirmative action in education was crucial in improving Latino access to the UC system. In 1980, Latinos comprised only 6 percent of the student body, but as a result of affirmative action that number had doubled to 12 percent by 1994. Over 35 percent of the state's college-age population, 18–24, is Latino. Even with affirmative action, black state workers in California still earn only 84 percent of what their white counterparts do. Latino workers earn even less. In 1995, according to the California Senate Office of Research, "White employees earn a median \$40,313; black employees \$33,774, and Latino employees \$32,978."[19]

Studies have also found that women and people of color hired under affirmative action programs tend to be more than qualified rather than less, as affirmative action opponents charge. A study by two Michigan State University economists, Harry Holzner and David Neumark, found that those minorities and women who were hired, at least in part due to affirmative action, performed as well as or better than white men in comparable positions. The study examined employers in Atlanta, Boston, Detroit, and Los Angeles, and found, contrary to widespread opinion, that "African American women generally outperformed white males on the job according to job evaluations filled out by their supervisors."[20]

As in the case of Proposition 187, a number of statewide organizations were formed to fight CCRI. One of the largest was Californians for Justice, a grassroots political movement founded in May 1995 by the Center for Third World Organizing (Oakland), Coalition for Immigrant Rights (San Francisco), and Agenda (Los Angeles).[21]

In terms of coalitions, the largest was the Campaign to Defeat 209, which involved hundreds of groups around the state. Differences over strategies between some of the feminist and civil rights organizations within the group led to a split a month or so before the vote and a new group was formed called STOP Prop. 209, which included the state chapter of the National Organization for Women, the Feminist Majority, and the Rainbow Coalition. Since the split was not driven by race or gender issues, some women and civil rights organizations, such as the NAACP Legal Defense Fund and the San Francisco-based Lawyers Committee for Civil Rights, stayed with the main group. While the Campaign to Defeat 209 tended to focus on media ads and building a statewide operation of speakers and surrogates, STOP Prop. 209 organized large protest events and grassroots mobilizations. As the groups noted, the differences actually complemented rather than opposed each other, and the two worked together throughout the campaign. Media buys were coordinated.[22]

At the same time, the inability of progressive and liberal activists to hold together the original coalition reflected real tensions over strategies, goals, and perhaps ideologies. Proposition 209 passed by a vote of 54 to 46 percent. It was overwhelmingly supported by whites (63 to 37 percent) and men (61 to 39 percent). Conversely, other racial and ethnic groups solidly rejected the proposition, such as African Americans (26 to 74 percent), Latinos (24 to 76 percent), and Asians (39 to 61 percent). Somewhat surprisingly, only slightly more women voted against it than for it (48 to 52 percent). In terms of age groups, the older the voter, the more likely they were to support 209. Those 18–29 split their vote (50 to 50 percent), while those 30–44 (51 to 49 percent), 45–64 (58 to 42 percent), and 65 and older (60 to 40 percent) voted for the proposition.[23]

In terms of class, income level and level of education did not correlate. Lower- and moderate-income individuals making less than $40,000 rejected 209 (45 to 55 percent), while those making above $40,000 strongly supported it (60 to 40 percent). On the other hand, except at the lower end, the higher the level of education, the less support 209 received. Those with some college did support 209 (60 to 40 percent) and, to a lesser extent, so did those with a college degree or more (54 to 46 percent). Those with a postgraduate degree, however, rebuked 209 (48 to 52 percent), as did those voters with a high school degree or less (54 to 46 percent).[24]

Studies and polls demonstrate that the rejection of affirmative action in California reflects a national trend. According U.S. News and World Report, 51 percent of whites agreed with the statement, "Equal rights have been pushed too far."[25] This was the first time ever that a majority has done so. In a poll of 248,000 teenagers, 90 percent opposed affirmative action in hiring and college admissions.[26] Much of the opposition to affirmative action is based on the false notion of "reverse discrimination." A 1992 study by People for the American Way found that young, white Americans felt more oppressed by reverse racism than had sympathy for racial bias.[27] The reality, however, is that so-called reverse discrimination carries virtually no legal or evidentiary weight. The U.S. Labor Department found that out of more than 3,000 discrimination cases between 1990 and 1994, less than 100 were about reverse discrimination and only 6 of those were decided in favor of the plaintiff. Rebecca Gordon of Californians for Justice stated, "Affirmative action is not quotas or remedies for past discrimination. It's narrowly tailored conservative remedies for current discrimination."[28]

In the final days of the campaign, President Clinton publicly joined the fray. According to White House Press Secretary Mike McCurry, the president believes that affirmative action must "remain available as a tool to address persistent discrimination in our society."[29] Other state politicians came out against 209, including U.S. Senators Dianne Feinstein and Barbara Boxer.

In April 1997, a three-judge panel of the 9th U.S. Circuit Court unanimously lifted the injunction on 209 that opponents had won in the days following the vote. That injunction had been imposed on December 23, 1996 by U.S. Chief District Judge Thelton Henderson, who is black and had been appointed by President Jimmy Carter. The three conservative judges who overturned Henderson's ruling—Diarmuid F. O'Scannlain, Edward Leavy, and Andrew J. Kleinfield—were all appointed by either President Reagan (the first two) or President Bush (the latter). Movements to end affirmation action are gathering steam in Arizona, Colorado, Florida, Ohio, Michigan, and Washington State.

Conclusion

Very few people are California dreaming these days. The state that should be a beacon of diversity and racial progress has been led by reactionary politicians concerned with their own ambitions and willing to stifle and obstruct opportunities under the guise of color blindness. They were able to exploit a populace predisposed to think in racist frameworks about social policy and economic opportunity.

The recent experiences in California also demonstrate that people of color are not immune to backsliding on issues that become racialized and polarized. African Americans who supported attacks on immigrants because they bought into constructed tales of job thievery, or Hispanics and Asians who opposed affirmative action because of the black mask placed on it, underscored the necessity of an honest dialogue on race that is inclusive of all.

Finally, California's integration into the national and global economy means that the intersection of race, economics, and politics must be understood beyond its local roots and ramifications. Its coastal location, size, and demographics make it a bellwether of social relations in an era of globalization. Perhaps no other state, with the exception of New York, will have the influx of immigrants of all backgrounds and have to rapidly make the economic, political, and cultural adjustments and transformations that will need to occur. An eye on California is an eye on the future, a future that is quickly and inexorably approaching.

4

To Be or Not to Be?: Race, Class, and Ebonics

"It is not the black child's language that is despised. It is his experience. A child cannot be taught by anyone who despises him, and a child cannot afford to be fooled. A child cannot be taught by anyone whose demand, essentially, is that the child repudiate his experience, and all that gives him sustenance, and enter a limbo in which he will no longer be black and in which he knows that he can never become white. Black people have lost too many children that way." [1] —James Baldwin

In the movie *Airplane*, two well-dressed black men are on a plane. Whenever they talk, in what appears to be a foreign language, subtitles are displayed below for the audience. In fact, they are actually speaking what is called in the movie "jive," that is, a mixture of black dialect and black ghetto slang. What this scene signals, *inter alia*, is the recognition that even in popular culture, class notwithstanding black folks and white folks do not talk alike.

Language is about power. It is about national power. It is about class power. It is also about racial and ethnic power. In South Africa, in the mid-1970s, Apartheid was brought to its knees in the resistance by black South African youth to the imposition of the Afrikaner language in the school system. In Canada, the country verged on civil war as French-speaking Canadians fought the domination of English and the English-speaking majority. Across the globe, the ability to determine and designate the position of language(s) in society reflects broader power systems that embody class, race, ethnic, and nationality issues.

This chapter argues several points generated by the concerns and controversy over Ebonics. The first point is that the fight over Ebonics is about more than just a particular educational practice. It is a manifestation of a broader struggle reflecting political and racial consciousness and the effort to promote and protect African-American cultural autonomy. The second point is the link between Ebonics and the conservative political backlash of the current period. The attack on Ebonics is part of an agenda of reaction that must be challenged and exposed. Finally, this chapter briefly examines the English globalization project that embraces the material and ideological interests of capital. Unfortunately, the response by many black leaders to the Ebonics discourse ignored these critical intersections and, in some cases, fed into the most negative dynamics of the debate.

Black English and Black Power

The 1960s witnessed the emergence of a black consciousness cultural movement that penetrated every facet of U.S. cultural life, including language. Black Power adherents, with vast support from the black community, challenged the imposition of standard English and the notion that black English vernacular (BEV) was inferior. While black linguists demonstrated the technical language qualities of BEV and traced its history to African speech patterns, Black Power nationalists fought the political battle of having black English, as William Van Deburg notes, "recognized as the lingua franca of the black nation."[2] BEV was viewed as part of the counter-oppositional culture of African Americans. At the same time, black student activists fought to have African languages—such as Swahili, Yoruba, and Hausa—accepted as legitimate for the language requirements that most colleges and universities demand.

This political struggle, unlike many of the period, had a mass character to it because broad swatches of the black community were affected by its outcome. The legitimizing of the culture of the black masses, the verification of their humanity and dignity, helped build the political mobilization necessary to win policy and political battles concerning education inequity. For those middle-class African Americans who had become bilingual in standard English and BEV, this struggle bridged, to some degree, the class cleavages that were growing in the black community during this period. The social dismissal of BEV was read by race-conscious, middle-class African Americans as the erasure of a critical part of their history, cultural ties, and indeed, even family connections. Working-class African Americans gained as the black English battle was merged into the black education reform movement that initiated black history courses and black studies, but more importantly, placed the issue of relevance at the center of the discourse regarding schooling.

In the end, while BEV was never officially recognized by most whites or policymakers as a full-blown language, activists were able to win an ideological point that language is neither a neutral political site nor unrelated to policy decisions.[3] As many African Americans rose to become members of school boards and elected officials, the issue of equal educational funding and the controversy over BEV was never far from the surface or the field of battle. Partly in reaction to the BEV movement as well as the growth of similar challenges from other language minorities, a conservative reaction sprouted under the banner of English-only. Given the historical and racial heritage at the base of it, English-only had and has a double meaning.

English-only, Por Favor

The English-only movement in the United States is generally defended by its proponents as simply concerned with practicality and preserving a cultural heritage. This rationalization, however, dissolves in the face of the fact that a single-language society has never been the heritage or history of the United States. Even among European descendants, one language has never been the rule. Many of the nation's founding documents, such as the Articles of Confederation, were printed in German and English, and multilingual education has always existed. From the beginning of the nation, the languages of Native Americans and Africans have always been present even as they have integrated, developed, and remapped the English language itself. According to the U.S. Census Bureau, in the 1990s, more than 300 first or second languages are spoken in the nation, reflecting the international character and diversity of contemporary society. According to the National Education Association (NEA), more than 185 languages are spoken in New York City schools, 187 languages are heard in schools in Fairfax County, VA, and in just one school in Los Angeles, at least 60 languages are spoken in the homes of the schoolchildren.

The attacks on non-English or nonstandard English speakers are part of the larger conservative agenda that seeks a homogenized (read: whitened) U.S. society and has an intolerance for diversity. Quite often the politics of the English-only movement are explicitly racist, the anti-Hispanic rhetoric is overt, and many of the groups in the movement are directly linked to right-wing, anti-immigration organizations. English First, one of the major English-only groups, is part of the ultra-conservative Committee to Preserve the Family, which created the U.S. Border Control that aims to stop what it defines as "illegal" Mexican border crossings. U.S. English, another English-only group, is organizationally linked with the Federation for American Immigration Reform, whose major focus is passing (more) restrictive immigration laws.

The battle to promote English-only has also taken place at the policy level as conservatives have attempted to legislate a struggle that is being lost in the streets and homes of the nation. They desire a constitutional amendment that would make English the official language of the United States, strengthening their case that educational institutions only be conducted in English. This would further stigmatize those U.S. born who do not speak so-called standard English as well as immigrants from non-English speaking nations. In 1981, the English Language Amendment was first introduced in Congress and has been a pet project of several of the most conservative Congressmembers. Although it has never been voted on, it stands as a token of the possibility of English hegemony over the nation. Since a Constitutional amendment is being sought, it requires approval by two-thirds of the members of the U.S. House of Representatives and the U.S. Senate, and must then be ratified by three-fourths of the states (38). There have been other English-only bills as well, which have also not gotten very far.

Clearly, much of the resistance to passing the legislation comes from the fact that Congress is a diverse body (though not enough) of Congressmembers from a wide range of ethnic and racial backgrounds and heritages. This includes Asian, African-American, Caribbean, European, and Latin American ancestry.

At the state level, the English-only movement has had more success. In those states where language minorities have fewer political resources to bring to the fight, a number of laws have passed—although in some instances, they have later been overturned. According to the NEA, states that have instituted such legislation include Alabama, Arizona (the law was ruled unconstitutional in 1995), Arkansas, California, Colorado, Florida, Georgia, Hawaii (a bilingual state), Illinois (the law was repealed in 1991), Indiana, Kentucky, Mississippi, Montana, Nebraska, New Hampshire, North Carolina, North Dakota, South Carolina, South Dakota, Tennessee, and Virginia.

In some states, the laws prohibit state and local governments from providing bilingual services to residents even if those residents have limited proficiency in English. While some states have passed laws that prevent legislatures from ignoring "the role of English," other states maintain that English is the official state language. The ideology of English-only, of course, is incompatible with the politics of an assertive black English promotion.

The Struggle over Black English

The battle over the role of black English in education is not separate from the politics of the discourse regarding the English-only movement. As often happens in the United States, the political discourse on race obscures underlying issues of class, national power, and other systems of oppression. Nowhere has this been so clear as in the historic debates over the educational role that nonstandard black English or BEV plays.[4] In 1996, this battle (re)surfaced due to the decision made by the Oakland Unified School District (OUSD) Board of Education to radically address the issue of how the school system was responding to the language and educational needs of poor black schoolchildren.

On December 18, 1996, following the recommendations of the Task Force on the Education of African American Students, the board voted unanimously to use whatever instructional strategies, were appropriate to raise the level of English proficiency among all students in the system, but particularly the students who spoke, at least in part, BEV or what has been termed "Ebonics," a fusion of the words "ebony" and "phonics."[4] Ebonics is *not* a teaching method, as some have mistakenly thought, but the descriptive term used to identify distinct black speech styles. The task force had been created by the OUSD board and had met and researched the issue for six months. Based on the task force's report, the board passed a resolution approving the systemwide teaching of black English speaking styles to teachers and concerned parents as a means of helping Ebonics speakers learn standard English. Helping teachers recognize the language structure of Ebonics, it was argued, would better prepare them to help students bridge between Ebonics and standard English.

For example, Ebonics speakers, similar to many Asian or French speakers, attempt to approximate some English sounds that are not natural to their language structure. The "th" sound, which does not exist in most African languages or with Ebonics speakers, is usually replaced with a "d," resulting in "dem" instead of "them" or "dey" instead of "they." These substitutions, and other well-documented linguistic differences, should not be demonized, but rather, the understanding of their operations should serve as a learning tool by which the transition to standard English occurs. It means conceptualizing the distinct way in which tenses are grasped by different languages, such that the Ebonics speaker use of "be" as a verb—as in "he be coming over."—is what linguists term an "aspectual" system. This system is found in parts of the Caribbean and elsewhere.

The Ebonics controversy highlights the disconnection that has grown regarding society's concern about the quality of education for the inner cities, and black inner cities in particular—a popular though misinformed equation. Long before the controversy, programs to teach black English to teachers already existed. These "bridge" programs were in several cities in Texas, Michigan, and even parts of California. Oakland had programs to teach black English to teachers in 26 of its schools; Los Angeles had programs in 31 schools.[6] These efforts were part of initiatives by black education activists and scholars—including voucher programs, all-black-male schools, Afrocentric curriculum, school decentralization, and military-style academies—to raise the educational level of black children in an era when social abandonment was the norm.

The search for alternative methods to help Oakland's black students achieve more was driven by the abysmal educational crisis that the children were facing. While black students constitute 53 percent of the Oakland school district, they make up the overwhelming proportions of those in special education (71 percent), suffering suspensions (80 percent), accused of truancy (67 percent), and those held back a grade (64 percent). Almost 20 percent of black 12th graders did not graduate. Most dramatically, in a system where 4.0 is the highest grade point average that can be obtained, black students averaged a dreadful and unacceptable rate of 1.8.

The decision to teach black English to teachers ignited a firestorm of opinions and dissentions from both black and white racial spokespeople. Clearly, part of the response was to the term Ebonics, a word most had never heard, but which was suddenly and ubiquitously popping up on the news and in headlines in every major newspaper. It is likely that many, black and nonblack, thought it was some new black cultural agent, like rap music or dreadlocks, that was being imposed on an unsuspecting white populace.

Politically, although not a single penny had been officially or unofficially requested, the Clinton administration issued a preemptive rejection from the Department of Education stating that it had no intention of classifying Ebonics as a foreign language and no federal funding would be released for any program having to do with it. In fact, the OUSD did not seek new funds, but new ways to use the funding already available. It should be emphasized, however, that the demand for more funding is quite legitimate.

It was clear that many of the people who were criticizing the decision had displayed little concern for Oakland's black children before December 1996. The response to Ebonics is more insightful in assessing the nexus of race and class than any of the facile and misinformed critiques of the approach. An outcry bordering on hysteria mounted as news of the board's decision spread. Black and white commentators condemned the decision. Black opponents went across the political spectrum from the Right to the Left including conservatives and moderates such as Shelby Steele, Clarence Page, and Ward Connerly, to liberals, nationalists, and progressives such as Kweisi Mfume, Jesse Jackson, and Maya Angelou. Journalist Carl T. Rowan wrote, "Telling troubled youngsters that a slang called 'black English' (dressed up as 'Ebonics') is good enough for them is the foulest of 'gifts' this holiday season. It is guaranteeing failure for all youngsters who swallow this cop-out from hard work and study."[7] Political activist Rev. Al Sharpton, who was contemplating a run for New York's mayor's seat, stated, "If I'm elected mayor, my inaugural address will not be delivered in broken black English. It will be clear."[8]

Civil rights leader Rev. Jackson initially opposed the Oakland decision. He stated, "I understand the attempt to reach out to these children, but this is an unacceptable surrender borderlining on disgrace....It's teaching down to our children and it must never happen."[9] Soon after, Jackson went to Oakland and talked with the board (amidst dozens of cameras). After the meeting, Jackson appeared to everyone to change his position and he stated that the board had been misunderstood. He did not say that he was the one who had done the misunderstanding. He also did not support the teaching plan, saying only, "I endorse the intent to make our children proficient in standard American English."[10] Jackson said later, in Jesse-speak, that regarding Ebonics, teachers needed to "detect, redirect, and correct."[11] After an endless round of reports about how Jackson had retreated, he found it necessary to point out in his newsletter that "Reverend Jackson did *not* change his position on Ebonics; rather, the Oakland School Board refined their initial position at which point they reached common ground."[12]

Maya Angelou, who has built a career on her use of Ebonics in her novels and poems, claims that she was "incensed" by the decision and that "The very idea that the African American language is a language separate and apart is very threatening, because it can encourage young men and women not to learn standard English."[13] Angelou's logic is faulty here in that her first premise (Why is the idea of a distinct black language threatening and who is it threatening to?) does not lead to her second (Where has it been shown that speaking Spanish or French discourages learning standard English?). This is reminiscent of her logic in supporting Clarence Thomas during his 1991 Supreme Court nomination battle, when she reasoned that his being black would ultimately lead him to reject his conservative anti-black views. There, too, she drew a conclusion devoid of evidence and wisdom.

Though given little press, some experts supported the Oakland decision. For many in the media, it was more newsworthy to discuss the controversial nature of the decision and the conflict surrounding it than its merits. No less than the Linguistic Society of America declared their endorsement of the proposal to use Ebonics as a teaching tool. In January 1997, the Chicago-based organization passed a resolution that said, in part:

> The variety known as 'Ebonics,' 'African American Vernacular English' (AAVE), and 'Vernacular Black English' and by other names is systematic and rule-governed like all natural speech varieties....Characterizations of Ebonics as 'slang,' 'mutant,' 'lazy,' 'defective,' 'ungrammatical,' or 'broken English' are incorrect and demeaning....There is evidence from Sweden, the US, and other countries that speakers of other varieties can be aided in their learning of the standard variety by pedagogical approaches which recognize the legitimacy of the other varieties of a language. From this perspective, the Oakland School Board's decision to recognize the vernacular of African American students in teaching them Standard English is linguistically and pedagogically sound.[14]

In response to the storm of criticism, the board initially made a tactical retreat and revised the resolution considerably. For example, the sentence that originally read, "Whereas, these studies have also demonstrated that African Language Systems are genetically based and not a dialect of English," was changed to, "Whereas, these studies have also demonstrated that African Language Systems have origins in West (African) and Niger-Congo languages and are not merely dialects of English."[15]

The resolution was also changed to make it clear that Ebonics was not being taught to students. The original language stated, "The Superintendent...shall immediately devise and implement the best possible academic program for imparting instructions to African-American students in their primary language for the combined purposes of maintaining the legitimacy and richness of such language." The revised sentence read, "The Superintendent...shall immediately devise and implement the best possible academic program for the combined purposes of facilitating the acquisition and mastery of English language skills, while respecting and embracing the legitimacy and richness of the language patterns."[16]

Another passage was changed for the same reason. It went from "Whereas, the standardized tests and grade scores...will be remedied by application of a program featuring African Language Systems principles instructing African American children both in their primary language and in English," to, "Whereas, the standardized tests and grade scores...will be remedied by application of a program featuring African Language Systems principles to move students from the language patterns they bring to school to English proficiency."[17] By late spring 1997, the board issued a final report in which the term Ebonics was completely exercised.

In the flurry to reject and rebuke the Oakland decision, the critical issue of the consequences of young black students speaking nonstandard English and the impact that will have on their educational, academic, and work careers was lost. The most salient issue concerning the controversy is not just that the black students who most strongly and consistently speak nonstandard English are black, but that they are disproportionately, perhaps overwhelmingly, poor and lower-income working class. It is their continuing and expanding social and economic isolation that is determinant of the language skills they do or do not possess.

The motivation to learn standard English by non-English speakers is premised on the assumption of upward economic and social mobility. In other words, there is a belief that learning standard English will lead to a better life. Nonstandard English is promoted more as an issue of personal responsibility than the consequences of a history of social and economic isolation and abandonment. The issue is not whether black youth can learn standard English (or for that matter, computer programming, physics, or accounting), but whether the resources and opportunities will exist or be made available to facilitate such learning in a meaningful way. This question, of course, is broader than the black community and goes to the heart of the poverty issue in the United States.

On a cultural level, few raised the question of whether the promotion of a "standard English" is in itself a racist presumption. Built on the debatable notion that such a standard holds merit or could even functionally exist without the authority of social power over "others," the rule of English seeks to lighten those who speak the standard while it darkens those, including even nonstandard English-speaking whites from the South or Appalachia, who do not. The English standard is also typically American chauvinism. As the joke goes, those who speak three languages are called trilingual, those who speak two are called bilingual, and those who speak only one are called Americans. It is not only black English that is looked down on, but Spanish, Farsi, Japanese, and other languages spoken by millions of U.S. citizens. English itself, of course, is a hybrid constantly reforming as words and terms from dozens of other languages and dialects, including the lexicon of black English speakers, become popularized and internalized into the language.

An alternative to this language imperialism is the English Plus program advocated by the NEA, which values the extension and growth of English as it encounters an increasingly multilingual world. The NEA argues that many in the United States "speak native languages other than English" and that these linguistic resources should be conserved and developed; that the United States was "founded on a commitment to democratic principles and diversity"; that "multilingualism is a tremendous resource and helps in American competitiveness and diplomatic efforts"; that "multilingualism has helped national security including the use of Native American languages in the development of codes during World War II, the Korean War, and the Vietnam War"; and that "there is no threat to the status of English in the United States since it is spoken by 94 percent of U.S. residents."

On July 13, 1995, Rep. Jose Serrano (D–NY) introduced the "English Plus Resolution" into Congress. The resolution read:

> Whereas English is the primary language of the United States, and all members of the society recognize the importance of English to national life and individual accomplishment;

> Whereas many residents of the United States speak native languages other than English, including many languages indigenous to this country, and these linguistic resources should be conserved and developed;

> Whereas this Nation was founded on a commitment to democratic principles, and not on racial, ethnic, or religious homoge-

neity, and has drawn strength from a diversity of languages and cultures and from a respect for individual liberties;

Whereas multilingualism, or the ability to speak languages in addition to English, is a tremendous resource to the United States because such ability enhances American competitiveness in global markets by permitting improved communication and cross-cultural understanding between producers and suppliers, vendors and clients, retailers and consumers;

Whereas multilingualism improves United States diplomatic efforts by fostering enhanced communication and greater understanding between nations;

Whereas multilingualism has historically been an essential element of national security, including the use of Native American languages in the development of coded communications during World War II, the Korean War, and the Vietnam War;

Whereas multilingualism promotes greater cross-cultural understanding between different racial and ethnic groups in the United States;

Whereas there is no threat to the status of English in the United States, a language that is spoken by 94 percent of United States residents, according to the 1990 United States Census, and there is no need to designate any official United States language or to adopt similar restrictionist legislation;

Whereas ''English-only'' measures, or proposals to designate English as the sole official language of the United States, would violate traditions of cultural pluralism, divide communities along ethnic lines, jeopardize the provision of law enforcement, public health, education, and other vital services to those whose English is limited, impair government efficiency, and undercut the national interest by hindering language skills needed to enhance international competitiveness and conduct diplomacy; and

Whereas such "English-only" measures would represent an unwarranted Federal regulation of self-expression, abrogate constitutional rights to freedom of expression and equal protection of the laws, violate international human rights treaties to which the United States is a signatory, and contradict the spirit of the 1923 Supreme Court case Meyer v. Nebraska, wherein the Court declared that "The protection of the Constitution extends to all; to those who speak other languages as well as to those born with English on the tongue."

Now, therefore, be it Resolved by the House of Representatives (the Senate concurring), That the United States Government should pursue policies that

- encourage all residents of this country to become fully proficient in English by expanding educational opportunities;

- conserve and develop the Nation's linguistic resources by encouraging all residents of this country to learn or maintain skills in a language other than English;

- assist Native Americans, Native Alaskans, Native Hawaiians, and other peoples indigenous to the United States, in their efforts to prevent the extinction of their languages and cultures;

- continue to provide services in languages other than English as needed to facilitate access to essential functions of government, promote public health and safety, ensure due process, promote equal educational opportunity, and protect fundamental rights; and

- recognize the importance of multilingualism to vital American interests and individual rights, and oppose "English-only" measures and similar language restrictionist measures.

English around the Globe

More than ever, English has gone global. The power of U.S. cultural and media industries reaches every corner of the earth and it does so in one language: English. Whether it is CNN broadcasting the news to hotel lobbies in Zimbabwe, Panama, or Toyko, or Madonna bellowing popular songs on radios and walkmans in China, Israel, or Chile, or the NBA promoting Michael Jordan or Shaquille O'Neal in South Africa, England, or Spain, English remains the language of first choice.

Perhaps the globalization of English is nowhere more pervasive than on the Internet. Dominated by U.S. corporations and users, the international connections that are touted as bringing the world together in cyberspace are not as multilingual as one would hope. Although the challenge to the English-dominated Net will grow, the increasing concentration of ownership indicates that democratizing the Net's language will not be easy. Countries, such as France and China, have already attempted to institute guidelines that would contain the hegemony of English, but these acts of defiance are having little impact on the overall growth of English as the language of choice and necessity.

Mitigating English globalization is the ever-changing character of the language. In the United States, England, Canada, and other English-speaking nations, the growing multicultural nature of those societies, and the political and cultural movements embodied in them, infuses English with new dimensions and influences. The struggle for democracy includes language rights and respect for linguistic diversity.

Finally, in terms of the United States, English as spoken by the whitest of whites embodies a fusion of words from all over the world, including Africa. According to PBS's Robert MacNeil, that most American of words, "okay," actually comes from the West African word "wakey."[18] So as we listen to the debates around Ebonics and English-only, first and last, it is instructive to remember the words of James Baldwin, who wrote, "Now, I do not know what white Americans would sound like if there had never been any black people in the United States, but they would not sound the way they sound."[19]

5

O.J. and the Symbolic Uses of Racial Exceptions

In spring 1996, fulfilling my civic duty and unable to come up with an acceptable excuse, I found myself on jury duty in Washington, D.C. On the surface, it appeared to be a rather straightforward case. A middle-aged, homeless black man had been arrested (and held in jail for several months) for the illegal possession of a rifle. According to the prosecution, a motorcycle cop had asked him to stop loitering in front of a liquor store. As the man was moving away, he began to take a large green trash can with him. The cop stated in court that, at that point, a woman came up to him and told him that the man had a weapon inside the trash can. The officer stopped the man, looked inside the can and saw a rifle, and then arrested him.

As the testimony portion of the trial began, however, this story started to unravel fairly quickly. First, because of budget cuts in the District of Columbus, the Crime Scene Unit was unavailable to come out and gather evidence, being reserved for more serious crimes such as murder and rape. Also, somehow there were no fingerprints taken off the gun. Second, the arresting officer, who had a striking resemblance to the infamous Mark Fuhrman, had not bothered to get the name of the alleged woman who told him that there was a gun in the trash can. Therefore, nothing that she theoretically told him was admissible since it was unverifiable hearsay. Third, a second officer who arrived to take the homeless man to jail failed to identify him while on the witness stand. Instead, he identified the man's lawyer as the guilty party. While the defendant was fiftyish, balding, and dark-skinned, his lawyer was tall, with a full head of hair, and fair-skinned. To the amusement of the jury and judge, the lawyer stood up to announce that he had an alibi for the time of the crime.

The jury consisted of 11 African Americans and one white. When we retired to the jury room to deliberate, there was an atmosphere of "this will soon be over." We decided to take a quick vote on the charges to see where we stood. Everyone wrote down their verdict and passed them to the jury forewoman. As she began to read the slips of paper, it became obvious where the sentiment lay. She read out loud, "Juror number one, not guilty; juror number two, not guilty; juror number three, not guilty;" and so on. That is until she got to juror slip number 12, she read, "Juror number 12;" hesitated for a second, and then said, "guilty."

In complete unison, everyone turned and looked at the one white male juror. He stated sheepishly that he was the guilty party, so to speak. There was an excruciatingly loud silence at that point. Without prodding, the white man stated that perhaps he could see his way clear to reverse his position. In short fashion, a unanimous verdict was reached and we all went home. Race and the U.S. justice system maintained their rocky marriage for at least one more day.

The O.J. Spiral

For most people in the United States and around the globe these days, when they hear the words "O.J.," they are not thinking of orange juice. Since the horrific murders of his wife, Nicole Brown Simpson, and her friend, Ronald Goldman, the trials (in both senses of the word) of ex-football legend, corporate shill, and sometimes actor Orenthal James "O.J." Simpson have never been far from the mass media and tabloids' front pages and lead stories. The case and the controversies around it highlighted the race, class, and gender issues of the period, and in a critical sense, our understanding of these concerns were mediated through a growing concentration of global media empires that determine much of what the world hears and sees.

While hyper-exploitation of the tragedy has known no bounds, it remains critical to explain and understand the O.J. story. It is difficult to underestimate the pervasiveness of the O.J. saga on a array of concerns and the important transformations and debates that have arisen as a result of the tragedy. This includes popular and scholarly discourses regarding the media, race relations, legal precedents, gender relations, the image of black males, and questions of class privileges. What can be called the O.J.-ing of America and the world signals a turning point in the popularization of contemporary racial meanings in public and private sites. The case has become a racial reference point for most Americans who struggle to grasp the increasingly complex race dynamics of late capitalism.

The pillorying of O.J. reflects the limits and contradictions of the philosophy of racial exceptionism. This philosophy posits the generation of black public figures who are cited as beyond racial boundaries, that is, deniggerized individuals who never become white, but land in a place that is far and away from the "other." These individuals are thus created as "another," nonthreatening and removed from the jungle terror that afflicts so many others of their hue and history. The O.J. stories scuttle this notion. The deniggerization and then reniggerization of O.J. Simpson exposes the racist underbelly of "color blindness" and its ultimate inability to be blind to color.

Beyond all the hoopla and hatred, of course, is the question of whether O.J. did it or not. It is quite likely that a constellation of racial factors, *inter alia*, conspired to frame a guilty man. In his criminal trial, a California jury of nine blacks, two whites, and one Latino said the prosecution did not prove its case and Simpson was found not guilty. In the civil trial, the jury of nine whites, one Asian, one Latino, and one person of mixed black and Asian ancestry found Simpson guilty. In the courtroom of public opinion, several mixed verdicts also appeared. During the criminal trial and since, most whites continue to believe that Simpson is guilty. Little coverage or analysis, however, has been given to those whites who think Simpson is innocent, a much more intriguing and provocative inquiry. What drove upwards of 40 percent of whites, according to some polls, to buck the racially logical trend and pronounce their view that O.J. should have been let loose? How did this break down in terms of gender, class, educational level, and region?

The views of African Americans were equally complex. In many parts of the black community, O.J. was viewed as innocent and a victim of a grand conspiracy. O.J. was seen as the latest in a long and documented history of white legal terror against African Americans, black men in particular. This included the classic cases of the Scottsboro boys and Emmett Till as well as their modern carnations in Rodney King or the even more racially and gender entangled rape, sexual harassment, and drug cases of Mike Tyson, Mel Reynolds, and

Marion Barry. Given the drama inherent in binary racial dispositions about the case, including media-staged events of white anger and black jubilation, it is not surprising that little attention was given to those blacks who were unequivocally convinced that O.J. was guilty.

In a *USA Today* poll in October 1995, at the time of the criminal verdict, 49 percent of whites, thought that the verdict was wrong. Conversely, only 10 percent of blacks surveyed thought the decision was wrong, while 78 percent of blacks thought it was right. A year later, whites' views on Simpson had hardened. In October 1996, 64 percent of whites, a rise of 15 percent, felt that the decision was a mistake. The number of whites who thought the verdict was correct dropped to 20 percent.[2] For blacks, the number of those who thought the decision was wrong rose 3 percent, while the number who thought it was correct dropped by 16 points to 62 percent. More than anything, it appeared that there was a growing doubt about the verdict rather than complete disagreement. The percentage of those who said they did not know or had no opinion doubled from 12 to 25 percent.[3]

These disparate views were used by racial cynics to highlight the obvious: that whites and blacks see the criminal justice system and its treatment of African Americans, even wealthy and estranged ones like Simpson, through vastly different lenses. Given that on the issue of race and criminal justice, blacks and whites have historically had vastly different opinions, why would the Simpson case be different?

By the civil trial, which began in August 1996, only 58 percent of African Americans thought that the verdict of not guilty was right. Whites who still agreed with the decision fell two points to 18 percent.[4] The symbolic use of Simpson for racial purposes and agendas was not restricted to whites and their revolt with pollsters. Incredibly, Simpson, who despite his reniggerization found little motivation to articulate even a black conservative politic, found strong support from some black nationalist groups and individuals that argued that Simpson had learned his lesson, no longer wanted to be estranged from the black community, and should be welcomed as a hero. Nationalist activists in Washington, D.C. even sponsored a visit by Simpson to the nation's capital.

The Many Narratives of O.J.

Several narratives of O.J. have been constructed over time. The first was O.J.. the athlete-hero. In the mid-1960s and early 1970s, as a college and pro football player Simpson was elevated to sports star status. It is here that O.J. began his transformation toward becoming a symbol of racial exception. In 1968, Muhammad Ali, Kareem Abdul Jabbar (then Lew Alcindor), Tommie Smith, John Carlos, and other black athletes were speaking out and protesting against racism inside and outside of sports—what sports scholar and organizer Harry Edwards called the year of the "Revolt of the Black Athlete"—challenging college, professional, and Olympic authorities. Militant black athletes, most notably those who organized the Olympic Project for Human Rights, sought greater black participation in key positions regarding the 1968 Olympics, but also called for the exclusion of racist Rhodesia and South Africa.[5] Simpson, preparing for a career of accommodation, denounced the protests. Radical politics has never been an element of the athlete-hero myth and Simpson was not about to break that tradition. According to Edwards, in 1967, Simpson was worth about $500,000 annually to the University of Southern California sports program. He was already commodified and politically contained.[6]

The athlete-hero narrative, as expressed through O.J, Michael Jordan, and others, also masks the reality that thousands of young men, particularly young black men, never become football (or basketball) pros. They waste years in college, where they end up not graduating in record numbers. According to *Emerge* 1995 annual report, the graduation rate for black male football players was only 42 percent.[7] The critical point here is that graduation was never the goal in the first place.

Finally, the athlete-hero construction in its non-white form manufactures a racial harmony that exists only so far as white hegemony remains unchallenged. From Jackie Robinson and Muhammad Ali to Dennis Rodman and Tiger Woods, the super "other" becomes a target of reconfigured racism in which one's athletic exceptionalism becomes the barrier behind which liberal white supremacy hides. It took O.J. 25 years to discover what Woods found out in the early stages of his acclaim: the "inevitability" of their blackness in public life.[8]

Following his retirement from football, the world witnessed the construction of O.J. as pitchman for corporate America. Here Simpson's duties were simple: grin and sell it. The idea, of course, was to associate narrative one with narrative two. Celebrities market their fame and link it to products that they have little knowledge of and could care less about how those products are produced, the producers, or the social impact of the product. Simpson expressed no more concern about the working conditions, salaries, or racial and gender issues faced by Hertz workers than Michael Jordan, a generation later, does about the horrible working conditions experienced by the international network of workers who make Nike products. Nike capitalism serves to not only produce sneakers, but also ideology, for Jordan's silence says much. To be like Mike is to conciliate to the worse that contemporary global capitalism has to offer, all the while embracing dreams of riches and fame that will for only an infinitesimal few remain just that.

The comparison with Jordan is appropriate for many reasons. Like Jordan in the 1990s, Simpson in the 1970s was the national and global embodiment of a vast number of products and services. Hertz, General Motors, Royal Crown Cola, Schick, and other companies fell over themselves to have the person called "the most watchable man in the world" hawk their goods.[9] In 1977, *Advertising Age* would designate him as the top celebrity spokesperson in the United States.[10] Also similar to Jordan, Simpson was projected as nonracial, as "another," his blackness was irrelevant to his appeal, or perhaps more accurately, he was to be seen as transracial, that is, his blackness had to be erased and disconnected from the popular conceptions of black usually seen as the negative.

The third construction was Simpson the actor and sports announcer. Reproducing a common image of black men in Hollywood films as mostly clowns, Simpson grinned his way through a number of movies, always playing a buffoon of some sort. In the *Naked Gun* movie series, Simpson actually played a Los Angeles police officer, albeit one that was abused and clowned by his fellow officers and his own cognitive limits. He tried dramatic roles in a few films, but that was not the image of Simpson that America wanted or that he was prepared to sustain. His role in *Roots,* another brick in the construction of the "we have overcome" black upward mobility rap, was stereotype and vapid. As a so-so sportscaster, Simpson was distinguished by a black diction and presentation style, yet played the role of sidekick to his white male counterparts.

All of these roles made Simpson wealthy, famous, and loved by a white population that was increasingly supporting the targeting of other black men (and women) for containment and marginalization, a project with unlimited media reinforcement. These roles also did not prepare America and the world for the fourth and decidedly sinister narrative of Simpson as the psychotic wife-killer. The scope of the feelings of betrayal were measured exactly in the perception of how far the door had been opened to let "one of them" in. Despite the entertainment value that Simpson had provided for three decades and the millions he had made sports programs, professional football teams, and multinational corporations, he was quickly thrown back over the fence. Ironically, Simpson's banishment would open new channels of wealth accumulation.

Minting the O.J. Industry

The political and financial exploitation of tragedy is as old as capitalism itself. In the O.J. era, however, this perversion rose to new heights. Making money off O.J.—not an unusual occurrence—went from a small cottage industry to a multi-million dollar spread of enterprises involving everything from T-shirt sales to product placement in the courtroom by *Fortune 500* transnationals. Within the first 100 days of the criminal trial, by March 1996, the *Wall Street Journal* cynically calculated that the profiteering from the " O.J. industry" had easily surpassed the Gross National Product of Grenada.[11]

From the very beginning of the case, money began to flow. Simpson's famous highway ride was watched for hours by an estimated 95 million people. Those people, glued to their television, did not bother to stop and cook or go out for dinner; they ordered pizza. Domino's Pizza reported that during the Bronco ride, "…was the single greatest hour for pizza delivery in national pizza history."[12]

Even the furniture in the hotel room where Simpson was contacted and informed by police that his wife had been murdered was sold at a huge profit. Wasfi Tolaymat paid $4,000 to the hotel manager who sold him 31 pieces of furniture and fittings. Tolaymat, in turn, had received and rejected an offer of $300,000 for the furnishings.[13]

Mezzaluna Restaurant, where Goldman worked and the site of the last public outing of Nicole Simpson before their killings, became more popular than ever. Within months of the murders, the restaurant was serving 240 more meals a day to curious tourists and local fans. Its profit line was expected to grow by $1 million.[14]

During the first trial, IBM, Coca-Cola, and Sony all managed to get essentially free product placements as their logos showed up regularly. The presiding judge in the trial was Lance Ito, whose ever present IBM Think Pad laptop computer was visible for all to see. IBM was enterprising enough to make sure that the logo was inverted so that those watching would see it the right way. Ito also had a taste for Diet Coke, which was usually prominently displayed in front of him. Even the specially designed chair, which sold for $1,250, that Ito had brought in to ease his back troubles saw a rise in popularity and sales. On one of the prominent monitors in the court, the Sony logo nearly leaped off the screen it was so huge. For some television-addicted watchers, the trial was one long commercial.

Desperate for funds, Simpson used his renewed fame to exploit his football glory years. He signed off on the issuance of commemorative coins in gold and silver celebrating his record-breaking 1973 pro football season when he became the first runner in history to gain more than 2,000 yards in one season. The 1,000 gold coins sold for $69.95 a piece; the 5,000 silver ones for $34.95.[15] There were an official 21-inch bronze statutes of Simpson in his football uniform, which sold for $3,395 each. More than $5 million worth of these had been sold halfway through the first trial.[16] The manufacturer expected to eventually make $85 million.[17]

Simpson did not let a little thing like being locked-down prevent him from make money off his troubles. While in jail, Simpson "wrote" a book titled, *I Want to Tell You*, autographed trading cards to be sold for $500 each, and even operated a 1-900 number. More than 600,000 copies of his book were printed along with 250,000 audiocassette versions of it.[18]

Simpson, of course, was not the only one to write a book about the case. Ghostwriters had a booming business. Dozens of books were produced including ones by prosecutors, defense lawyers, dismissed jurors, jurors who endured, witnesses from both sides, family members, friends and acquaintances, journalists, detectives, and nearly anyone who had only peripherally been touched by the trial. Simpson attorney Johnnie Cochran's ex-wife and Simpson's mother both had books. Kato Kaelin, the nation's best-known houseboy, sold 800,000 copies of his book, *The Whole Truth,* which at $20 each was a potential gross of $16 million.[19]

The commodifying of the Simpson tragedy was carried on the context of exploiting the racial tensions, indeed, racial rage, already inherent in the public sphere. This rage found relief in the grand media-built and promoted narrative that cared little about seeking the truth, but a great deal about mining the multiple opportunities available for sensation in a case that involved celebrities, interracial relationships, wealth, two gruesome homicides, and gender conflicts. As Anne DuCille writes, "the Simpson scandal is good news precisely because it is good business."[20] It is hard to imagine a case more ripe for media exploitation.

Media Circus or Media Bonanza?

What appeared to be an exceptional media circus of the highest order was an icon of things to come. The O.J. trial and aftermath has been great for the media conglomerates. From the cable networks to the tabloids, they have seen their profiles and bottom lines grow and grow. Who really watched Court TV before the trial? The drive for profits means that O.J.-type trial coverage will become more the norm, given the technologies, competition, and increasingly desperate acts that define modern society. The construction of hyper-media hegemony that engulfs the public sphere and increasingly the private sphere, is well on its way.

The Simpson saga coincided with these changes and, in turn, became an opportunity for the growth and hegemonic objectives of media conglomerates. A true story involving a fallen hero, race, sex, Hollywood, and sports wrapped in a murder mystery with two brutal slayings could not have been better scripted by the best fiction writers. The revolution in media—new technologies and new global reaches—fostered an already predisposed national and international interest, an opening that the cable channels were more than prepared to meet. It was reported, during the height of the criminal trial in 1995, that for the first time ever more people watched cable channels in the first quarter of that year than watched the three major networks. This, of course, gave a massive boost to the ratings and profits of CNN and Court TV.[21] CNN charged $24,000 for a 30-second commercial slot and made more than $45 million on its coverage of the trial. Geraldo Rivera's cable show was about to be canceled prior to the Simpson criminal trial. By having his show become a platform for white anger and black defensiveness about the case, he turned his ratings around and prospered. Meanwhile, the networks took a beating as their daytime soap opera and game shows were little competition for the drama of Marcia Clark, Johnnie Cochran, and Judge Ito.

O.J. through the Prism of Race

Though discreetly avoided and deftly denied in the media and public discussions, race was at the center of the Simpson drama. He was not just a famous athlete suspected of killing his wife. Simpson was a hero, accepted into white society as a safe African American, who was now being accused of brutally and viciously murdering his young white wife and her Jewish friend. The contemplation of such betrayal was stunning. The nation has never been comfortable with interracial marriages and relations. Indeed, it was only a generation ago that such links were outlawed in many states. U.S. history is filled with the bodies of black men who have been accused of affronting white women, let alone marrying them.

Simpson's fondness for white women was well-known. His leaving his black wife for the young and blond Nicole was public knowledge and perhaps a critical part of the O.J. legend. It signaled to Simpson and others the completion of his transition from black sports figure to transracial American hero. Simpson was the racial exception embraced by white America, a black man who did not raise social or political issues, who was willing to market his fame to sell any product, who played golf, and who caused no one trouble but himself.

Many commentators only saw racism manifested in the trial when Los Angeles police officer Mark Fuhrman was exposed as a liar and racist. Ignored was years and years of black community-police tension in the Los Angeles area, so profound that any situation involving African Americans and the L.A. Police Department (LAPD) or Sheriff's Department was suspect from the beginning. Well-documented cases of police brutality, planted evidence, murders, and racist organizing found a black community predisposed to believe little and suspect all related to the prosecution's case. This was, after all, the city of Rodney King. The so-called race card was a whole deck dealt by the LAPD long before Fuhrman took the witness stand. Apologists sought to individualize racism in Fuhrman and not ascribe it to the police department that hired, promoted, and sent him to court repeatedly to "testi-lie," nor to the prosecutor's office that was aware of Fuhrman's racist proclivities, nor to local and state officials that aggressively resisted progressive reform of the police department.

Fuhrman's brand of racism was more than just an occasional racial epithet. Cochran's comparison of Fuhrman to Adolf Hitler, which brought Cochran condemnation, was entirely appropriate in that Fuhrman advocated black genocide. As it came out in court, Fuhrman stated that he wished "nothing more than to see all niggers gathered together and killed."[22] Replace the word "niggers" with Jews or Greeks or women or any other group and there is little doubt that Fuhrman would be seen and projected as the villain he is. But complete indictment of Fuhrman undermined the official story and, therefore, the indictment itself had to be undermined. So prosecutor Clark and others continued to defend Fuhrman, relegating his statements to little more than hyperbole and zeal. The legal system saw otherwise. Exactly one year after the first Simpson trial, Fuhrman pleaded no contest to perjury charges, was fined $200, and given three years probation.[23] Media coverage was limited.

The trial was potentially Simpson's passage back to blackness. This was not because Simpson was going to change due to his exposure to a racist criminal justice system experienced by so many other black men, or his drubbing in the media where infamy in this era is not necessarily a negative thing. Rather, the trial served as a transformation in white attitude, probably permanent, towards Simpson. He became a modern black outlaw, a Bigger Thomas, an Othello, a murderer of white women. And, whether he wanted to go that route or not, Simpson and his lawyers were forced into a defense that further polarized him from his betrayed and furious white fans. Symbolically, the sight of Simpson being protected by the Nation of Islam's Fruit of Islam security force enhanced the racial divide that the case turned into signaling that this was not the Simpson of earlier narratives. Leaving one point, however, does not necessarily get you to another, so Simpson's race consciousness was still elusive.

One further racial dimension that garnered little exploration was the public perception of Judge Ito. Asian Americans have often been portrayed as one of the in-between "races" in U.S. society—certainly not white, but also not black. But more than that, in the media and popular imagination, Asian Americans have been painted as the "model minority," i.e., an acquiescent community that does not aggressively struggle for equality, political power, or civil rights, preferring to quietly melt into the pot. This false picture belies decades of struggle by the Asian-American community for inclusion, an inclusion and equality that has been resisted at both the mass and state level. Ito, at one level, was the "model judge." Clearly, either a black or white judge would have only fanned the racial flames of the trial no matter what posture they took. Given the place that Asian Americans are constricted to in the popular racial hierarchies, Ito's role was seen by some as comic relief, a tension breaker, for the more stubborn and explosive black-white conflict. Racist parodies of Ito—Jay Leno's "dancing Itos" and Sen. Al D'Mato's sick Japanese accent impression—did exist and should have been criticized, but were relegated to sideshow status as the big event unfolded. More seriously, Ito was also given his share of the blame (along with the mostly black, mostly female jury) for the not guilty verdict feeding the argument that non-whites have little business being placed in charge of serious · matters.[24] Clark's incompetence, unprofessionalism, and inebriation on a newly acquired celebrity status were dismissed as possible causes for the decision. Coincidentally, the judge in Simpson's civil trial was also an Asian American, Hiroshi Fujisaki.

O.J. through the Prism of Class

It was estimated by the Associated Press that Simpson spent between $3 and $6 million on his defense in the criminal trial (the prosecution spent $9 million).[25] Simpson's fortune guaranteed that he would not simply be railroaded as so many poor and working-class black men and women have been. Few, black or white, could afford the "Dream Team" of lawyers, researchers, and experts hired by Simpson for his defense. Although some were for show and their infighting became legendary, Simpson's assembly of legal power brought down the best that the state had to offer. Few, if any, of Cochran's critics would have turned down his talents should they have found themselves in a situation similar to Simpson's.

It was Simpson's wealth and fame that protected him in previous brushes with the law over his physical abuse of his wife. While male-controlled structures and ideologies reinforce the oppressions that women face domestically, class provides another cushion on which men escape responsibility and punishment for exploitative and violent treatment of women. To the degree that poor men face a judge on spousal abuse charges, they more often than not get something beyond just community service.

Though lambasted in the media, Simpson also enjoyed what could be called a celebrity credit card, where he was given the benefit of the doubt simply because he was famous and rich. Personal identification with Simpson, mediated through public relations and professional marketing, led many to accept his version of the story with little investigation or exploration into the contradictory evidence. Note the multiracial cheering that occurred on the bypasses and streets of Los Angeles as Simpson made his aborted freedom ride.

Even if Simpson had been convicted in the criminal trial, he was guaranteed an appeal virtually before the first witness took the stand. While thousands of his black and poor fans are falling victim to three-strikes provisions, the death penalty, and mandatory minimums, none of which Simpson has ever expressed an opinion regarding let alone done anything about—wealth and financial power make one thing clear: class matters. Despite the racial edges of the trial, Simpson's court experience was one of privilege and power.

O.J. through the Prism of Gender

The case, of course, also raised a number of issues related to gender inequality and oppression. Whether Simpson was guilty of killing Nicole and Goldman may never be truly known. There is little doubt, however, about his activities regarding spousal abuse. Pictures of a battered Nicole, the 911 tape of her screaming as O.J. attempts to break into her home, and other witnesses' claims that he physically mistreated her erased any allegations to piety that he might have. The grinning, affable O.J. known to millions was transformed into a battering monster before everyone's very eyes.

His brutal and brutalizing relationship with Nicole raised some perplexing and confounding questions related to the nexus of race, class, and gender. Was there a basis for black and white sisterhood on the issue of abuse even though that was not what the trial was about? Was the ferocity toward Simpson by many white feminists a response shaped by racism and the failure to entertain the thought that the whole case might have been a racist frame-up? How should progressives, even those who thought Simpson not guilty, respond to the demonizing of Nicole as a cocaine-abusing, money-grubbing whore, implying that she probably got what she deserved (although not from Simpson)? One also has to wonder how strong the white outcry would have been from the black and white communities had Nicole been black.

The Simpson trial, like the trials of Mike Tyson, Mel Reynolds, and Clarence Thomas, again provided a glimpse into the state of the debate on gender relations among African Americans. Those cases are distinct from O.J., however, in that they do not involve interraciality, that is, the accused and the victim were of the same race. Yet similar themes do appear, such as uncritical defense of the black male and the demonizing of the woman who is involved. Given the daily rapes, spousal beatings and murders, and general violence experienced by black women, their erasure from the mass and black media makes it clear that the popularity factor is also a strong motivation in deciding whose story gets told. As many black feminists have pointed out, only interracial rape (or charges thereof) mobilize, not the more ordinary and pervasive intraracial kind.

It is telling that the organizers of the Million Man March sought to have Simpson superlawyer Cochran appear at the event, in effect, as a way to celebrate the acquittal of a spouse abuser who had demonstrated little interest in the problems of the black community. They were turned down not because Cochran professed any outrage at the exclusion of women, but because it was exclusive of other racial and ethnic groups. Cochran has a lengthy history of speaking out on racial concerns and, in a sterling follow up to his Simpson case, managed to free imprisoned Black Panther Geronimo Pratt, who had been incarcerated for more than two decades on what many believe was a state frame-up.

Clearly missing, in any organized or relevant way, are the voices of black male feminists or even what scholar Joy James calls black women nationalist feminists in a debate that often seems to be only between black women feminists and male nationalists. Black feminists have been branded traitors by some nationalists and generally have been fighting an uphill battle to have black women's issues seen as of equal importance to these of black men.[26]

O.J. Forever

In 1997, Simpson lost the civil case brought against him by the families of Nicole and Goldman. O.J. was ordered by the court to pay $33.5 million to the families, a sum that he had little apparent ability to pay, according to his lawyers, and court appeals are in the works. Judge Fujisaki was criticized for making several huge legal mistakes, such as allowing into evidence a lie detector test by Simpson and the tape of a phone call to a battered women's shelter by someone claiming to be named Nicole (though not proven to be Nicole Simpson). In addition, a juror who was discovered to have lied about her ties to the prosecutor's office was dismissed after jury deliberation had begun, creating more grounds for an appeal. Finally, unlike the criminal case, the judge would not allow the testimony and behavior of racist cop Fuhrman to be discussed, a cornerstone of the defense in the first trial. Fuhrman was a central figure from the very beginning of police involvement in the case: Fuhrman found the bloody glove, discovered the knit cap, and was the first officer to enter the Simpson compound.

There are also more books, films, and inevitable Simpson-related scandals and news events on the way. The case made household names of previously unknown lawyers, sports figures, family members, and people who happened to be jurors, store clerks, forensic specialists, and so on. Whether we like it or not, these people will remain in our lives for a very long time to come.

More critically, the case brought into sharp relief the race, gender, and class tensions that refuse to go away and, in fact, are intensifying in this period. O.J. was a global sensation made available by new technologies and expanded media networks. Unlike other famous legal cases that found an international audience—such as the Scottsboro case in the 1930s, Angela Davis in the 1970s, and Mumia Abu Jamal in the 1990s —the politics of O.J. were not about an obvious injustice and, therefore, nothing approaching global support for Simpson emerged. Indeed, given the image of blackness, and black males in particular, that has been projected on the global scale, Simpson's demonization was simply one more incident in a long string of such.

O.J. the phenomena provides a platform, at an emotive level, for nearly everyone's anxieties about race, gender relations, violence, privilege, and postindustrial capitalism. What is liberating (and disturbing) about the Simpson case is that it allows for and encourages absolutes. Either you think Simpson is guilty or not. Either you think the criminal justice system is fair or not. The complexities of the intersection of race, gender, class, the criminal justice system, and the media demand much more rigorous analysis and attention than emerged around the Simpson case, even as that case set the tone and has become a reference point for those interactions for many years to come. The multiracial dimensions of U.S. society deserve and require a seriousness of analysis from intellectuals, policymakers, journalists, and activists that took a walk regarding O.J. and the tragic circumstances of his life. Yet more than anything, the Simpson case moves beyond Simpson the individual—who lived a life of luxury and isolation, privilege and wealth—to challenge the ideology of racial exception. In the end, he said it best in his suicide note, "Don't feel sorry for me, I've had a great life, great friends." Guilty or not, Simpson achieved in infamy what he was unwilling to do otherwise: expose the racist underbelly of the myth of color blindness and the limited value of racial exceptions.

6

Thug Life:
The Rap on Capitalism

How many brothas fell victim to tha streetz
Rest 'n peace young nigga
There's a Heaven for a 'G
Be a lie if I told ya that
I never thought of death. My niggas
We tha last ones left. But Life Goes on.[1] —Tupac Shakur

In the film *Juice,* rapper Tupac "2-Pac" Shakur's signature cinematic turn, his character Bishop cold-bloodedly guns down two people in less than five minutes, one of whom is his best friend. In that pivotal moment, Bishop obtains "juice," the street term for power. Having street juice, however, is a fluid circumstance, and not too long after, in the inevitable cycle of destruction brought on by a philosophy of take-no-prisoners, Bishop suffers a violent death and juice passes on to the next unlucky soul.

As a rapper and one of the most visible commodified global black male images, Tupac had juice.[2] As a leading signifier in the world of rap music, Tupac's controversial life provided a platform of debate for both the proponents and opponents of the genre. Posturing as an unrepentant thug, Tupac shamelessly celebrated and acted out as his generation's Stagolee—a national outlaw unrestrained by social conventions or rules, pointing a ring-adorned middle finger at both the streets that attracted him so strongly and the social system that (often successfully) sought to exploit and contain him. With an artist's irony, he relished the belief that he would die young, violently, and with street glory. In his song "Life Goes On," he discusses the death of his friend as well as his own death and funeral, a premonition that now appears as inevitable as it was chilling. His murder at the age of 25 also pushed buttons and graphically linked studio gangsta fantasies with lived ghetto realities.

By all accounts, Tupac was a gifted artist at a young age, and enjoyed acting, dancing, and writing poetry as a high school student at the Baltimore School for the Arts. Hope was alive and possibilities appeared limitless. But these were the Reagan years and crack was king. Tupac's mother, like countless others, became addicted to the drug, which made for an unstable home life. In response to this situation, Tupac took off for the West Coast, where he would eventually build his rap career. He would also become fascinated with black gangster culture. The child of a Panther, Tupac's rearticulated militancy found expression in his hard core raps and in the lifestyle of "don't give a fuck" that he embraced. Over the years, he gained gangsta rap credibility through his troubles outside the studio: a shoot-out with police in Atlanta; a shooting in Marin near San Francisco; his own robbery and shooting in New York; and most determinant, his conviction and imprisonment for his alleged part in a gang rape.

The fan-driven notion that gangsta rappers must be more than "studio" hoodlums has a disturbing quality to it. While few expect Arnold Schwarzenegger, Bruce Willis, or Jean-Claude Van Damme to act out their tough guy roles in daily encounters, quite the opposite is true in the rap game. To their legions of fans, the legitimacy of gangsta rappers is conditioned on the real troubles that they find themselves in. While actors can play prisoners convincingly without ever having been locked down, for too many rap fans, it is illegit to rap about prison if one has never been imprisoned. This is a perverse, and indeed racist, expectation that too many young rappers have adopted themselves.

It should be noted that this "authenticity anxiety" is not just felt by black youth wannabees, but has also been appropriated by a number of black intellectuals. In their desire to link with roots that many do not have—a charge often hurled at "studio" gangsta rappers—some scholars, such as Harvard University's Henry Louis Gates, have muted their criticism of the misogynist, self-destructive, and pro-capitalist character of certain subgenres of rap in their defense of rappers' first amendment rights and black essentialist proclivities.[3] This has been done at the expense of more politically critical rappers, who are increasingly finding little space or place for their music. The authenticity anxiety is also grounded in definitions of community and black life that segue into conservative notions of social and cultural pathology as the root cause of black strife. The black community is thus defined by its most destructive, dangerous, and debilitating elements.

At the same time, opposition to gangsta rap does not by definition signal a progressive turn. This is most vivid in the confluence of opportunism in the alliance concocted by civil rights activist and president of the National Political Congress of Black Women, C. Delores Tucker, and former Reagan official and national drug czar, William Bennett. While taking on the easy target of rap's most banal and base performers, they project a false community of interests between a civil rights agenda and conservative cause. Politics paraded as morality feeds an agenda that negates state responsibility for the crisis in the black community while promoting a cultural project that retards and restricts the resistance so needed in this period.

Is the inevitability of living a thug life dying a thug death? In many ways, Tupac mirrored his cinematic and audio bad boy image. On September 7, 1996, in a street scene scripted from dozens of gangster movies—*Scarface, Bonnie and Clyde, Goodfellas, The Godfather I, II,* and *III, Menace II Society, New Jack City,* and *King of the City*—Tupac was gunned down in a shower of bullets, his legacy rising almost immediately as a site for contestation over the intersection of rap, race, and reality. His shooting, and subsequent death one week later, once again raised questions and queries about the importance and significance of black marginalized cultural styles on everyday life. As this chapter argues, in the saga of Tupac Shakur are embodied the unresolved dilemmas of community, gender, and commodified relations that haunt the black community.

Black Cultural Challenge

Contemporary black oppositional popular cultures express the complexities of race matters. Neither wholly liberating nor unmitigatingly depraved, rap music challenges and embraces bourgeoisie notions. Rap music and hip hop life-styles and practitioners continue to challenge prevailing orthodoxies even as they succumb to the corporate and conservative tendencies inherent in popular culture.

Tupac's dramatic death elevated the pivotal question: exactly what and who is the hip hop generation and where does its authenticity lie? How much of contemporary black popular culture is driven by market dynamics over which the black community has virtually no control? What is the relationship between hip hop culture and the criminalization of black youth? How is hip hop gendered and what are the implications of that? The answers to these questions gain new urgency every day as scores of black youth, in the words of Bone, Thugs, and Harmony's *Crossroads,* "keep passing away" in orgies of violence and retribution.

Scholar Mark Naison argues that the "outlaw culture" running rabid in black neighborhoods represents a new phenomena in black life. He writes:

> an 'outlaw culture' has emerged among low-income black youth that has rejected African American communal norms in favor of the predatory individualism of the capitalist market-place. These youngsters living in neighborhoods bereft of resources and hope, have embraced a doctrine of 'might makes right' that converts everyone into a potential victim.[4]

These dynamics, increasingly mirrored in other communities, preoccupy much of the thrust of social activism in the 1990s. In some sense, Naison's thesis compares with Cornel West's concern about the increasing "nihilism" engulfing the black community. Although West greatly overstates his case and many criticize the cultural determinist character of his thesis, he raises a significant point when he writes that the "loss of hope and absence of meaning" for so many is the breeding ground for self- and community-directed destruction.[5] This loss of hope and absence of meaning must be grounded in the durability of racism and the broader state and corporate assaults on dispossessed communities.

Naison does not say that every young black person is engaged in gangsterish and destructive behavior. What he does argue, however, is that predatory styles are increasingly dominant and perhaps soon will have a hegemonic edge in far too many communities. There are some serious implications here. One is that the contestation for the moral soul of black youth, including many of those in the middle class, is being won by the streets despite the heroic efforts of parents and others. Lumpen street culture, with its masculinist dimensions on full throttle, criss-crosses the black community at a number of class and social levels. From the high school dropout to the college senior, contemporary black street culture weaves in and out of the lives of young blacks. Most important, however, this battle is not primarily or simply over behavior. It is the fight to recapture and reposition a value system and world outlook that emancipates rather than oppresses, that values service over materialism.

Outlaw culture is not the defining character of inner-city black neighborhoods. For every shooting that occurs, there is a teenage mother going back to school to finish her education. For every crack sale, there is a black couple taking in a foster child. For every drive-by, there are thousands of black workers who get up and go to work every day, to church on Sundays, and volunteer when possible.

Unfortunately, it is true that a small, relatively organized minority can terrorize a disarmed and ill-prepared majority. Many black neighborhoods are entrenched in fear, all too ready to surrender civil liberties and political rights because there are, indeed, drive-bys, crack sales, and brazen shootings. Among some black youth, the fusion of lumpen street culture with prison culture has created a new and spreading subculture that is passionately violent and without social or moral restraints.

The high unemployment rate for black youth, which is generally triple the official rate for white youth, exacerbates and feeds the economic desperation felt by so many. College opportunities for the poor and lower income of all races have been severely reduced since the Reagan era, with little prospects for a change. Even service in the military, once a way out, if not up, for many young black men is no longer the option it used to be in these downsized days when criminal records and low educational attainment become means for military rejection. Finally, the virtual absence of a vibrant black leadership contributes to a crisis of direction for the black community as a whole and youth in particular. Out-of-style civil rights leaders carry little leadership weight and black conservatives even less. The Nation of Islam is perhaps closest in the imagination of many black youth to a legacy of resistance, as evidenced in the closeness and even membership of some rappers in the group. Yet the Nation finds it difficult to sell—to an impatient black youth—the group's high demands for discipline, piety, and rectitude, and ultimately its conservative social and political agenda.

The dominance narratives existent in rap, which celebrate patriarchy, consumerism, and thuggery, do not emerge simply from the creative and misguided genius of black youth nor just the imperative of corporate profit and its exploitation of social depravities. These dynamics intersect and constantly reform their relationship, nurtured by the external demands of capital and the internal exigencies of black social and cultural life. Furthermore, the music reflects and generates broader discourses about power and capitalism filtered through race, gender, and class fulcrums. Shakur's music and life personified these debates and the struggle to resolve the conflictual tendencies of hope and struggle with despair and surrender.

Commodified

What role and responsibility do rap and rap artists like Tupac have to this set of circumstances? Popular music, including rap, plays a pedagogical role in the socializing of society. Rappers, particularly gangsta rappers, claim that they are only telling the truth when they describe the black community as a war zone where only the strong survive, a place where no one is to be trusted and where it is all about the love of money. In the rapper-constructed world, everyone is a commodity to be exploited and then discarded when used up. Women are "hos," commodified sex objects devoid of humanity, or bitches, too willing to confront males on heretofore sacred grounds, or mommas, nurturers whose priority is male protection and security. Those who work every day are suckers and prey for getting "jacked," that is, robbed and victimized.

This notion of community, however, must be rigorously interrogated because it manifests a narrow and, indeed, racist perspective that reduces black life to the worst pathologies of modern society. As an imagined and real community defined by historically and socially derived identities, African Americans reflect a broad array of class, gender, ideological, political, and social differences. Bourgeois blacks are as much a product of the racial history of the West as are working-class blacks and the black lumpen. To limit black authenticity to predatory life-styles remains a conservative vision that unites black rappers with white conservatives in an unholy alliance.

If the world created by rappers is a construct, the questions that need to be answered are who is doing the construction and for whose consumption? The near monopolization and concentration of the production and distribution of cultural commodities by forces far removed from the black community or its authority means that a small, unaccountable, and generally white elite is making decisions about the content of the music and where it will ultimately end up.

The most critical market for rap music is, of course, the hip hop niche—one that is studied by cultural theorists, sociologists, and market analysts alike. According to a study by public relations firm Yankelovich Partners, Inc., hip hoppers watch more game shows, award shows, music video shows, and late night entertainment, and fewer dramas and sitcoms, than the rest of society. In general, hip hoppers are loosely and popularly defined as those inner-city black youth aged 15 to 19. This group, however, comprises only 1.4 million—or 8 percent of all U.S. teens. In addition, it is disproportionately lower income with relatively little disposal income. Even if inner-city African Americans between 20 and 24 are added, they constitute only another 1.6 million. A potential market that maxes out at about three million at most is too small—and in reality much, much smaller—to be economically feasible in this era of global economies, which move billions of dollars and millions of commodities per hour.

The power over the development, production, and distribution of popular music is supremely concentrated. Six transnational corporations—Time Warner, Sony, Philips, Bertelsmann, Thorn-EMI, and Matsushita—account for more than 90 percent of all albums, cassettes, music videos, and compact discs sold in the world.[6] Their international aspirations are captured in their marketing slogans—Time Warner's "The World is Our Audience," Sony's "Think Globally-Act Locally," or Thorn-EMI's "A Truly Global Organization"—as well as in market shares.[7] Critics are painfully naive to think that these transnationals's target audience is black youth.

The real target is the market niche that seeks to bond and appropriate hip hop's constructed black inner-city authenticity. As one analyst noted, the apparent appeal to black youth is really a stepping stone to white youth who search for their own identity in the popular-ized cultural images of the inner city. These images are symbolized in material expressions that are easily reproduced and, most pivotally, sold in the form of baseball caps, designer sneakers, oversized, off-the-butt jeans, and compact discs. While nonmaterial signifiers, such as a walk or a snarl, cannot be sold, their link to real commodities can. All of this is done to the rhythms of rap, particularly gangsta rap. MTV's *Yo! MTV Raps* is a critical cog in the national and global mar-keting machine. The cunning genius of MTV is that it is a network made up entirely of promotional commercials for music successfully masquerading as entertainment and even news.

In 1993, MTV was beamed to 210 million households in 71 na-tions. On the air 24 hours a day, MTV through its *Yo! MTV Raps* pro-gram has sent videos of black rappers to the far corners of the earth. For many around the world, this constitutes their sole contact with black youth other than that perceived in feature films. The globaliza-tion of American culture also means the globalization of American racial and racist images.[8] Those images are in no small part images of gangsta rappers.

Gangsta rappers do not challenge the horror that many black communities face; indeed, they revel in and exploit it and, more often than not, advocate greater exploitation. They only resemble—in the words of Public Enemy's Chuck D's famous quip—a "black CNN" to the degree that they reproduce a media distortion that is normative. It is the media and corporate construction of ghetto and poverty myths that is more in line with the pedagogic value of most gangsta rap songs than the liberation ethos of the freedom songs of the past.

Capitalist mass media has always been receptive to outlaws. Af-ter all, since the days of Jesse James, Al Capone, and John Cotti, the "bad man" icon has fascinated and repulsed millions of viewers worldwide of Hollywood westerns and gangsta movies at one and the same time. Clint Eastwood's 1992 *Unforgiven* was designated best movie of the year with a message that essentially advocated that out-laws must challenge a corrupt and savage state apparatus, particularly one that sanctions the oppression and brutality of women and African Americans. While Eastwood should not be seen as a progressive or even a liberal, his film embodies a politics that celebrates individual initiative against perceived social injustice, albeit an initiative that promotes violence as the first and last weapon of choice. Gangsta rappers, with their rhetoric of lawlessness, anti-police themes, and espousal of violence, make connections with this legacy in many ways.

Naison also argues that contemporary black outlaw culture embraces many of the symbols of black nationalism of the 1960s combined with that period's glorification of the lumpen proletariat.[9] He contends that black activists and writers glorified criminal behavior, giving it a revolutionary character that it clearly did not deserve. The Black Panther Party is cited by Naison and others as being guilty of expressing these tendencies even as it attempted, in some cases, to eliminate or control such behavior. Ironically, Tupac was born into this Panther-lumpen nexus.

Tupac's mother is Afeni Shakur, a former New York City Panther and member of the infamous Panther 21, a group accused of conspiring to blow up stores in the New York area. She was acquitted of those charges. Afeni and Tupac had close ties with a few famous black political prisoners, including Mutulu Shakur (no relation), Assata Shakur (no relation), and Elmer "Geronimo" Pratt. Mutulu functioned as Tupac's stepfather and political mentor, Assata was close enough to be seen as a play "aunt," and Pratt is Tupac's godfather. Unfortunately, while many ex-Panthers are vigorously involved in various productive and progressive activities, for Tupac, by the time he came of age, most of the Panthers in his life were either in prison, in exile, or in the case of his mother, strung out on drugs and alcohol, unable to realistically pass on the urgency and commitment to struggle that had shaped their youth.

The Panther legacy and relationships haunted Tupac all his life as it carried unresolved political and personal issues that he played out in family relations and through his music. The lack of a popularized theoretical and political closure on the significance of the Black Panther Party for black politics was not Tupac's cross to bear alone, but that of the broader scholarly and political black community. It is only now, three decades after the founding of the Panthers, that serious, nonautobiographical scholarship has begun to emerge.[10] It is too late for Tupac, but not for a generation of black youth looking to the past for political guidance for the present. Unless a compelling summation is offered and struggled with, the mistakes of the past will be revisited time and time again.

Contained

> It ain't a secret, don't conceal tha fact
> Tha penitentiary is packed and it's filled with blacks
> I wake up in tha morning and I ask myself
> is life worth liven, should I blast myself?
> I'm tired of being poor, and even worse I'm black
> My stomach hurts, so I'm looking for a bud sack.[11]
> —Tupac Shakur

So what is the agenda for black youth if their roles as producers and consumers are limited and dissolving? In a word: containment. In the last quarter of the 20th century, the United States has become a nation of prisons. Most significantly, as the country's jail population has tripled since 1980, that population has also become darker. This intersection is neither incidental nor accidental. It is a systemic response from above and below to social transformations that are rapidly creating a growing surplus labor force determined to survive by any means necessary. African-American males, particularly young ones, are going into the criminal justice system in unprecedented numbers. As of 1996, the Sentencing Project concluded that 32.2 percent of all young African-American males between 20 and 29 (827,440) are either incarcerated, on parole, or on probation nationwide. According to their report, in the period between 1989 and 1994, the number of black women in that situation increased 78 percent. Much of that increase had to do with changes in state and federal drug laws that had the impact of disproportionately hurting African Americans. According to federal records, while African Americans make up 13 percent of all illegal drug users, they constitute 35 percent of all drug arrests, 55 percent of all drug convictions, and 74 percent of all those who go to prison on drug convictions. Between 1986 and 1991, the number of black women incarcerated for drug offenses in state prisons increased by 828 percent. According to the Justice Department, at the end of 1994, there were 992,000 men and women prisoners in state and federal prisons; 94 percent men, 6 percent women, 47 percent white, and 51 percent black.[12]

Tupac not only rapped about going to jail and prison life, but had these experiences himself. His encounters the criminal justice system became part of his living legend. From his involvement in a shooting in Marin County in northern California that left a young black child dead to an altercation with police in Atlanta to his conviction and jailing on rape charges in New York, Tupac embodied a thug-life ethos. His street reputation, and perhaps the beginning of the inevitability of a violent end, grew considerably when he was shot five times and robbed and still survived during the middle of his rape trial. He was bailed out of prison, for about $1 million, by Marion "Suge" Knight, the CEO of Death Row records. Moving to southern California where Death Row is located and where it enjoys its own hoodlum reputation for being linked to some of the area's notorious street gangs, Tupac completed his transition to full-time outlaw.

Death Row is the record label started by Andre "Dr. Dre" Young (who is no longer with the company), the most creative mind and influential producer in gangsta rap. It is home to Snoop Doggy Dog, gangsta rap's one other true superstar. Dr. Dre, Snoop, and other Death Row artists have all had high-profile criminal trials in the short history of the company. The notoriety, however, only built the company's fame and infamy, allowing it to sell millions of records. In 1996, Death Row revenues came to $75 million.[13]

Despite its entrepreneurial success, Death Row has fallen on hard times since Tupac's murder. Suge Knight went to jail in October 1996 for parole violation and was sentenced to nine years in February 1997. More critically, the company is under ongoing federal and state investigations to determine if it is what the government calls a "criminal enterprise" dealing in drugs, money laundering, extortion, gunrunning, murder, and gangbanging. While Surge Knight and Dr. Dre received millions in financing from Sony, Time Warner, MCA, and Interscope Records to start Death Row in 1992, some investigators are alleging that the seed money, at least in part, came from drug dealers associated with Knight.[14]

On March 9, 1997, gangsta rap suffered another traumatic event with the drive-by slaying of Biggie Smalls (aka the Notorious B.I.G.) in Los Angeles six months after Tupac's killing. Smalls, 24, whose real name is Christopher Wallace, had once been close to Tupac, but later had a bitter falling out and was accused by Tupac of being involved in his earlier shooting in New York. A former drug dealer, Wallace also rapped about using women, thugging on the streets, and dying young. His first album is titled *Ready to Die,* while his last, released after his murder, is titled, *Life After Death... 'Til Death Do Us Part.* Both Tupac and Wallace's murders occurred amid street rumors and actual incidents of a "war" between East and West Coast gangsta rappers, more specifically, those affiliated with Death Row in the West and those affiliated with New York's Bad Boy records and its owner Sean "Puffy" Combs in the East. Although rap emerged first on the East Coast in New York City, by the late 1980s, hard-core gangsta rap from Los Angeles, Oakland, and Houston not only challenged the East Coast in popularity, but also in bravado. Initial insults traded in studios turned into ugly confrontations at music concerts, awards ceremonies, and in the streets. These feuds were fed by fans and rap media, as well as reputation-seeking rappers themselves.

Whether real or not, the "beef" between East and West Coast rappers—proclaimed and promoted in rap and mainstream media despite acclamations to the contrary—helps to sell long-sought hoodlum reputations, which helps to sell products. Incarceration is not a badge of dishonor but a rite of passage to the higher echelons of the gangsta rap financial ladder. Containment, thus, on a grand scale functions as a marketing device that pushes the "other" further from the mainstream which then serves to make even more attractive and abstract the commodified black identification politics of white youth. This interpretation is held by music corporate executives and authenticity-seeking homeboys and homegirls alike. Its ultimate social and human costs are simply bottomed-lined away.

Conclusion

The collaboration between some of the largest transnational corporations in the world and inner-city black youth is not as strange as it may appear. The creation of global market niches in this era is a driving force in the contemporary exploitation of black American cultural forms. The marketing of the "other" as entertainment, an opportunity to experience the dangerously exotic, even if only abstractly, motivates both corporate producer and nonblack consumer. In the middle are "declassed" poor black youth—that is, those who are marginalized perhaps permanently out of the labor force—whose efforts to avoid what are clearly unpleasant destinies generate innovative ways to prosper and survive. Those ways have become new modes of capital accumulation.

Rap has reached a crossroads. Far removed from its roots as principally a cultural expression of urban resistance and political rebellion, it is now in the possession of global corporations whose interest is market expansion and profit maximization. It was the genius and curse of Tupac and other rappers that they could merge their creative impulses with the imperatives of capital, and as a by-product, become global articulators of the plight and predicament of black youth, perhaps youth the world over. At the same time, a harsh judgment must be rendered on the project as a whole. Neither Tupac nor other gangsta rappers joined the struggle against the powers that exploit, oppress, jail, and otherwise marginalize African Americans, other people of color, and working and poor people in the United States and beyond. Indeed, their commitment to individual glory and success may have helped those processes along. Ultimately, as Tupac discovered, the commodification of thug life fails to resolve the underlying causes reproducing it in the first place and creates just one more arena of necessary struggle for African Americans to engage in against hegemonic corporate and state powers.

> I'll never die
> Thug niggas multiply.[15]
> —Tupac Shakur,

7

Globalizing the Black Image

"Monopoly is a terrible thing until you have it.[1]*"*
—Rupert Murdoch

Only a few short years ago, when the Internet was an infant, an attorney couple sent out a message over the Net advertising their law firm. Within a matter of hours, they were flooded with messages by outraged Internet users who felt that the "nonprofit" character and ethos of the Net had been violated. In a massive protest rarely seen in or out of cyberspace, they received so many E-mails that they were forced to give up their account and go underground, never to be heard from again. Millions celebrated what appeared to be a complete and vindicating victory against the commercialization of the Net. That incident now seems almost mythical.

The electronic revolution that has combined media, telecommunications, and computers—generally referred to as information technologies (IT)—has forever changed how information will be generated, distributed, and consumed. Some have heralded this era as an "information age" that will witness unparalleled democracy, shared prosperity, and harmonized social relations. For some this will be true. In many ways, however, far from challenging the status quo, the electronic revolution is a central component in the growth of an increasingly unfettered global capitalism. Information technologies open up new markets and new marketing opportunities. In ways unimagined by even the most free-minded free market thinkers, the century is ending with corporate power and control expanding into nearly every facet of life.

Economic globalization has led to the depression of wages, the permanent elimination of millions of jobs, the curtailment and erosion of the welfare state, extensive government deregulation, and unlimited access to markets worldwide. New technologies, robotics, computers, satellite technologies, and information technologies, such as the Internet and the World Wide Web, have transformed our path to the future. They have fed a process popularly known as globalization that is changing the economic, political, and cultural life of humankind.

All the while, working and nonworking people in the United States and the world over are being misinformed about the real relations of power underlying these changes by corporate-mediated news and by entertainment diversions from corporate-owned cultural industries. On the cultural front, what is being exported is more than just capital and industry. In particular, racist images of a media-constructed, African-American life, unmonitored and uncontrolled by that very same community, are transmitted around the world through a wide range of mediums. From rap videos to Hollywood gangsta films to television entertainment and news programs, the black image as corporate construction has been globalized. The ideological character of these images reflects dominate racial paradigms that convey a popular though flawed narrative where African Americans are their own worst enemies; racism exists only in the individualized expressions of white and black extremists, and black cultural pathologies and biological "limits" are normative. At the same time, the pervasiveness of blackness in U.S. popular culture—Michael Jordan and the Dream Team, *The Bill Cosby Show,* film stars Denzel Washington and Eddie Murphy, etc.—also falsely signals an integration and success that has little currency in the real world, but allows for broad denial that racism still exists in the United States.

Who owns and controls these media monopolies? What role do they play in globalization? How will they impact democratic participation? How do they affect race relations on a global scale? Understanding and seeking answers to these questions are critical for progressives involved in contemporary social movements.

The argument of this chapter is that the global media, dominated by U.S.-based firms, assumes a critical, if not decisive, role in the construction of contemporary images of race. The internationalization of the black image, filtered through conservative ideological fulcrums, has been facilitated rather than challenged by new media technologies and expanded media markets. While the popular images of whites in the United States reflect a broad diversity of characters, black images are stereotypical. As scholar Polly McLean notes, "Despite various restrictions imposed by some countries, the United States continues to be the major player in the international cultural marketplace. Therefore, it is important to examine the stereotypes prevalent in media culture that have helped shape the construction of social reality on both the domestic and the international fronts."[2] What gives these concerns new urgency is the speed, breadth, and pervasiveness of distribution in this period, which is unlike any in the past.

All the News that's Fit to Be Owned

Concentration in the media and entertainment industry has meant that a few people control most of the airwaves and other channels of communication. Those in control are primarily white males. One study has concluded that 8 individuals, families, and foundations control 91 television stations and networks, 71 radio stations and networks, 145 daily newspapers, and several dozen magazines, book distributors, film production businesses, and record production companies.[3] This includes the three major networks, ABC, CBS, and NBC, as well as the major newspapers such as the *Wall Street Journal* and *Washington Post*. These media conglomerates form interlocking boards of directors with multinational oil, banking, and industrial corporations, including Chase Manhattan, Coca-Cola, Chemical Bank, Xerox Corporation, AT&T, IBM, and American Express.

All of these corporations also have interlocking directorships with high-powered policy organizations, such as the Trilateral Commission, Business Roundtable, Business Council, Council on Foreign Relations, and Committee for Economic Development. The networks shamelessly flaunt their government links, raising serious questions about their "objective" reporting standards. For example, ex-President Ronald Reagan served as chief spokesperson for General Electric which owns NBC; deceased CIA Director William Casey was a major stockholder in Capital Cities, which owns ABC; and former Secretary of State Henry Kissinger sits on the board of CBS.

The mid-1990s saw a merger mania, where huge transnational corporations gobbled up media conglomerates. Mass media increasingly came to resemble an octopus with a few heads and many, many arms. In a brief one-year period, ABC, NBC, and CBS all underwent radical ownership changes as they were either bought or merged with even larger corporate powers. In the cutthroat world of corporate takeovers, even the biggest media operations are fish food for larger, imperial-minded enterprises. In 1995, in a pivotal two-day period, the Walt Disney Company acquired Capital Cities/ABC Inc, the number one television network, for a record $19 billion, while less than 24 hours later, CBS agreed to be bought out by Westinghouse Electric Corporation for $5.4 billion. It was only a decade ago that ABC was bought by Capital Cities. This further concentration of media power into a smaller number of hands continues the trend of placing much of the world's popular cultural agenda into the claws of corporate barons and executives.

The range of control of media that is held by only few hands is nothing short of astounding. In 1996, *The Nation* published a map of what it appropriately termed "The National Entertainment State" showing the various links of media ownership and control involving the three big networks.[4] General Electric, which was ranked number one with General Motors on the Forbes 500 list, along with its ownership of NBC controls a large number of television stations, news programs *(The Today Show, Meet the Press, Dateline NBC),* and cable shows and networks *(Court TV,* which it shares with Time Warner, which now owns Turner Broadcasting, American Movie Classics, Bravo, and A&E, which it shares with Disney and Hearst). Westinghouse, already a powerful multilayered, multinational nuclear corporation, by taking control of CBS gained authority over its news division *(60 Minutes, Face the Nation, 48 Hours,* and *CBS Morning News),* television stations, CBS Radio (21 FM and 18 AM stations), and cable outlets (Home Team Sports, The Nashville Network, and Country Music Television). Disney, a corporate media behemoth itself, in acquiring ABC, got ABC Radio (21 stations), ABC Network News *(Good Morning America, Nightline, 20/20,* and *Prime Time Live),* and nearly 20 television stations.

This assessment does not even include Time Warner, the largest media conglomerate, or Rupert Murdoch, who owns the Fox network and sprawling international media outlets. By bringing Ted Turner's Turner Broadcasting under its wing, Time Warner gained control over CNN, which is increasingly the world's most dominant news machine, replacing local news from Austria to Zimbabwe. Murdoch's empire continues to grow, linking communication outlets of many types from New York to New Zealand. News Corporation, Murdoch's parent company in which he owns about 30 percent of the stock, controls or owns, *inter alia,* HarperCollins and Basic Books (publishing); the *New York Post*, the (London) *Times*, and the (London) *Sun* (newspapers); *Premiere, TV Guide,* and *The Weekly Standard* (magazines); the Fox Network and Twentieth Century Fox Television, which produces *The X-Files* and *Chicago Hope* (television); and Fox Sports Net, Fox Sports International, FX, and Fox News Channel (cable). In addition, Murdoch owns 22 television stations in the United States and the film studio Twentieth Century Fox. In 1995, News Corp brought home $9 billion in revenues.[5]

The power of Murdoch and others is not just about a growing concentration of economic power. It also highlights the dangerous trend of information control in a few hands shaping the social and political consciousness of tens of millions. As longtime media critic Herbert Schiller notes, "Packaged consciousness—a one-dimensional, smooth-edged cultural product—is made by the ever-expanding goliaths of the message and image business. Gigantic entertainment-information complexes exercise a near-seamless and unified private corporate control over what we think and think about."[6]

Black ownership of broadcast facilities is minuscule, resulting in little and limited ability by African Americans to shape national debates regarding race and other concerns. In 1995, according to the Department of Commerce, African Americans owned 2 percent of 4,929 AM stations, 1.4 percent of 5,044 radio stations, and 1.7 percent of 1,155 television stations.[7]

In the past, the news media and entertainment industry have often been criticized for being on the wrong side of issues facing people of color, the poor, and working people. In fact, it is increasingly clear that the mass media is not as much on the wrong side as they *are* wrong side. Tighter corporate control and concentration of the media—interlocked with the industrial, financial, and telecommunication industries—means that the news is being delivered by the same forces whose interests more and more diverge from that of the majority of working people.

Entertainment Concentration

Along with the concentration of the news into a few corporate hands, the entertainment and cultural industries are also increasingly controlled by a small economic elite. As entertainment has grown to become a multi-billion dollar industry, globalization has also penetrated the cultural sphere. In the United States, entertainment provided the third largest trade surplus in 1989, with sales of $8 billion, behind only food and aerospace products. Internationally, entertainment sales were about $150 billion. In every major area of popular culture, capital has gone global.

According to researcher Robert W. McChesney, there are five global entertainment giants: News Corporation, Disney, Time Warner, Viacom, and TCI. These five vertically integrate their ownership of film, television, cable, music, newspaper, radio, and advertising firms into one seamless, global operation such that the whole is indeed greater than what are already substantive parts.[8] There are perhaps a dozen more whose global reach is unrelenting. In every field, from music to films to video, the presence of transnational corporations is pervasive and they are encroaching on local cultures with brutal dominance.

In the 1990s, there were six major record companies that determine much of the world's music choices: Sony, Bertelsmann, Thorn-EMI, Polygram, MCA, and Time Warner. While only Time Warner is still a U.S.-based operation, U.S. popular music dominates, marketed on a global scale that takes full advantage of technical advances. In 1990, the world recording industry had sales of over $20 billion, including $6.5 billion in the United States, $8 billion in Europe, and $3 billion in Japan. Contrary to the popular image, it is not just the earphone-wearing, boom box-carrying ghetto youth who is tranquilized by the music. More than 100 million walkmans have been sold around the world and more than a million are still produced monthly.

Hollywood, of course, has also gone international. Of the seven major Hollywood studios, two are owned by Japanese (Columbia and Universal), one by Australians (Twentieth Century), and one by Italians (MGM-UA). Only Warner Brothers, Walt Disney Studios, and Paramount can lay claim to U.S. citizenship. Hollywood films have become dependent on the global market because only 20 percent earn back their initial investment on domestic sales.[9] American violence, and increasingly, American inner-city, black violence, is a universal language that sells well in both the developed and developing worlds. Black-oriented films such as *New Jack City, Malcolm X,* and *Boyz 'N the Hood* can be seen in countries as diverse as Guadeloupe, Chile, and the Peoples Republic of China. Black films, which almost always return a profit because they are so cheaply produced, do even better outside the United States, where they share longer runs with minimal advertisement and promotion costs.

The bulk of Hollywood's profits on these films are from non-blacks. Global and domestic film (and television) sales total about $137 billion annually.[10] In 1993, Hollywood films by black directors sold 29 million tickets.[11] This included *Hollywood Shuffle,* directed by Robert Townsend, which cost $100,000 to produce, but made at least $10 million in return.

MTV, which functions as one long 24-hour commercial for the record industry, is owned by Sumner Redstone. In 1993, MTV was beamed to 210 million households in 71 nations. In addition to MTV, Redstone also owns Viacom as well as VH-1, the Comedy Cannel, USA Network, Lifetime, Showtime, The Movie Channel, Nickelodian, and UPN. Redstone owns Simon & Schuster publishing house, Blockbuster video rental chain, controlling interest in Para-mount (*Forrest Gump, Primal Fear,* and *Mission Impossible*) plus 5 television stations and 12 radio stations. In 1995, Viacom had reve-nues of $11.7 billion, employed 80,000, and had operations in over 100 nations. Viacom's motto is "Exceptional Content, Global Reach.

MTV is not just exporting videos, it is also exporting images that convey particular messages and stereotypes. Through its *Yo! MTV Raps* program, MTV has sent videos of black rappers to the far cor-ners of the earth. For many around the world, this constitutes their sole contact with black youth other than that perceived in feature films. In effect, in the United States, Redstone impacts how black and Latino youth dress, their musical tastes, their views on gender rela-tions, their political ideas, and even their language, the lexicon by which they articulate their worldview; globally, it shapes the world's views of African Americans and youth culture, while imposing those views on dozens and dozens of nations.

Entertainment consumption is high in the black community. According to a recent report, compared to whites, blacks watch television "90 percent more in late night, 59 percent more in daytime, and 55 percent more in early morning."[12] The average U.S. household has the television on 50.1 hours a week. In black households, the average is 77.3 hours a week.[13]

Although the corporate boardrooms and executive suites of the multinational multi-media are filled with mostly white males, some blacks have penetrated these enclaves of financial and cultural power. In 1994, for example, Time Warner—the world's largest producer of music in the world and the largest magazine publisher in the United States—named Richard Parsons company president.[14] Parsons sat on the board of directors before his appointment. Other blacks that have made it big in the mainstream cultural industry include Lamont Boles, Epic Records senior vice president of black music; Tony Anderson, Arista Records vice president of black promotion; Benny Medina, senior vice president and general manager of black music; Sylvia Rhone, Elektra/EastWest Records chairperson and CEO; Michael Moye, writer and *Married With Children* executive producer; and Kim Fleary, ABC Entertainment vice president of comedy series development.[15]

Overall, people of color constitute a smaller fraction of employment in the entertainment industry than in the workforce in general. While blacks, Latinos, and Asians are 22.6 percent of the nation's labor force, they are 16.1 percent of the high-level jobs in broadcasting and 13.2 percent in the cable television industry.[16] Complaints of biased images by African Americans, other people of color, and women are understandable when it is revealed that white males are 95 percent of all writers for television and that only a half dozen black directors can find consistent work.[17]

Several black entrepreneurs have benefited from the growth in black cultural commodities. A number of blacks have formed film production companies. These include Jackson/McHenry Entertainment, which produced *New Jack City* and *House Party II*; Denzel Washington's Mundy Lane Entertainment; and, of course, Spike

Lee's 40 Acres and a Mule. The most visible and successful beneficiary has been Oprah Winfrey. As a result of the financial success of her show and her film and television production company, Harpo Productions, Winfrey has earned well over $100 million annually for a number of years.

Other notable successes include Black Entertainment Television (BET) (cable television and music videos), Rush Communications (rap music), DPC, Inc. (hats), and Threads for Life (clothing). Robert Johnson, founder of BET, has big dreams. His hope is that the BET empire "become the focal point of black entertainment in this country" and internationally.[18] Already, the company has branches outside of the United States: BET International, which coordinates and develops programs for global consumption, and Identity Television, its London-based cable service that targets blacks in England. Currently, the BET business network includes: Black Entertainment Television, which reaches 39.7 million homes and accounts for 86 percent of the parent company's (BET Holdings, Inc.) $72 million in sales; Action Pay-Per-View, a cable network that has 7 million subscribers; the black monthly magazines *YSB* (Young Sisters & Brothers) and *Emerge*; a cable network that focuses on jazz; and United Image Entertainment, a joint effort with actor Tim Reid to produce black-oriented television programs.[19]

Future BET plans include building a sports arena in Washington, D.C., and launching several feature film production and distribution companies.[20] BET is looking to form its home shopping venture with the leader in the field, Home Shopping Network (HSN). The program would feature clothes, appliances, cosmetics, and other consumer items with a black emphasis to them. According to one study, black women spend $1.2 billion on beauty aids. This is the market that BET and HSN want to tap into. HSN brings in about $1 billion annually.[21]

Johnson began BET in 1979 with $15,000 of his own money and $500,000 from Tele-Communications Inc. (TCI). He owns 55 percent of BET's public stock, which is reported to be worth $130 million. TCI owns 21 percent and Time Warner owns 18 percent of the stock.[22] In 1991, BET had sales of $50 million and, in 1992, sales rose to over $60 million.

Much of BET's cable programming is dominated by music videos. These programs are cheap to produce and highly profitable. Similar to MTV's *Yo! MTV Raps*, BET's *Rap City* is very popular among young black viewers. These videos tend to be high in abuse and degradation of women and unnecessarily violent. According to one researcher, there is an average of 18 violent acts per hour in music videos.[23] Although BET and some other networks that broadcast rap videos have created policies to prohibit videos that show violence, profanity, or weapons, there has been no censoring of the portrayal women as whores or the glorification of gangster lifestyles.

No one better symbolizes the contradictory aspirations of the rappers than Russell Simmons and his phenomenal achievements with Rush Communications and its rap label, Def Jam. By any estimation, Rush Communications is huge. Home to legendary rap groups such as Public Enemy, Run DMC, and Big Daddy Kane, and producer of the highly-rated, hip hopish cable comedy series *Def Comedy Jam* on HBO, Simmons has transformed what was essentially a small basement operation into a $34 million conglomerate.[24] Rap artists at Rush have earned, at least, 10 gold records, 6 platinum records, and 2 multiplatinum records. Plans are afoot to expand the conglomerate into film production and even sell public stock. In 1994, Rush Communications was the 32nd largest black-owned business in the United States and the 2nd largest black-owned entertainment company, and is likely to grow larger due to a distribution deal signed with Poly-Gram in 1994.[25]

As CEO, Simmons earns about $5 million annually.[26] Usually attired in sneakers, a sweatsuit and a baseball cap, Simmons is a major driving force behind the music and in often attacking the racist structures of the popular music business that have historically reduced the role of African Americans to that of powerless entertainers. Simmons' success and efforts are as laudable as they are remarkable. They do not, however, represent a break from the economic system that is responsible for the misery that forms the substance of the music that Rush produces. The commodification of black resistance is not the same as resistance to a society built on commodification. Rap artists, even those who obtain some economic power and independence, are still slaves to a market system that requires an economic elite and mass deprivation.

There are other players in the television image game. Since the demise of the racially sugarcoated *The Cosby Show* in the early 1990s on NBC, the major networks have gotten out of the black sitcom business. In fact, they have gotten out of the black shows business altogether. The void was initially filled by Rupert Murdoch's Fox Network. The upstart network put a steady stream of black sitcoms on the air, including *In Living Color, Living Single,* and *Martin,* among others. The Fox strategy was to corner the inner-city, urban market that is disproportionately young, consumer-oriented, and black. The approach was highly successful as Fox's black programs shot to the top of the list for black viewers.

In the mid-1990s, Fox shifted its strategy. Having established itself, the network was now ready to take on the big three networks on their own turf. Murdoch paid $1.6 billion for the rights to broadcast National Football League games and $575 million for professional baseball.[27] In 1996, in a decisive move away from black-oriented programs, Fox attempted to emulate the success of shows like *Seinfeld* and *Friends,* popular sitcoms with no black characters. Yet Fox shows like *Party Girl, Lush Life,* and others bombed completely and were quickly withdrawn. Fox had more success, phenomenal success in fact, with cynical dramas like *The X-Files,* and *Millennium.*

Picking up the slack on black programs have been the syndicated networks Warner Brothers and UPN. Virtually overnight, these two networks captured the black market with shows like *Moesha, Homeboys in Outer Space, In the House, Parent 'Hood, Jamie Foxx, Steve Harvey, Sister, Sister,* and *Wayan Brothers.* Despite differences in tone and level of silliness, these shows have several factors in common. Aimed at a black hip-hop audience, they are all comedies that send a deceptive message: essentially, the conditions facing African Americans are humorous and always good for a laugh. Black men are buffoonish, roguish, immature, and always in trouble. Black women are loud, domineering, oversexed, and always taking care of black men. The black elderly and black children are never without quirks and behave abnormally. On the surface, these shows advocate nonviolence, tolerance, the Protestant work ethic, what are popularly perceived to be middle-class values, and a love-thy-neighbor ethos. Underneath, however, lies an ideological order that dismisses alternative, radical political action, sanctions corporate authority, promotes consumerism and materialism, and reinforces status quo social relations.

The comedies developed by Fox, Warner Brothers, and UPN have a global audience. *Martin* is produced by HBO which in turn is owned by media Hercules Time Warner. *Sister, Sister, Jamie Foxx,* and *Wayan Brothers* are all on the Warner Brothers network which is also owned by Time Warner. From London to Cape Town to Port-au-Prince to Mexico City, these programs are watched by millions. MTV's black thugs and the other networks' black jesters are two sides of the same coin. The complexities and multidimensional character of black life rarely appear on television. The few sitcoms that miraculously make it to the air and attempt a more genuine reflection of the dynamics of the black community, such as *Roc* or *Frank's Place,* do not last long.

The global market is key and transnational entertainment corporations are spending billions to reach consumers the world over. In 1995, global advertising was $335 billion. It is projected to be $2 trillion by 2020.[28] Time Warner receives at least 25 percent of its revenues outside the United States.[29]

Does the Net Work?

The Internet has increasingly become one of our most important means of communications and research. In a few short years, it has gone from obscurity to addiction for many. Some have called it electronic heroin. Even more have hailed it as the next stage in democracy. Whatever the Internet and the World Wide Web represent, they do not represent democracy. This can be seen not only in the history of the Internet, but in its growing commercialization.

The Internet was initially designed by the U.S. Department of Defense—not exactly what most would call a democratic institution. In 1969, the Pentagon's Advanced Research Projects Agency (ARPA) created ARPANET, essentially the first network of computers that could talk to each other. ARPANET was turned over to the Defense Communications Agency in 1975. In the 1980s, academic networks tied to military and defense-related research began to develop nodes (networks) under the auspices of the National Science Foundation. The NSFNET replaced ARPANET in 1990. By the early 1990s, nearly every college and university was connected to the Internet as well as most government agencies and departments. Although the Internet still functioned as a system used primarily by the economically and educationally privileged, it was overwhelmingly for nonprofit purposes.

The invention and spread of the World Wide Web, which allows easy use of the Internet, as well as audio and video enhancements, popularized the Net to millions. The Web was started in 1989 at the European Center for Particle Research, a military-connected institute, but did not emerge to be the force that it has become until the invention of Web browsers that allowed any user to easily access and surf the Web. With the popularity of the Web came the hyper-commercialization. In 1993, only 4.6 percent of the Web sites had extensions that ended in "com," the signature designating a commercial site. By 1995, "com" far outnumbered all the "edu" and "gov" sites combined.[30] Many studies have shown that anywhere from 60 to 80 percent of what is on the Internet is controlled by major corporations, and that percentage is growing. It has been predicted that by the year 2000, the Internet will account for at least $1 trillion in commercial transactions.[31] The *Playboy* magazine Web site, which was receiving over three million visits or "hits" a day, was charging and getting $100,000 for businesses to have a link on their Web screen.[32]

Rather than becoming the new engine for democratic input naively hoped for by progressives and others, the Internet has increasingly become a new vehicle for capital accumulation. As *Monthly Review* notes, "Although the Internet clearly has opened up important space for progressive and democratic communication, the notion that the Internet will permit humanity to leapfrog over capitalism and corporate communications seems dubious unless public policy forcefully restricts the present capitalist colonization of cyberspace."[33] In a similar vein, the American Libraries Association depressingly predicts that, in spite of its democratic potential, the Internet "will be owned, controlled, and dominated by unregulated media giants that are driven by profits, not the hope for cultural understanding, greater democracy, the decrease of poverty, or educational enhancement."[34]

The black presence on the World Wide Web has grown substantially in the last few years. Web sites, such as "The Black World Today," "Black America On-Line," and dozens of others, provide critical news and information regarding black life. There are thousands of personal, business, community organizations and professional black home pages. In other words, the opportunity to get accurate and extensive information about African Americans exists.

There are also numerous sites on the Web regarding Africa as well as the Caribbean, Latin America, and other parts of the African diaspora. Clearly, a strength of the Internet is the ease and speed with which it unites distant activists, scholars, and researchers, rapidly creating new bodies of information and new channels of exchange. The images and discourses found on the black Internet flow are counternarratives to the dominant portrayals expressed in other mediums, where black input is limited or nonexistent.

At the same time, racist propaganda and advocacy have a growing presence on the Internet. A long list of right-wing militias, fascists, white nationalists, skinheads, neo-Nazis, Ku Klux Klan, white supremacists, and racists of all sorts are spreading their messages and building their networks through the use of Web pages, E-mail networks, list servers, and news groups. The racist right has had a presence on the Internet for a number of years, dating back to at least the late 1980s. Hate groups have also engaged in sabotage over the Internet, attacking progressive and black sites in a number of cases by rewriting code and posting racist messages. Some black sites have been inundated with racist jokes while others have had pictures of African Americans being lynched or killed sent to them from somewhere on the Internet. While conservatives and censors from the White House to the Republicans and Democrats in Congress have taken on the issue of pornography on the Internet, they have been loudly silent on the issue of cyberhate. Conservatives are stressed that children may see nude pictures or read profanity, but are quite relaxed that those same children may first learn the word "nigger" from the Internet or be told that African Americans and Latinos are less intelligent than whites.

The fight-back against cyberhate has grown, however. At the forefront has been Atlanta's Center for Democratic Renewal,

Montgomery, Alabama's Klanwatch, Los Angeles' Simon Wiesenthal Center, the National Bar Association, and New York's Anti-Defamation League. There are also a number of World Wibe Web sites that are dedicated to exposing racism and fascism on the Internet. Unfortunately, most civil rights organizations have ignored this arena of struggle. In part, it has to do with the lack of technological skills, computer accessibility, efficiency, and orientation by these groups. It also has to do with not taking seriously enough the threat posed by cyberhate.

More than ever, there is a need for public intervention in the development of the Internet. Left to the free market, the Internet will soon disappear into simply an instrument of commercials and entertainment, only occasionally interrupted by relevant information and news. At a minimum, there needs to be a federally sponsored "Corporation for Public Networking" that ensures diversity, access, and an alternative to corporate networking. Public television and radio, as weak as they may be on issues of diversity of content and management control, were created to counter the corporate and exclusionary nature of those commercial mediums.

Activism in the Globalization Age

This era is being defined by the globalization of corporate power concentrated in fewer and fewer hands. A 1996 study by the Institute for Policy Studies found that global corporations now constitute 51 of the world's largest 100 economies.[35] The combined revenues of the top 200 corporations, according to the study, are larger than the combined economies of 182 countries; all but the top nine.[36]

This growth in power by the transnational corporations has paradoxically not translated into global job expansion. The top 200 corporations employed only 18.8 million globally, less than one-third of one one-hundredth of one percent of the world's labor force.[37] Today, the world economy is being driven by only a few transnationals. The 300 richest corporations in the world account for 70 percent of all foreign investments and 25 percent of the world's capital assets.[38] Left out of this phenomenal growth and prosperity are large regions of the world that are being sacrificed and marginalized. Here at the millennium, about one billion people live in absolute poverty around the world.

When it comes to real-world equality, unlike the much celebrated "virtual equality," the World Wide Web is not so worldly. The electronic and information revolutions have failed to make much of a progressive impact on many, if not most, parts of the developing world, especially Africa. More than 90 percent of the world does not have telephones.[39] Two-thirds of the globe's televisions and radios are owned and controlled in Europe and North America though these two regions constitute only 20 percent of the world's population.[40] Sub-Saharan Africa, which has 12.1 percent of the world's population, has only 3.7 percent of the world's televisions and 1.3 percent of its radios.[41] North America has 798 televisions per 1,000 residents; Africa has only 37 per 1,000.[42] South Africa, the most developed nation in Africa, has 60 telephones per 100 white residents, but only 1 per 100 black residents.[43] Assessing the Internet and advanced telecommunications technologies reaching the masses of African people, South African Deputy President Thabo Mbeki states, "The reality is that there are more telephone lines in Manhattan, New York than in Sub-Saharan Africa."[44]

In the United States, economic inequity has also increased and is starker than it has ever been. According to the U.S. Census Bureau, 94 percent of all financial wealth in the United States is owned by the top 20 percent of the population, while the top 1 percent owns 48 percent. The top 200 U.S. manufacturing corporations own 60 percent of all manufacturing assets in this country, with the top 710 owning 80 percent.

This economic power has led to powerful and growing corporate influence over public policy, particularly that related to corporate interests. American corporations won significant victories with the passage of NAFTA in 1993, the General Agreement on Tariffs and Trade (GATT) in 1994, and the Telecommunications Act of 1996. These legislative wins smashed all illusions that control of the globalization process and corporate development of cyberspace would be ceded to democratic input without a battle. Computer nerds, academics, political activists, undergraduates, and those looking for dates notwithstanding, the struggle to accentuate the democratic potential of the Internet will be fierce and long term.

One of the most critical concerns of this period is that of governance. In an era where international economic, political, ecological, and cultural relations increasingly dominate the national and local, there is an urgent need for international political bodies with the authority to manage those relations.

All of these issues must be taken up by progressives and others fighting for a more democratic world. The technical revolution in information production, distribution, and consumption must be accompanied by a social revolution to increase democratic participation and control unchecked corporate power. Movement organizers must address the contradiction that people need to be informed in order to fight back against the consequences of media concentration and economic globalization, but that the means by which most people are informed are by those very media corporations in the first place.

All progressive organizations, including women's groups, civil rights organizations, environmental organizations, and labor unions, have critical roles to play in these struggles. Trade unions, in particular, with their broad base, economic interests, and experience, hold a potentially strong leadership role in this new era. As University of Wisconsin journalism professor Robert McChesney wrote, "Organized labor has a crucial role to play. It is uniquely situated with the resources and the perspective to battle the media and communication status quo....Labor needs to devote significant resources to the policy battles against profit-driven communication and for public broadcasting. It needs to subsidize a healthy independent non-commercial journalism and media. It needs to learn the conventions of mainstream journalism well enough to improve the amount and quality of its coverage. In sum, the labor movement needs to learn from its enemies and take ideological warfare as seriously as economic warfare."[45]

Fighting the power means fighting racist images. Working-class unity, national and global, has consistently shattered on the grounds of racial equality and opportunity. One step in breaking with that tragic past is the construction of new ideologies that challenge assumptions and prejudices. The Internet and other mediums can be used to foster this development or retard it.

If the problem of capitalism has shifted from how to manufacture goods to how to distribute and market them, then the roles of the new information technologies and media concentration become strategic, in different ways, both for capital and labor. For some, such as Bill Gates, who wrote, "The information highway will be able to sort consumers according to much finer individual distinctions, and to deliver to each a different stream of advertising," the era is only the latest stage in capitalism.[46] For the billions around the world, however, who seek development, employment, and democracy, this new era must be break with the past and truly build a world unified for peace and prosperity for all.

8

How Cracked is the CIA-Contra Drug Connection?

As the debate raged over who introduced crack cocaine into the U.S. black community, the super-addictive drug was discovering new global markets. From Soweto to Brixton to the city of Bluefields in Nicaragua, black communities are being inundated with rocks of concentrated cocaine as drug cartels solidify international channels of production and distribution. Crack cocaine is a perfect symbol of the new commodities of the global era. Cocaine capitalism involves international channels of production, distribution, and consumption, unregulated and disrespectful of national borders. While the drug trade has always been international in scope, the expansion of the Colombian cartel operations has given it the power and reach of transnational corporations.[1] The cartels, along with the Italian Mafia, the Russian gangs, the Japanese *Yakuza,* and the Chinese triads, have developed networks of economic interests that rival the capacities and drive of the traditional corporate world. Increasingly, these organizations collaborate as they, too, take advantage of the new technologies and opportunities opened up by economic globalization.

In writing about the global drug trade, French journalist Roger Faligot noted, "The Colombian cartels produce the cocaine, the Chinese take it in exchange for heroin that can then be smuggled into the U.S. The triads bring cocaine to Japan and distribute it with the help of the Yakuzas. Then the Asian mafiosi launder their drug money in Europe."[2] The market focus of the global drug networks are, first and foremost, those communities most economically and politically vulnerable. In this context, drug concerns intersect with those of race and class. For the drug moguls, in the words of the 1970s' rock group War, "the world is a ghetto."

U.S. drug policies and problems have reverberated to the rest of the world and black communities are being the most devastated. Drug profits from U.S. consumers built the international drug conglomerates that are opening new markets in poor black communities in South Africa, Nicaragua, England, France, and elsewhere. In sensational fashion, crack cocaine has come to South Africa. Freed from decades of apartheid segregation, the people of South Africa, particularly those in the black townships, face a new enemy and find that their budding democracy is now threatened by the politics of a drug war that has quickly gotten out of control.

In August 1996, the very public burning and shooting of a drug dealer in the Cape Town area dramatized that South Africa had arrived in the modern era. Confronted by a 500-car caravan, drug dealer Rashaad Staggie, leader of the notorious Hard Living drug gang, was killed by members of the anti-drug group People Against Gangsterism and Drugs (PAGAD). The entire incident, broadcast live, divided a nation already frustrated by growing street crime and insecurity. While many condemn the vigilantism of PAGAD, its take-no-prisoner tactic also has wide support, particularly among Indians. A political and racial division has transpired as the black government finds itself on the defensive regarding the drug issue. One consequence of the Staggie killing was the emergence of a united front of drug dealers. About a week after Staggie's death, 150 drug gangs from the western Cape met and formed an umbrella group called "The Firm," which, in a surreal move, issued a press statement that it would fight back against PAGAD. A few days later, a shoot-out happened between PAGAD and The Firm.

The rise in drug trafficking in South Africa is driven by the gruesome economic and social conditions facing millions of black South Africans. The unemployment rate for black South Africans, for example, is officially about 48 percent. These dire economic times coincide with a dramatic rise in cocaine imports into the country. In 1992, authorities seized 24 pounds of cocaine; in 1995, that number rose to 411 pounds. It is no wonder that the *Washington Post* called South Africa "one of the hottest new transshipment points and domestic markets in the world."

In Nicaragua, crack is devastating the black and Indian populations of the Atlantic coast. The bags of cocaine that routinely wash up on shore, dumped by planes and boats along the trafficking routes that go from South America to the United States, are 90 to 95 percent pure. But since at least 1993, that cocaine has been processed into crack and sold for less than $1 per rock, which is starting to result in growing overdose deaths. One Miskito Indian community estimates that as many as half their young men may be addicted to the drug. In 1997, in Bluefields, a largely black community, police conservatively estimate that there are over 100 crack houses in a city with a population of only 50,000.[3] In the region, unemployment runs as high as 90 percent in most areas.

The intersection of race, politics, and drugs has been most salient in the United States. For a number of years, black activists and leaders have charged that the federal war on drugs has been a war on communities of color and the poor. It would take the controversy of one reporter's dogged determination, however, before these concerns would reach a popular level.

Spies, Lies, and Ghetto Ties

The politics of drug trafficking reached banner headlines in the United States in fall 1996 when a relatively unknown regional newspaper decided that the lead story on the inauguration of its Web site would be a tale of the links between Los Angeles' black street gangs, drug trafficking counter-revolutionaries, and one of the United States' most surreptitious agencies. Few media stories in recent years have generated as much response from the black community as the *San Jose Mercury News*'s investigative series published on the CIA-backed Contras' involvement in crack cocaine trafficking.[4] Written by investigative reporter Gary Webb, the series makes several allegations concerning the relationship between drug dealers tied to the CIA-backed Contras and the spread of crack cocaine in the black community of Los Angeles. Webb asserts that U.S.-backed Contras and Contra supporters imported cocaine into the United States; that the cocaine was sold to at least one major Los Angeles' black drug dealer with ties or membership in the Crips street gang; and that the

CIA was aware of the Contra drug activities and choose to either ignore them or protect the traffickers.

The response to the series has been phenomenal and is an instruction in the power of the intersection of race, new technologies, and foreign policy politics. Internet access to the series meant that a rapid and national, indeed global, exposure of the stories occurred and spread like wildfire. Reprints of the story have been put together and are being sold on the streets of Harlem, Washington, D.C., and other U.S. cities as well as Cape Town, Kingston, and Paris. Forums and meetings along with demonstrations and other protests have also taken place. Calls for investigative hearings have come from Congressmembers and black leaders.

Major broadcast media responded to the series by either ignoring its existence or, as in the cases of the *Los Angeles Times, New York Times,* and *Washington Post,* doing stories imputing Webb's motives and research skills. The Department of Justice, the CIA, and other U.S. agencies also denied the validity of Webb's allegations, and promised internal investigations. The backlash was so strong that even Webb's editors at the *Mercury News* began to speak with some hesitancy in their support for his work and even launched their own investigation of Webb's charges.[5]

This is a complicated story with many layers and serious implications for African Americans, the nation, and the global community. It would be a grave mistake to simply reduce the issue of the CIA's role in drug trafficking to conspiratorial legend or to the excessive activities of some of its operatives or the groups that it has employed over the decades. While all of these things are true, a much larger concern exists. Only by framing the discussion in the context of a critique of the political and economic foreign policy objectives of Congress and U.S. presidents since the mid-1940s can a genuine appreciation of the link between international affairs, racism, and illegal drugs be grasped. This framework can only be discussed briefly here, but it is a necessary discourse for sorting through the media and policy defenders of the status quo and assumptions of legitimacy that are accorded the CIA and government officials in general.

Under the cover of anti-communism, every U.S. administration from Truman to Bush justified global covert operations that directly led to the opening and expansion of trafficking routes for illegal narcotics, whose trafficking was then either ignored or even supported by operatives associated with U.S. intelligence agencies.[6] The role of U.S. intelligence agencies in narcotics trafficking has been a direct function of U.S. foreign policy both during and after the Cold War.

These policies were not race neutral. People of color in both the United States and the developing world have been the victims. The consequences of drug trafficking to and in the black community, and the subsequent growth in substance addiction, have been devastating. In this light, the black community has a deep vested interest in uncovering the truth behind the forces of drug trafficking as well as demanding that appropriate remedies and policies be instituted to rectify the problems created by the drug crisis.

Further, the growth and harvesting of cocoa leaves, opium, hashish and other crops essential to illegal drug production are also driven by global capitalist economics that have relegated developing nations to producing, under profoundly inequitable circumstances, for the developed world. Trade policies, such as NAFTA and GATT, also facilitate the spread of drugs. These policies have made not only the movement of money more efficient and faster, but have also made importation and distribution easier as inspection barriers have been relaxed. Since NAFTA was implemented in 1993, 70 percent of the cocaine that comes into the United States and one-half of the marijuana comes through Mexico. Government experts attribute this growth to a vast increase in trucking traffic from Mexico and limited inspections, both derived from NAFTA implementation.[7] The "NAFTA Accountability Act," H.R. 978, was introduced in the U.S. Congress in 1997 in an effort to address this problem.

Virtually all of the media stories, including the *Mercury News* series, have ignored the economic imperative driving the production of illegal drugs in the developing world and retail trafficking in the United States. In conjunction with whatever role the CIA and other intelligence agencies have played in narcotics trafficking, the corporate-driven international policies of the U.S. government are central to the economic woes of the masses of workers and peasants in the developing world and in the inner city and rural poverty belts of the United States.

What the *Mercury News* Articles Say and Don't Say

Webb asserts that U.S.-backed Contras and Contra supporters imported cocaine into the United States and sold that cocaine to black street gangs in Los Angeles. The Contra drug dealers, according to the *Mercury News,* "met with CIA agents both before and during the time they were selling the drugs in L.A."[8]

More specifically, Webb's investigation states that from 1982 until 1986, L.A. cocaine trafficker Danilo Blandon and his San Francisco-based supplier Norwin Meneses sold hundreds of kilos of cocaine to "Freeway" Rick Ross, a then 22-year-old, black street dealer with ties to the Crips gang in Los Angeles.[9] Ross, according to Webb, turned the cocaine that he received from Blandon and Meneses into crack. Ross grew to be a major dealer and, therefore, had broad influence over the spread of crack in Los Angeles because he was able to receive kilos from Blandon and Meneses at prices well below normal.

The millions in profits made from the drugs sold to Ross, according to court records obtained by the *Mercury News,* were "then used to buy weapons and equipment for a guerrilla army" created by the CIA to overthrow the Sandinista government in Nicaragua.[10] The Nicaraguan Democratic Force (FDN), a coalition of several groups waging war against the Sandinistas, was created in mid-1981, and authorized by the Reagan administration in its fight against communism.

Although the CIA and Contra leaders now state that Meneses was a key player in the Contra war and that they are surprised to find out that he was involved in drug trafficking, those disclaimers don't ring true. Meneses says that, for at least five years, he raised funds for the Contras, visited Contra camps, and sent people to Honduras to work for the Contras.[11] Although Adolfo Calero, the U.S.-based political leader of the FDN, downplays Meneses and says that he was unaware of his drug trafficking, Meneses and Calero were photographed together at a Contra fund-raiser in San Francisco and Calero concedes that Meneses visited Contra camps numerous times during the 1980s.[12] Also, Calero's denial of knowledge about Meneses' trafficking activities is not credible. The *Los Angeles Times* noted earlier linkages had been reported between Meneses' drug trafficking and his Contra connections.[13] Not only was Meneses well-known in the

United States as a large dealer, as the *Mercury News* pointed out, but he was heralded in Nicaraguan newspapers as "Rey de la Droga" (King of Drugs).[14]

Webb writes that the cocaine sold to Ross and later turned into crack created "the first mass market in America" for the drug with which the black community is all too familiar.[15] It is generally agreed that the eruption and broad growth of crack in Los Angeles occurred around this time. While Webb perhaps over enthusiastically writes at one point that Ross was "the Johnny Appleseed of crack in California," which led the *Washington Post* to charge in its attack on the articles that Webb claimed that Ross was the key to the crack epidemic, Webb never states that Ross was solely responsible for the spread of crack.

The series does not state, as some in the media have accused, that the CIA, Blandon, or Ross initiated or invented crack. Webb clearly states that crack existed before the Blandon-Ross relationship. As one of the *Mercury News* articles notes, Blandon's entry into cocaine trafficking coincided with a time period in which "street-level drug users were figuring out how to make cocaine affordable...by changing the pricey white powder into powerful little nuggets that could be smoked—crack."[16]

The series also does not say that the CIA as an agency or any identifiable employees of the CIA directly sold drugs in the United States or specifically targeted the black community. These charges have been made by both critics and proponents of the series.

The series raises two key questions that the black community has long sought answers for: did the CIA and other officials of the United States authorize and participate in the marketing and distribution of crack cocaine to the black community as a matter of policy or strategy?; and has the CIA and other U.S. intelligence agencies through their covert operations and other activities facilitated the flow of drugs into the United States, generating the greater narcotics trafficking that has resulted in increased drug use and sales in the black community?

On the first question, neither the series nor other reports and studies provide evidence of such high-level authorization or a targeting of the black community. While there are examples of U.S. officials being arrested and convicted of illegal narcotics trafficking, no conspiratorial network of top officials inside the CIA has ever been identified. This is not to clean the moral or political slate of the CIA, however. The record shows that high CIA officials did nothing to stop, and often protected, traffickers. No official sanctions or authorities were necessary for the events being charged to have happened.

On the second question, there is plenty of evidence and a long, documented history of CIA involvement in the facilitation of illegal narcotics trafficking. In addition to the CIA, the FBI, National Security Agency, State Department, Justice Department, Military Intelligence, and other agencies have also been shown to be aware of narcotics trafficking on the part of operatives and agents employed and used by these entities. This knowledge went all the way to the top of these agencies, and many believe, to the White House and the presidents.

Jack Blum, chief investigator for the Senate Subcommitete on Terrorism, Narcotics, and International Operations, told the *Los Angeles Times,* "If you ask: In the process of fighting a war against the Sandinistas, did people connected with the U.S. government open channels which allowed drug traffickers to move drugs to the United States, did they know the drug traffickers were doing it, and did they protect them from law enforcement? The answer to all those questions is yes."[17]

A Long History of Involvement

Official collaboration between U.S. government entities and known drug traffickers dates back to at least the World War II era. The Office of Strategic Services (OSS), the predecessor to the CIA, made deals with the Corsican heroin traffickers as well as with gangster Lucky Luciano in the U.S. effort to prevent communists from gaining a political foothold in postwar France and Italy. Luciano had dealt heroin in the United States since 1915.[18] The OSS's Operation Underworld would negotiate a deal that would eventually free Luciano from prison in 1946 in exchange for his role in helping to secure the docks of New York from Nazi sabotage and using his mob contacts in Sicily to attack the Italian Communist Party.[19]

From 1924 to 1944, the U.S. heroin addict population dropped from 200,000 to about 20,000.[20] These numbers would begin to grow again after the war and after Luciano established a worldwide network of traffickers, distributors, and retailers for heroin.[21] The U.S. government, "through the CIA and its wartime predecessor, the Office of Strategic Services, created a situation that made it possible for the Sicilian-American Mafia and the Corsican underworld to revive the international narcotics traffic."[22]

Similar alliances led to similar consequences in Southeast Asia. In Laos, beginning around 1960, the CIA created a secret army of 30,000 Hmong people to fight the communist in charge of the nation. Hmong Gen. Vang Pao was allowed to use the CIA's Air America planes to traffic opium, the Hmong's major cash crop. This heroin would not only be used to addict thousands of U.S. soldiers fighting in Vietnam, including a disproportionate number of African Americans, but it would eventually comprise about one-third of all heroin in the United States by the end of the war in the mid-1970s.[23] By 1989, 73 percent of the world's heroin was being produced in Southeast Asia.[24]

Beginning in the late 1970s, in Southwest Asia, in the area known as the Golden Crescent where Afghanistan, Pakistan, and Iran come together, the United States supported the anti-communist Mujahedeen guerrillas fighting to overthrow their Soviet-backed government. The covert activities of the CIA would create trafficking lines that did not previously exist. A tremendous spurt in heroin production occurred that would have a direct impact on heroin use in the United States. As researcher Alfred McCoy notes, "As heroin from Afghanistan and Pakistan poured into America throughout 1979...the number of drug-related deaths in New York City rose by 77 percent."[25]

The trafficking surge would also directly impact the black community. Although heroin in Harlem had traditionally come from Southeast Asia, by the early 1980s, as a result of trafficking routes opened by U.S. intelligence operations in Afghanistan and Pakistan, about 42 percent of Harlem's heroin was now coming from southern Asia.[26] As McCoy notes, by late 1980, heroin from the region "had captured 60 percent of the U.S. market."[27] Between 1982 and 1985, covering the first Reagan term, the number of cocaine users grew to 5.8 million, a 38 percent rise.[28]

The pattern of exploding narcotics trafficking would be repeated when the Reagan administration made the decision to support anticommunist rebels in Central America. From Honduras to Costa Rica to Panama to Nicaragua, the CIA and other agencies would employ numerous drug traffickers to assist their covert wars against the Sandinistas in Nicaragua and guerrillas fighting to overthrow military and political dictatorships in El Salvador and Guatemala. The rationale for these unsavory alliances is captured by Gen. Paul F. Gorman, former head of the U.S. Southern Command, who said, "The fact is, if you want to go into the subversion business, collect intelligence, and move arms, you deal with drug movers."[29]

It is critical to note that it was not just the CIA but the entire U.S. foreign policy apparatus that was brought into play in implementing the covert war. This included all branches of the military, the National Security Agency, and the U.S. State Department. All of these activities and connections would be revealed in the investigations and hearings held by Senator John Kerry (D-MA) in the late 1980s. The report issued by the Subcommittee on Terrorism, Narcotics, and International Operations of the Committee on Foreign Relations in the U.S. Senate stated, for example, that "The U.S. State Department paid four contractors $806,401.20 to supply humanitarian aid to the Contra forces in Central America. All four of these companies were owned by known drug traffickers."[30] It went on to say that the U.S. State Department made "payments to drug traffickers...for humanitarian assistance to the Contras, in some cases after the traffickers had been indicted...on drug charges."[31]

Although the *Washington Post* attempted to imply that the Kerry report was ambiguous, a careful read reveals fairly clear conclusions. It states, for instance, that "on the basis of this evidence, it is clear that....elements of the contras....knowingly received financial and material assistance from drug traffickers....In each case, one or another agency of the United States government had information about the involvement."[32]

The Kerry report also concluded, "The logic of having drug money pay for the pressing needs of the contras appealed to a number of people who became involved in the covert war. Indeed, senior U.S. policymakers were not immune to the idea that drug money was a perfect solution to the contras' funding problems."[33]

The increased influx of drugs into the United States, whether Contra carried or otherwise, had a devastating impact on the black community. The harmful effects of drug trafficking and growing substance abuse would be compounded by Reagan, Bush, and Clinton's war on drugs, which has disproportionately been aimed at African Americans.

Racism and the War on Drugs

Historically, U.S. wars on drugs have without exception singled out and accused communities of color of being the main traffickers and users of drugs. Although this has never been the case, since the mid-1960s, drug use by African Americans has grown as heroin, cocaine, and other illegal narcotics have flooded the inner cities.

In the 1980s and into the 1990s, the black community has been ravaged by a drug crisis of historic proportions. The drug crisis among African Americans has resulted in "crack" babies, record drug overdoses, unprecedented numbers of black male youth incarcerations, a rise in AIDS cases, and numerous other harms. In Los Angeles County alone, according to the *Mercury News,* there are more than 70,000 children in foster care for drug-related reasons.[34] In Washington, D.C., of the thousands of neglected and abused children that had to be removed from homes, 90 percent of those cases have involved crack mothers.[35]

The war on drugs has exacerbated the drug crisis in the black community. As scholar Michael Tonry writes, "The war on drugs foreseeably and unnecessarily blighted the lives of hundreds of thousands of young, disadvantaged Americans, especially black Americans, and undetermined decades of efforts to improve the life chances of members of the urban black underclass."[36] One aspect of the racialized drug war that has received the most attention is the sentencing discrepancy between the laws regarding crack cocaine as opposed to the ones regarding cocaine powder. Under the Omnibus Anti-Drug Abuse Act of 1988, possession of five grams of crack cocaine nets a mandatory sentence of five years. For an equal amount of cocaine powder, there is no minimum sentence and, indeed, many offenders receive probation. It takes trafficking of 500 grams of cocaine powder to receive a sentence of five years.[37]

According to the U.S. Sentencing Commission, there are three times as many users of powder cocaine as crack cocaine. Meanwhile, there are far more prosecutions for crack than for powder. Although 91 percent of those who use cocaine snort it, 31 percent smoke it, and 10 percent swallow it, most of the law enforcement focus is on the 31 percent who smoke the substance, according to the 1992 National Household Survey on Drug Abuse.[38] In 1992, of those arrested for federal crack cocaine offenses, 92.6 percent were black. According to one sampling by the U.S. Sentencing Commission, of the defendants charged with simple possession of crack cocaine in the second quarter of 1992, all were black.[39] The disproportionate targeting of African Americans for drug crimes is fostered by a mass media perspective that demonizes and racializes crack users while steadfastly refusing to conduct serious investigation into the genesis of drug importation into black communities or the connections between U.S. foreign economic and political policies and global trafficking.

Media Misinformation

The thunder of response to the *Mercury News* articles forced other major newspapers to reluctantly address the issue and do their own investigations. The big three newspapers—the *Washington Post, Los Angeles Times,* and *New York Times*—all did stories about the series and how other news outlets were covering the controversy. The outrage in the black community—manifest in black newspapers, black talk radio, cable programs, and C-SPAN-broadcasted forums—became too strong to ignore and left the big three with little choice but to put their own spin on a story that the upstart *Mercury News* had scooped them on.

At one level, it is not surprising that the major media organizations would not report about an issue in 1996 that they were given information about in 1986. Despite Senate hearings and the work of the former Christic Institute to bring the stories of Contra drug trafficking to light, major media outlets dismissed the accusations and gave scant attention to these issues.

In their coverage of the story, the major papers—most notably the *Washington Post, New York Times,* and *Los Angeles Times*—had a number of objectives. First, they sought to prove that Ross was not a major dealer and, thus, not the catalyst for the spread of crack. Second, they argued that the Nicaraguans who were involved were marginally, if at all, tied to the Contras. Third, they contended that the amount of cocaine trafficked by the Contras was relatively minuscule. Finally, without questioning the veracity of the CIA, they supported the view that CIA officials had no knowledge of and gave no support to those Contras who were involved in drug trafficking. All of these objectives were in sharp variance with the facts and even these newspapers' own histories of reporting.

As *The Nation* discovered, the *Los Angeles Times* published stories critiquing the *Mercury News* series that contradicted other reports that had appeared in their own paper. In an effort to rebut the *Mercury News* assertions that Ross was the central figure in the distribution of crack cocaine in the Los Angeles area, *Los Angeles Times* reporter Jesse Katz attempted to downplay Ross' role. He quoted a source that stated, "Even on the best day Ricky Ross had, there was way more crack cocaine out there than he could ever control."[40] In fact, this is a rather sensible statement and it is doubtful that Webb or anyone else would disagree with it. Yet, in 1994, in grand hyperbole, Katz wrote in the *Los Angeles Times,* "If there was an eye to the storm, if there was a criminal mastermind behind crack's decade-long reign, if there was one outlaw capitalist most responsible for flooding Los Angeles' streets with mass-marketed cocaine, his name was Freeway Rick."[41] Katz went on to write, "[Ross] was a favorite son of the Colombian cartels, South-Central's first millionaire crack lord."[42]

The purpose of the attacks on the *Mercury News* series by the majors was to refocus the debate away from the more general charge of U.S. government complicity in what many consider the nation's most pressing social problem to a concentration on trivial details and the questionable character of the drug dealers and street operatives that Webb interviewed.

The *Washington Post* asserts that the CIA's role in illegal narcotics smuggling is only alleged and not proven. The *Post* fails, however, to cite any reference to research by academics and journalists that challenge that position.[43] As shown earlier, there is ample evidence of a long history. The *Post* and other papers not only failed to expose the illegal activities of the Contras, but served as a cheerleader for Reagan's wars in Central America and Bush's drug war on the black community. In fact, the reporting was so slanted that the newspaper's ombudsperson, Geneva Overholser, wrote a pointed criticism of the coverage: "The *Post* (and the others) showed more passion for sniffing out the flaws in *San Jose* [*Mercury News*]'s answer than for sniffing out a better answer themselves....Overall, the *Post*'s focus seems to have been misplaced. A principal responsibility of the press is to protect the people from government excesses. The *Post* (among others) showed more energy for protecting the CIA from someone else's journalistic excesses."[44]

The media has diverted attention from the main point of the allegations: the Contras were involved in drug trafficking. Even if the Contras, created by U.S. intelligence agencies and paid for by tax dollars, only dealt one rock of crack, and that had the tacit approval of U.S. officials, then serious policy and ethical problems must be raised (not to mention legal ones) that cannot easily be dismissed because there were other larger drug dealers operating.

Finally, the approach of the major media regarding the black community's response has been to chalk it up to "black paranoia."[45] While noting that a long history of government-sponsored activities against the black community have justified suspicion, the majors have categorized those suspicions as baseless theories about government conspiracies not that different from the rantings about UFOs and tales that the earth is flat.

Policy Implications and Ramifications

Outrage characterized the black community's response to the series. Given the devastation that crack trafficking and addiction has wrecked on the African-American community, it is more than understandable that the discovery that U.S. officials were involved at any level in the spread of crack would initiate a fury that flows from centuries of memories of transgressions.

As a consequence, a mass movement emerged to distribute the *Mercury News* series as widely as possible and to force investigations into the validity of the allegations. Black political leaders and activists called for hearings and investigations. Representative Maxine Waters (D-CA) in a letter to Attorney General Janet Reno wrote:

> In addition to the stress caused by crack cocaine use, I am also terribly disturbed by the heavy-handed, arbitrary, and discriminatory mandatory minimum sentences which politicians have attached to crack cocaine use and possession. These sentences have the effect of severely punishing small-time users, and are prosecuted in a discriminatory way which disproportionately impacts African American males....I would like to request a full and complete investigation into the connection between law enforcement agencies, most particularly the CIA, and the early 1980s importation of crack cocaine. In addition, I would like to know what actions may have allowed these drug shipments to continue. I would also like to know the status of any efforts to investigate, punish, or prosecute those involved in this matter.[46]

Letters were also written by Senators Barbara Boxer (D-CA) and Dianne Feinstein (D-CA) to the Justice Department.[47] San Francisco Mayor Willie Brown and Los Angeles Mayor Richard Riordan expressed outrage over the series allegations and sent letters to President Clinton and other U.S. officials asking for a federal investigation.

Outside of Congress, Rev. Jesse Jackson and other black leaders demanded that Clinton order a complete and independent investigation into the issue by his Intelligence Oversight Board. Jackson also called for the release of all classified documents on the CIA's involvement in the Contra war, all Drug Enforcement Agency (DEA) records related to the Contras, and all DEA files on Meneses and Blandon.[48]

What catalyzed the movement was grassroots activism and black talk radio. Other activists have been arrested in acts of civil disobedience. Longtime civil rights organizer Dick Gregory, radio host Joe Madison, activist Mark Thompson, and Rev. Joe Lowery, president of the Southern Christian Leadership Conference, were arrested for demonstrating at the CIA headquarters in Langley, Virginia and at the Justice Department. Gregory and Madison also went on hunger strikes. From Washington, D.C. to California, there were protests, rallies, and forums. Howard University law students held a march and rally on the U.S. Capitol steps.[49] More than 1,500 people showed up at a Congressional Black Caucus forum on the issue.[50] In Los Angeles, 1,000 people turned out for a forum held by a local coalition that included Waters and city leaders, while 1,500 more waited outside.[51] In many cities, ongoing multiracial coalitions formed to distribute updates on the story and hold community meetings to link the issues raised in the *Mercury News* series with other local, national, and even international concerns.

Madison, through his syndicated radio show, and other black radio personalities from Washington, D.C. and New York to Oakland and Houston, not only kept the black community informed and updated on the ever-unfolding story, but also provided a platform for a counter-oppositional dialogue where the black community could voice its views. Just as black talk radio became the medium through which a popular black voice could offer alternative narratives regarding the O.J. Simpson case, the Clarence Thomas nomination, the Rodney King beating, and the Million Man March, so too did it become the megaphone of opposition to the institutional and mass media denials and attacks.

Conclusion

On October 23, 1996, at a U.S. Senate hearing, CIA Inspector General Frederick P. Hitz testified that, based on their investigation, there was "no credible information" to support the *Mercury News* stories.[52] That pretty much sums up the position that the agency, other government bodies, the major media, and most white lawmakers embraced and continue to stand behind.

Incredibly, that also became the position that Webb's editors at the *Mercury News* would take. On May 11, 1997, *Mercury News* Executive Editor Jerry Ceppos published an editorial directed to the readers of the Webb series. He wrote, after months of criticism and internal evaluation, that "the series did not meet our standards" and that the paper was, in effect, disowning the reportage.[53] Ceppos contended that Webb and *Mercury News* editors exaggerated Webb's findings and, "Through imprecise language and graphics, we created impressions that were open to misinterpretation."[54] He also wrote that the series was often one-sided and that many of those accused of being involved with Contra drug trafficking were not given an opportunity to present their side of the story. Ceppos wrote, for example, "We also did not include CIA comment about our findings, and I think we should have."[55]

The rebuking of Webb, indeed, of the very paper itself, was widely applauded by the major papers. Newspapers that were initially reluctant to cover the story at all, within days of Ceppos' retreat, published editorials essentially celebrating their journalistic victory over the now-humbled *Mercury News*. Among the editorial headlines that appeared after Ceppos' statements were: "Editorial: A newspaper says 'mea culpa'" (*Chicago Tribune*, 14 May 1997); "Editorial: A destructive newspaper series," (Scripps Howard News Service, 14 May 1997); "Editorial: The *Mercury News* comes clean" (*New York Times*, 14 May 1997); "Expose on Crack Was Flawed, Paper Says" (*New York Times*, 13 May 1997); and "CIA Series 'Fell Short,' Editor Says" (*Washington Post*, 13 May 1997). None of these editorials mentioned that even as Ceppos was apologizing, he noted in the same editorial, "Our series solidly documented disturbing information: A drug ring associated with the Contras sold large quantities of cocaine in inner-city Los Angeles in the 1980s at the time of the crack explosion there. Some of the drug profits from those sales went to the Contras."[56] The real journalistic failure here is not the recantation on the part of the *Mercury News*, but the complete disregard by the major papers to pursue the answers to the questions raised by the series as they focused more on battering their upstart competitor.

The *Mercury News*'s turnaround was more than just on the paper's editorial page. In June 1997, Webb was transferred from the paper's office in Sacramento, the state capital, to Cupertino. This obvious demotion was preceded by months of rancor inside the paper, with many staffers and other reporters calling for Webb's dismissal. Apparently, many reporters and editors felt that their careers were jeopardized by Webb's continued tenure with the *Mercury News*.[57]

Despite Ceppos' statement, the Department of Justice and the CIA pledged that their investigations would continue. This had less to do with the search for truth by these government officials than the ongoing pressure from the Congressional Black Caucus, and grassroots activists, as well as continuing media attention to the issue. Few believe that these investigations will result in anything close to the truth, let alone indictments.

The controversy around this issue underscores the necessity of black community awareness and involvement in U.S. foreign policy. The creation of the Contras was a policy initiative that emanated from a Republican White House and was supported by both Democratic and Republican policymakers. It is more disturbing that the CIA-Contra activities were not rogue operations, but, in fact, sanctioned and sustained by the highest U.S. officials.

Black leaders must move beyond merely criticizing the possible role that the Contras had in drug trafficking to questioning a foreign policy that shows little regard for democratic processes or the interests of poor and working people in the developing world. It is not enough that those involved in Contra narcotics trafficking be brought to justice—an unlikely prospect at this point—but that a larger critique be advanced that calls for an overhaul of the mission and practices of U.S. intelligence agencies.

It is also timely for black leaders to renew the call for major reform of the nation's drug laws. Numerous studies have demonstrated that the current laws and policing practices are racially discriminatory in regards to arrest patterns, sentencing, imposition of mandatory minimums, the aforementioned crack-powder sentencing discrepancy, and the punitive character of laws such as the "three strikes you're out" provisions in a number of state and federal statutes. It is also important to reiterate the demand that treatment access be given a higher priority in the federal drug budget. Under Reagan and Bush, 70 percent of the drug budget was aimed at law enforcement, while only 30 percent was focused on education, prevention, and treatment. Under Clinton, two-thirds of the budget is still focused on law enforcement. If the concerns raised by the *Mercury News* series and the U.S. war on drugs in general are to be seriously addressed, major reforms in U.S. drug policies and their links to domestic and foreign political and economic concerns are a necessary beginning.

9

The Souls of White Folk

In *White Man's Burden*, a film in which race *and* class roles in the contemporary United States are reversed, a subtle but sophisticated point is underscored: race and class are shown to be inexorably connected in a system of discrimination that is institutionalized, socialized, and systematic. It becomes impossible, in other words, to portray even a mythologized white oppression without constructing a profound and pervasive class oppression.

In the film, the dominant positive images on television are those of African Americans except for the news coverage, where the criminals are white. Cops beat up on white people for no apparent reason other than harassment. In one scene, a charity fashion show is held in which all the models are black and the money raised goes to help poor, inner-city white children. Racial privilege, petty and broad, is reversed. Even more intriguing, the film struggles to identify the racist mind. Racism is not only a way of acting and benefiting, but of thinking and imaging. It is what African Americans think about whites in the movie that is most compelling, and perhaps most chilling, to watch. Whites are without redemption for most blacks in the film; doomed to a ghetto existence without reprieve, whites are forever shackled by their own limits and irresponsible behavior. These moments, played to great dramatic effects, tease out the multilevel dimensions of racism. Racist attitudes become a material force generating frustration and even hatred among its recipients.

What really drives the point of white oppression home, however, are the class images that pervade the film: all the servants are white, the unemployment office is overwhelmingly filled with whites, and blacks drink expensive wine while pontificating on the genetic and cultural limits of whites. It is African Americans who do the hiring and, often on a whim or an irrational fear, the firing. The filmmakers even create a predatory white underclass that plays loud and irritating music.

Despite the fact that, in the end, it degenerates into classic liberalism of the "can't we all just get along" kind, the richness of the movie is that it overthrows the categories of race and class as they are articulated in popular culture, thereby exposing a necessary link between what is often projected as unrelated identities. In the rhetoric of intolerance that passes for mainstream political discourse today, the individualizing of race and class relations weakens the social response while perpetuating the notion that all discrimination is personal.

What makes the film science "faction" is the reality that there are poor, working-class whites who do suffer from class oppression, albeit a class oppression that travels through the funnel of race. In that funnel, a great transference happens. The concrete material reality of class power is replaced by the abstract threat of racial and ethnic social groups. These perceived threats become hardened views that are easily and repeatedly reinforced.

One issue avoided in the film is the role of those who are perceived to be neither black nor white. In this sense, the film embraces a politically outdated paradigm that whitens or blackens all others. While the social construction of race varies incredibly from nation to nation, the United States has perhaps been the most stubborn in adhering to a simplistic white/black bipolar racial scheme even when the obvious social participation of Native Americans, Asian Americans, and Latinos has always existed. This framework is even more problematic and complicated when one considers the notion of a multiblack African-American community that incorporates the distinctiveness of blacks whose ancestry of the last few hundred years is located in the United States and blacks who have most recently migrated from the Caribbean, or from the many nations of Africa.

The Whiteness of the Ideology of Color Blindness

In the 1990s, the ideology of officialized segregation has been superseded by the ideology of color blindness, which brands racial categories as inherently without merit and relics of the past. It asserts boldly that society is not organized into social groups, but rather individuals with individual strengths and weaknesses, individual talents and limits, and individual value systems and cultural behaviors. Color blindness also jettisons the ramifications of a long history of racial oppression marked not only by the oppression of people of color, but significantly, by substantial white privilege. The view that race is not biological or essentialist—that is, the recognition that racial categories are social and ideological constructs—appears at first blush as progressive, but in fact, color blindness as advocated in the mainstream attempts to neutralize rather than explain the social power of race.

The ideology of color blindness is a smoke screen for a more dangerous and disturbing mission, however, than just to make race neutral. Within the framework of color blindness, all colors of value become white. As legal theorist Kimberlé Williams Crenshaw notes, "Neutral functions here as a euphemism for white."[1] Underneath the progressive notion that race is a social construct and should not matter is an insistence that race will not matter even in circumstances where racial inequities prevail, that is, color blindness becomes racial blindness. In the post-civil rights era where open defense of racial privilege is impolitic, both sides of the ideological spectrum succumb to this theoretical non sequitur. While liberals and some progressives defend color blindness and selectively blind themselves to real racial issues, contemporary conservatives use the rhetoric of color blindness to justify the elimination of social programs and policies deemed to remedy problems that disproportionately affect racial minorities. The conservative appropriation of a term historically associated with progressive politics is rooted in the current dislocation and marginalization of the Left, the lack of a popular radical discourse that argues that the eradication of racism is a social responsibility, and leftist concessions to theories of pathology and personal responsibility.

Despite appropriation of the term and its dominance in popular debate by some well-known conservatives, there is a growing conservative critique of the ideology of color blindness. Theorists, such as Charles Murray, Dinesh D'Souza, and their national and international counterparts, argue that there are determinant cultural and even biological differences between the "races."[2] Their view is that race does, indeed, matter. They offer models, of course, that give supremacy to whiteness. While they claim objectivity and scholarly investigation, their project is thoroughly political in nature and their goal is to influence public policy. It is not social inequities that they seek to eradicate, but rather the societal responsibility and white sacrifice required to do so. Murray and D'Souza get to the same spot via different roads. Initially wedded to the idea that black cultural behavior and social pathology are the causes of black problems, Murray subsequently migrated to building his case on neoeugenics in *The Bell Curve.* D'Souza, who when convenient lays claims to third worldness, argues against multiculturalism, in defense of slavery, and for the abolishment of all government programs that foster "dependency" and perpetuate "victim mentalities."

Race at the Millennium

What are white folks thinking about in these days of great transitions when they think about race? If national opinion polls, academic papers and books, the pabulum of the mass media, and the rhetoric of elected officials are any indication, then they are thinking some pretty appalling, disturbing, and wrong ideas. Recent polls show that not only are whites (and other groups) factually misinformed on a wide range of questions related to race and perceptions of the "other," but that those views shape attitudes and beliefs that rationalize and support racial discrimination.

Media-derived views of race, for example, have led many to believe that African Americans constitute a larger percentage of society than they really do. According to a survey done by the *Washington Post,* whites believe that they are being swamped by a dark plague. Most whites, Hispanics, Asian Americans, and even African Americans said they believe the black population, which is officially about 12 percent, to be twice that size.[3]

More important than just incorrectly guessing the percentage of African Americans in the United States, are views by a majority of white Americans that blacks have made it economically and are doing equal to or better than whites when it comes to employment and education opportunities. The survey found that most whites believed that blacks have reached parity. About 58 percent of whites said African Americans had jobs that were equal to (46 percent), a little better (6 percent), or a substantially better (6 percent) than those held by whites. Only 41 percent said that black jobs were either a little worse (26 percent) or a lot worse (15 percent) than white jobs.[4]

Ignorance was pretty evenly distributed. As the *Washington Post* noted, "White men were as misinformed as white women, wealthy whites were only slightly more informed than lower-income whites and white Republicans surveyed were slightly more informed than white Democrats."

Not surprisingly, African Americans had different views on whether parity had been reached. A vast majority of blacks, 68 percent, stated that racism is alive and kicking and remains "a big problem in our society today." African Americans surveyed believe that not only was racism real, but that it also was a major cause for the deteriorating economic and social conditions faced by millions of blacks. Only 38 percent of whites felt that racism was significant.

The view that blacks have reached parity or equality with whites has far-reaching implications. First, it means that there is little reason to feel sympathy with or special concern for the plight of poor blacks. If inequality and discrimination are not the cause of black poverty, then the problem is clearly African Americans themselves, the reasoning goes. Sure, there was discrimination in the past, but those days are gone. Whether whites' views were generated by images culled from the mass media, nativist fears of a black plague, overgeneralized personal experiences, or ideological predisposition and affinity, the bottom line is that historically derived and socially perpetuated black subjugation is no longer canon.

A second implication of these views, which propelled conservative Republicans into control of Congress in 1994, is that government can not and should not attempt to intervene and address the problems of blacks. According to the survey, "two-thirds of whites interviewed said the federal government had no responsibility to make certain minorities have jobs and incomes equal to whites." The message here, of course, is that programs like affirmative action and minority set-asides are no longer needed.

Significantly, both blacks and whites expressed deep fear and anxiety about the future. Economic dislocations—sparked by runaway shops, depressed wages, downsizing, new technologies that replace workers, and other factors—have people searching for answers and solutions. Although sharing the same fears, the survey shows that whites and blacks have opposing perspectives on what to do. A majority of whites conclude that efforts such as affirmative action and government welfare programs, as well as the growth in immigrants of color, have all contributed to diminishing their quality of life and should be abolished or halted. On the other hand, an overwhelmingly number of blacks who felt concern about the future favor programs like affirmative action and felt that government has a role and responsibility to intervene where possible to alleviate economic and social problems.

In 1997, a poll by the Gallup Organization on race drew major media attention. The poll, conducted between January 4 and February 28, interviewed 1,680 whites and 1,269 African Americans, a significant number given the usual underrepresentation of blacks even in surveys that are about race. The 1997 poll traced the opinions of blacks and whites on issues of race that compared with previous polls. What is important to note about the poll is that it reflects the subjective perspectives of those interviewed rather than the reality of race relations. Gallup notes in the executive summary:

> Whites are more positive than blacks on a variety of perceptual measures of how well blacks are faring in our society, and how they are treated in the local community....Whites also tend to view themselves as having very little personal prejudice against blacks, but perceive that "other" whites in their area have much higher levels of prejudice against blacks. Blacks also ascribe to whites significantly higher levels of racial prejudice than whites give themselves. Blacks claim that they have little prejudice against whites.

On issues of personal relations between blacks and whites, the poll found evidence of a significant decline regarding some racial prejudices held by whites, such as living and working with blacks or sending their children to school with blacks. It also documented amazing changes in whites' attitudes toward interracial marriages and their expressed support for voting for a black candidate for president. In 1958, only 4 percent of whites approved of interracial marriages; in 1994, the number had risen to 45 percent, and in the 1997 poll, the number was 61 percent.[5] Similarly, in 1958, 35 percent of whites said they would vote for a black presidential candidate; in 1987, the number was 77 percent, and in the 1997 poll, 93 percent.[6]

These numbers are not coterminous with the reality of race relations. Residential and school segregation is strong and growing. And, while the number of interracial marriages has grown, many couples still face discrimination and individual prejudice. There is also little evidence that whites will actually vote for a black presidential candidate when given the chance as opposed to being asked an abstract question. Studies have shown, for example, that the responses of people in surveys often reflect what appears to be the right thing to say rather than what they really believe or how they will actually behave. That people believe that the right thing to say is not to express open prejudice can be seen as progress and a result of the influence of the movement against racism.

Even with the popular hesitation to be seen as prejudiced, whites had little trouble in stating their opposition to programs such as affirmative action. There were also big gaps in the perception of how much race relations have advanced. More than three-quarters of whites, 76 percent, say that blacks are treated equally in local communities, while only 49 percent of blacks felt the same way. While 59 percent of blacks felt that "government should make every effort to improve conditions of blacks and minorities," only 34 percent of whites thought so. Overall, a majority of blacks, 56 percent of those without a college degree and 76 percent of those with one, felt that racism would always be a problem in the United States. Fifty-five percent of whites felt the same way.

The differences in perception about race between whites and blacks grows out of the distinct realities that the two communities face. Those differences are also fostered by the wide dissemination of conservative and racist views on race, in the form of books, films, news programs, television shows, and other popular outlets. Much of this work comes from those ensconced in academia.

Writing Racism

The disparate views of whites and blacks are, in part, massaged by contemporary academic discourses regarding the nature and function of race as a determinant of social and cultural outcomes. Conservative academics have increasingly taken on the role of creating racial scapegoats and providing "scholarly" cover to justify social attacks on people of color and the poor. In the United States in the 1990s, under the guise of scholarly inquiry, racism has taken on an academic veneer in books such as *The Bell Curve* and *The End of Racism* that have dramatically helped to shift the popular debate on race (and racism) to a debate on genetics and personal responsibility. Funded by conservative and right-wing think tanks, these works have political agendas that have been ignored by the mass media as it legitimizes them as works worthy of intellectual debate. Other academics who engage in what one writer called "scientific pornography" include City College of New York's Michael Levin, Johns Hopkins University's Robert Gordon, University of California at Santa Barbara's Garrett Hardin, University of Delaware's Linda Gottfredson, University of Pennsylvania's Daniel Vining Jr., University of California at Berkeley's retired Arthur Jensen, and University of Georgia's R. Travis Osborne.[7]

Views, ostensibly scientific in nature, about the intellectual inferiority of African Americans (and other blacks in the diaspora) are not limited to the United States. A global backlash has emerged as marginalized and oppressed communities have contested social status quos in all the major industrialized nations. As in the United States, rationalizing state cutbacks and a reduced welfare state on the backs of people of color and ethnic minorities is a task that has been embraced by some academics, which serves the purpose of diverting critical focus by the majority population on genuine power centers while allowing racialized targeting to occur unchallenged.

Social scientists, in particular, have rushed to meet this task. Canada, which has become increasingly multicultural due to large immigrant populations from the Caribbean, Africa, and India, has produced a number of racial theorists in *The Bell Curve* mode. Canadian psychologist J. Phillipe Rushton has long been notorious for his crackpot studies on the relationship between race and intelligence. In his *Race, Intelligence, and Behavior,* he echoes a long history of scientific rationales for racist views about blacks as well as the intellectual and even physical superiority of whites.

In 1996, in England, a similar controversy about race and intelligence arose around the book *The G Factor: General Intelligence and Its Implications*, written by a little-known psychology professor at Edinburgh University named Christopher Brand. At a press conference to promote the book, Brand boldly stated that "I am perfectly proud to be a racist in the scientific sense. It is a scientific fact that black Americans are less intelligent than white Americans." That Brand would cite African Americans as his racial target of choice is significant in two ways. First, it reflects the globalized perception of the racial struggle in the United States. Second, it denotes the media power—unaccountable, unmitigated, and discursive—underlying global articulations of race. After broad outrage, John Wiley & Sons, the publisher of the book, withdrew it from circulation, stating belatedly that they recognized that the book was "making assertions we find repellent."[8] Brand also suffered the indignity of students boycotting his lectures and organizing rallies demanding his ouster.

The eugenics argument is old, very old, and not worth dignifying as an intellectual function. Stephen Gould's *The Mismeasure of Man,* Barry Mehler's *The New Eugenics Movement in the United States,* Daniel Kevles' *In the Name of Eugenics,* and other books have thoroughly repudiated the argument. The question that really has to be raised, as Harvard scholar Henry Louis Gates and *Harper* editor Michael Lind both noted in a special issue of *The New Republic* that published critiques of *The Bell Curve,* why are these works being published now and given such widespread exposure? The agenda of these writers and the foundations that fund them is social and political, not academic. It is not about "ending racism," it is about ending welfare and other distributive economic programs. It is not about issues of intelligence; it is about reform that punishes legal immigrants of color and attacks those who are undocumented. It is not about "less qualified" blacks and Latinos taking white jobs; it is about less aid to the cities and abolishing all social programs.

A clear message is being sent to whites, blacks, Latinos, Native Americans, Asians, and other sectors of society. Whites are being told not to feel guilty about being less sympathetic to the plight of the poor, especially the poor of color. First, it is their own fault, due to their social and cultural predispositions, and perhaps even their genes.

Second, government would do better to reallocate funds for social spending to other projects since "those people" cannot be helped anyway. The message to groups of color is that you are on your own, and that you need to accept your intellectual and social limits and remain as isolated from the rest of society as you can.

White Politicians and the "Constant Curse"

In 1997, Representative Tony Hall and a number of other white Congressmembers proposed that the government apologize to African Americans for slavery. The apology would involve no reparations or any programs that would compensate African Americans for not only the experience of slavery, but the legacy that has crippled the economic and social life of the black community up to this very day. The response of Harvard Law Professor and former Clinton aide Christopher Edley to the proposed apology was appropriate. He stated, "Our problem is the lingering ideology of racial difference and caste along with the inherited economic disadvantages of slavery and segregation. So long as that subtle legacy of slavery remains, an apology would be superficial, not reflective of the moral change truly required of America."[9] The idea was rejected by House Speaker Newt Gingrich and other Republican Congressmembers as unnecessary since, in effect, racism was no longer a problem in the United States. Meanwhile, Clinton was constructing an intervention of his own.

President Clinton has given a number of speeches related to race since he has been in office and two stand out: his second inaugural speech on January 20, 1996, and his June 14, 1997 speech launching a national race relations initiative. These speeches were markers of Clinton's views on race and the legacy he seeks to leave behind. They were attended by well-known civil rights leaders and black elected officials, and received broad media coverage. Neither speech was a breakthrough regarding policy, but both capture Clinton's struggle to balance his stated desire to bridge the nation's great racial divide with his centrist political sensibilities that proffer unnecessary concessions to the rhetoric of personal responsibility and equal culpability.

Clinton's celebration of his second inauguration was planned to occur on Martin Luther King Jr.'s birthday holiday. Appropriately, in his remarks, Clinton spoke about racial divisiveness in the United

States. He stated, "The divide of race has been America's constant curse. Each new wave of immigrants gives new targets to old prejudices." He also referred to race when he said, "We cannot—we will not—succumb to the dark impulses that lurk in the far regions of the soul, everywhere."[10] Like most liberal interpretations of King that seek to de-radicalize him, Clinton's references that day to the slain civil rights leader focused on his "I Have a Dream" speech from 1963. He said of King, "Like a prophet of old, he told of his dream that one day America would rise up and treat all its citizens as equals before the law and in the heart. Martin Luther King's dream was the American dream. His quest is our quest—the ceaseless striving to live out our true creed."

It is likely that King would have appreciated having a president, from the South no less, acknowledge that racial discrimination is still a problem in the United States *and* that the government has some responsibility to intervene to end that discrimination where necessary and possible. King also would have likely seen the value of the diversity of men and women of all races and backgrounds—entertainers, civil rights leaders, business leaders, and elected officials—standing with Clinton.

In spite of those acknowledgments, it seems highly probable that, based on Clinton's policies and politics, King would not have been found anywhere near Washington on inauguration day. Just as he challenged Presidents Dwight Eisenhower, John Kennedy, and Lyndon Johnson, and other white moderates, I seriously doubt if he would have given Clinton any easier time. Given that Clinton has taken positions that, at best, could be called moderate Republicanism—such as welfare and crime, whose impact on millions of African Americans, Latinos, and the poor is nothing short of long-term disaster—if King's record is any indication, he would have consistently called for resistance. While many black leaders today have found accommodation with Clinton, preferring to grouse about his duplicitous politics and then return to the fold, King operated in a period where strong black leftist and nationalist trends helped to radicalize otherwise moderate civil rights leaders, forcing them to strongly challenge presidential initiatives deemed harmful to African Americans.

This is speculation, of course. No one knows where King would be today if he had lived. Indeed, as the Discovery Channel showed on its historically hypothetical program *What If?* King might have even become president of the United States, given the right historical configurations. In any case, we do have King's own words as guidelines to where he stood on issues of race, poverty, democracy, and equality. In the last years and days of his life, King was passionately devoted to ending the nation's shameful poverty as well as racial discrimination against African Americans, two interlinked but distinct social concerns. He died before the term "affirmative action" came into vogue, but he made it clear that he did support special government programs to remedy the centuries of oppression of African Americans. King wrote, "Whenever the issue of compensatory treatment for the Negro is raised, some of our friends recoil in horror. The Negro should be granted equality, they agree; but he should ask nothing more. On the surface, this appears reasonable, but it is not realistic." King, who did not merely dream about a "color-blind" society, argued that something aggressive had to be done to actualize it. He stated, "A society that has done something special against the Negro for hundreds of years must now do something special for the Negro"[11] if competition on a just and equal basis is ever to occur. King also did not bifurcate radical politics from the struggle for equality. Those who would evoke King's words in the name of a conservative or neoliberal agenda, as Clinton did, profoundly misread King's revolutionary vision of a society reconstituted and reconstructed along the lines of radical social democracy.

The de-liberalizing of Clinton's cabinet in his second term demonstrates the hypocrisy embedded in evoking King while moving to implement a political agenda that countered all that King stood for. Behind the symbolism of having a cabinet that "looked like America," was the reality of a cabinet that thought like big business. By all appearances and, indeed, in preinaugural rhetoric, Clinton seemed all too ready to accommodate the Republican Congress on a wide range of issues. Clinton's notion of a "vital center," his explanation of the core politics of the Democratic Party, is significantly to the Right of the liberal Democratic politics of most of the last 30 years. Vital centers do not make radical change. Clinton's political equivocations underscore that a leadership of vision and audacity—exemplified by King—is sorely missing on the national political scene from politicians of all races.

On the issue of race, King would have sadly witnessed over the years, by both Republican and Democratic political leaders, including Clinton, the twisting of his notion of a color-blind society to mean a society in which history is erased, group experiences are meaningless, and the burden of addressing concerns of ongoing institutional and systemic discrimination are placed on the individual. King's vision of a society where people are not judged on the basis of the color of their skin or the shape of their eyes or the familiarity of their tongue presumed the *a priori* existence of equality, justice, and opportunity.

In his speech, Clinton talked mainly in generalities when he addressed issues of race and he proposed no programs or initiatives to address America's racial divide. By not speaking to the wide range of racial incidents that have occurred during his tenure in the White House, from the exposure of corporate racism to the militias to attacks on affirmative action, he left the impression that responsibility for the racial divide is evenly tasked out between whites and people of color. This fits into the conservative bromide that African Americans can be just as racist as whites, dismissing the fact that racist violence is overwhelmingly targeted at African Americans, Asians, and Latinos; that the perpetrators of these acts are almost universally white; and that institutional and systemic racism are still relevant and critical factors. Clinton also did not discuss the urgent crisis facing America's cities that disproportionately inflict injuries on the African-American and Latino poor. In his first term, Clinton avoided serious discussion of the cities, growing economic disparities, and public school abandonment. Finally, in the speech, he also avoided any criticism of the real sources of racist power that reside in the social institutions, political structures, economic configurations, and popular media of this society.

In June 1997, Clinton launched his "Race Initiative" project, which has five goals: "to articulate the President's vision of racial reconciliation"; "to help educate the nation about facts surrounding the issue of race"; "to promote a constructive dialogue" about race; "to recruit and encourage leadership...to help bridge racial divides";

and "to find, develop, and implement solutions" in the area of race relations. To achieve these goals, an Advisory Board was created to "assist the President in outreach efforts," such as holding town hall meetings and other efforts. The Advisory Board is headed up by imminent scholar and historian John Hope Franklin, who is African American. He is joined by Linda Chavez-Thompson, an executive vice president with the AFL-CIO; Rev. Suzan D. Johnson Cook of New York's Bronx Christian Fellowship Church; Thomas H. Kean, former Republican governor of New Jersey; Los Angeles attorney Angela E. Oh; Robert Thomas, CEO of Nissan Motor Corporation; and William Winter, former Democratic governor of Mississippi. Chavez-Thompson is Latino, Oh is Asian American, Kean, Thomas, and Winter are white, and Cook is black. Clinton's former adviser on affirmative action policies Christopher Edley, who is black, will serve as consultant to the board.

After weeks of buildup, where the White House fed the press numerous stories about Clinton's sincerity and life experiences regarding race relations, Clinton delivered a commencement speech at the University of California at San Diego where he talked about race and his proposal to generate a national dialogue on the issue. Attending the speech were a large number of African Americans from Congress and Clinton's administration, including Labor Secretary Alexis Herman, Transportation Secretary Rodney Slater, Veteran Affairs Secretary Jesse Brown, Congressional Black Caucus Chairperson Representative Maxine Waters (D-CA), Representative Jim Clyburn (D-SC), Representative John Lewis (D-GA), and Representative Juanita Millender-McDonald (D-CA).

Overall, Clinton's speech revisits common ground. It came at a pivotal time in the nation's angst over race, creating a rare opportunity for leadership and vision, neither of which Clinton was able to furnish. Never straying from the center, Clinton moderates the excesses of the Right while keeping an arm's length from even the liberals in his own party. His remarks, thus, continue the evasion and denial of responsibility for the nation's race problems that must be assumed, at least in part, by policymakers and politicians. The speech begins with a candid acknowledgment of the sordid and murderous racist history of the United States, tracing a spring of incidents and themes from the slave sanctions ensconced in the Constitution up to the present era. Clinton declared, "We were born with a Declaration of Independence which asserted that we were all created equal and a Constitution that enshrined slavery....We pushed Native Americans off their land....Japanese Americans...were herded into internment camps....Though minorities have more opportunities than ever today, we still see evidence of bigotry—from the desecration of houses of worship, whether they be churches, synagogues or mosques, to demeaning talk in corporate suites."[12] Significantly, the word "racism" is never mentioned in connection with these events. Euphemisms, acting in the interests of Clinton's color blindness perspective, are employed—such as "discrimination," "demeaning talk," or "disturbing tendency"—underscoring Kimberlé Williams Crenshaw's insight that the "triumph of the ideology of colorblindness has effectively rendered explicit racist discourse entirely unsuitable within mainstream political debate."[13] Clinton stays on safe and acceptable turf and, as further described below, never lets himself be put in the position of seeming to unduly blame whites for the nation's problems regarding race.

He next asks the rhetorical question, "Can we become one America in the 21st century?" It is a question complicated not so much by the growing diversity of the nation, as hyped in the mass media, academia, and political circles, but by the policies of the state and the unchecked power of corporate America. It is easier to fret and rant over what conservatives and many whites view as an invasion of nonwhites than identify and address straightforwardly the ideological and power foundations on which inequality stand in the United States. Clinton then explains why diversity should be seen as in the interests of the nation. He states, "We understand the benefits of our racial, linguistic, and cultural diversity in a global society, where networks of commerce and communications draw us closer and bring rich rewards to those who truly understand life beyond their nation's borders." Here, again, Clinton equivocates the differences in interests from the majority of working people, who are not benefiting necessarily from globalization, and the transnationals, which truly do receive benefits "beyond the nation's borders."

Clinton defends his record on race and again underlines his theme of personal responsibility by stating, "For four and a half years now, I have worked to prepare America for the 21st century with a strategy of opportunity for all, responsibility from all, and an American community of all our citizens." He then addresses what many view as his most controversial and certainly enduring decision regarding concerns about race and poverty: welfare reform. To the cheers of the mostly white crowd, he stated, "We must press forward to move millions from poverty and welfare to work."[14] This is Clinton at his sophistic best. Analyst after analyst has shown that welfare reform, as fashioned by Clinton and the Republican Congress, will move millions, including perhaps a million children, from welfare to poverty. Welfare reform is doing more to create a class of sub-minimum wage workers who are forced to endure menial work, with virtually no opportunities for obtaining skills or advancing their educational level, than any other legislative reform in the last 50 years. The fact that the momentum behind the reform was built, to a great degree, by racializing conceptions of welfare recipients only makes Clinton's signature on the bill and ongoing rationalizations even that more hypocritical.

Even in his support for affirmative action in the speech, he selected moderation. He first choose to not sharply criticize the 1996 vote in California to eliminate affirmative action by stating that Californians who voted for the repeal possess no "ill motive." He then goes on to say that for "those who oppose affirmative action, I ask you to come up with an alternative. I would embrace it if I could find a better way." Here, Clinton is signaling that he feels trapped by the present policy, that perhaps it does harm whites, and that he does not really have a deep commitment to the policy. This is a message to both conservatives and neoliberals that he is about realpolitiks and not necessarily won over to a program of racial remediation. He implores those who support affirmative action to reach out to those who disagree with it and to point out the *practical impact* of the policy. A moral imperative to racial justice, as far as Clinton is concerned, has no place in this debate.

There are several schools of thought as to why Clinton created his Race Initiative. One belief is that he sincerely wants to improve race relations in the nation. Certainly no president since Lyndon

Johnson has spoken so publicly and often on the subject of race. Unfortunately, sincerity has little to do with the development of public policy or the urgency of personal political agendas. A second view is that Clinton is responding to the polls and surveys that demonstrate that race relations in the United States are strained and that presidential leadership is wanting. A third view is that Clinton is concerned about what the historical record will show about his presidency in the years ahead. As he faces his legacy, despite his bombast to the contrary, Clinton must recognize that his record on race is mixed at best and that little that he has done has mitigated the nation's racial discord. While his policies on civil rights and other racial matters can arguably be seen as better than those of Reagan and Bush, few black or Latino leaders are ready to cheer the work that he has done thus far and many see little difference. The list of issues in which he has adopted policies and positions inimical to the black community is long, including: his treatment of Haitian refugees, the Lani Guinier nomination, his jettisoning of Joycelyn Elders, his refusal to end the crack cocaine/cocaine powder sentencing disparity, his support for draconian Republican budget cuts, his back and forth on affirmative action, his signing of NAFTA and the 1994 Crime Bill, his support for the death penalty, and the bungling of the Henry Foster surgeon general nomination. Above all, as previously noted, Clinton's signature on a Republican welfare reform bill, which wiped out 60 years of guaranteed assistance to the nation's poor, who are disproportionately black, potentially sending millions into destitution, has consolidated for many African Americans a negative appraisal of his terms in office. Whether Clinton's Race Initiative can partially rescue what may ultimately be seen as a poor, perhaps even disastrous record on race—from the president who promised to be a leader on the issue—remains to be seen.

It is doubtful. The Race Initiative is much too little, much too late. Clinton made clear in his remarks before and after the speech that he was not going to initiate any new programs or address any of the concerns that civil rights leaders and others have been proposing for years. As he noted, the Race Initiative was primarily about dialogue, an exchange of ideas. When pushed against the wall, he simply would not go any further than the moderate program that had characterized his whole presidency. Clinton's White House was long on symbolism and short on substance when it came to race relations actions. As even Harvard University Law Professor Randall Kennedy, who has fashioned a career on wringing his hands about the overemphasis on race, noted, "The tribute to Jackie Robinson, the medals for the long-ignored black heroes of World War II, the apology for the Tuskegee experiment, and the condemnation of racially motivated violence were all politically safe gestures rendered according to wholly conventional formulas."[15]

Ideologically, even as Clinton noted the long history of brutality against African Americans, Latinos, Asian Americans, and Native Americans, and a continuing disparity on a wide range of measurements, he fell back on the conservative mantra of "personal responsibility." He stated in the speech, "Beyond opportunity, we must demand responsibility from every American. Our strength as a society depends upon both—upon people taking responsibility for themselves and their families, teaching their children good values, working hard and obeying the law, and giving back to those around us."[16] Note that Clinton lays down no challenge to the corporate powers that determine much of who works, where they work, how they work, and the nature and viability of communities from coast to coast. The devolution of the welfare state under Clinton's watch has continued with little trouble. Conservative policymakers and the transnational corporations have had a friend in the Clinton White House that has supported virtually every demand that has arisen from the global economic powers based in the United States.

Following the speech, the Advisory Board had hardly begun its work when internal division arose. A public and embarrassing debate emerged among board members over how the race question in the United States should be framed and addressed. Asian-American board member Angela Oh argued that the discussion and the project should move beyond what she calls the traditional "black-white paradigm." She contended that the United States has become too racially and ethnically complex to define the race issue in dichotomous black-and-white terms. The two African-American members of the board Franklin and Cook, countered that the foundation of racial conflict in the United States and its legacy arise from slavery and the experiences of blacks. The dialogue, argued Franklin, must begin and be framed by coming to terms with the historical racism against African Americans.

In a number of ways, the debate misses the point. Franklin and Cook would certainly agree that the race issue in the United States has never been simply black and white. To believe that would mean erasure of the memories of the murderous land grab against Native Americans and Latinos. It would also mean obscuring the history of brutality perpetrated against Asian Americans, as manifested by the internment camps for Japanese Americans during World War II. These are concerns that Franklin has himself written about and is more than capable of discussing. At the same time, Oh should have been astute enough to recognize that the pervasive racist images associated with issues such as crime, welfare, and affirmative action are overwhelmingly, if not exclusively, black, and this is not accidental or incidental. The complicated configurations of race relations in the United States, where ethnicity and skin color find multiple and overlapping representations in how race is conceived have not diminished, in the minds of most, the notion that the conflicts between blacks and whites are the most intense, persistent, and immediate. Full integration of African Americans into mainstream society has stalled in many areas even as it has opened up for Latinos and Asian Americans in some ways. Indeed, a conservative retrenchment against African Americans is in process, and, in the end, that retrenchment hurts all people of color.

There are other factors that color the debate on race in the United States that the Advisory Board did not seem to identify. The changing racial demographics of the nation have been noted, but important subtleties have been overlooked. While it is true that Latinos will become the largest group of color in the decades ahead, public perception of that growth will be affected by Latinos disproportionate concentration in certain states, such as California, Texas, and New York. For the most part, African Americans will continue to have significantly disproportionate and often decisive influence in most of the nation's major cities by virtue of not only their numbers, but also their history, political experience, and demographics. This particular configuration will mean that both African Americans and Latinos must engage in coalitions if both groups are to progress. At the same time, it must be recognized that the differences between African Americans, Latinos, Asian Americans, and Native Americans have not disappeared. None of these groups are excluded from the racial socializing process that occurs through the media, education system, and other institutions that instruct us on how to think about race.

It is interesting to note that neither side of this debate raised the issue of Native-American participation on the Advisory Board. If there is any group in the United States that has been marginalized and dispossessed, it has been Native Americans. As Clinton even noted in his remarks, the native population was robbed of its land through the most brutal program of genocide in the nation's history. Yet, when he put together his board, representation from the Native-American community was overlooked. Perhaps that oversight alone is more telling about the ultimate worth of the Race Initiative than its stated concern of racial reconciliation. African-American leaders, scholars, and policymakers must go beyond Clinton in finding white leaders who are prepared to honestly poise and answer the hard questions of race that the nation faces.

On January 11, 1996, a different kind of speech was given by former Senator Bill Bradley at a gathering in Los Angeles. Titled "Race Relations in America: The Best and Worst of Times," Bradley located the nation's racial problems in both its past and future. He stated, "Slavery was America's original sin, and race remains its unresolved dilemma."[17] Unlike Clinton and others, Bradley did not avoid the touchy subject whose consequences resonate down to the present era. He does not claim that slavery is an irrelevant relic; rather, he sees it as a central part of the nation's history and a shaper of its development.

Bradley also talked about the racial tensions of the current era and what is driving those tensions. He stated, "So what is the state of black-white relations in America? Both black and white America is caught in a traumatic economic transformation in which millions of Americans feel insecure about their future for good reason."[18]

He called for a new racial paradigm and for whites to reconceptualize how they think about race relations in the United States. In his challenge to whites he said, "We have to recognize that the flip side of racial discrimination is racial privilege, which consists of all those things that come to white Americans in the normal course of living; all the things they take for granted that a black person must never take for granted....As long as white America believes that the race problem is primarily a black problem of meeting white standards to gain admittance to white society, things will never stabilize and endure."[19]

In the end, Bradley called for a new political vision for the nation. Implicit in his words was a critique of the current configuration of political leadership. By most measures, neither party has played a progressive role in race politics in recent years. He stated:

> Above all it will take a new biracial political vision that acts....A new political vision requires people to engage each other, endure the pain of candor, learn from each other's history, absorb each other's humanity and move on to higher ground. Such is the task of racial healing. It won't happen overnight nor will one person bring it however illustrative his career, nor will one person destroy it, however heinous his crime or poisonous his rhetoric.[20]

1 0

Old Stories from the New South

More than 13 decades after the end of the Civil War, the South still holds a peculiar fascination in the imagination of the people of the United States. Following the destruction of the first Reconstruction, the South led the nation in the creation of an encompassing segregation. It took 70 years between the 1895 *Plessey* decision and the 1965 Voting Rights Act for a second Reconstruction to occur. In this reincarnation, the mythology of a New South was constructed that argued that the old way of doing things and the old way of thinking were in the past. In this New South, whites no longer defend Jim Crow and African Americans have unprecedented opportunities.

The South has risen again, at least in terms of national politics. In a remarkable political flip, white southerners have switched in increasing numbers to the party that defeated them in the Civil War. If that was not notable enough, add the Republican takeover of Congress in 1994, the growth in the number of Republican mayors and governors, and the southernization of the White House.

Among the southern national leaders are President Bill Clinton (former Arkansas governor), Vice President Al Gore (former Tennessee senator), Speaker of the House Newt Gingrich (Georgia), House Majority leader Dick Armey (Texas), and Senate Majority Leader Trent Lott (Louisiana). In the 104th and 105th Congresses, southerners also chaired critical committees: Jesse Helms (North Carolina), Senate Foreign Relations; Strom Thurmond (South Carolina), Senate Armed Services; John Warner (Virginia), Senate Rules and Administration; Robert Livingston (Louisiana), House Appropriations; Thomas Bliley (Virginia), House Commerce; Larry Combest (Texas), House Intelligence; Floyd Spence (South Carolina), House National Security; and Bill Archer (Texas), House Ways and Means.

For African Americans, where the South has historically been the bane of racial progress, the southernization of American politics has significant and worrisome meaning. Polls and surveys consistently show that the South remains the most politically conservative region in the nation. It is no surprise, therefore, that as the Democratic Party moves to the Right, it moves South.

Not coincidentally, the South is also the poorest region in the country. It boasts the highest unemployment and poverty levels, and the lowest incomes. Southern states are very stingy when it comes to income transfers to the poor. Combined state welfare benefits and Food Stamps in many states—Alabama (46 percent), Louisiana (49 percent), Mississippi (42 percent), Tennessee (48 percent), and Texas (48 percent)—do not bring recipients up to even half the official poverty line.[1] The southern economy is also being battered by NAFTA. As researchers Sarah Anderson and Karen Harris write, "Layoffs related to the trade pact are accelerating throughout rural America, especially in the South. Rural workers comprise only 21 percent of the U.S. workforce, yet they have suffered 46 percent of NAFTA-related job losses. Of the rural layoffs, 42 percent occurred in the South."[2]

Seeking new opportunities, African Americans in the 1990s are returning to the South in record numbers. In places such as the suburbs of Atlanta, Montgomery County, Alabama, and the small city of Petersburg, Virginia, the black population is growing. A number of factors are contributing to this return, including African Americans in the army who have relocated, and a flow of immigrants from the Caribbean and Latin America to agricultural regions in Florida and other southern states.

Yet economic progress has been elusive for most African Americans in the South. Take the case of black farmers. As John Zippert, director of program operations for the Federation of Southern Cooperatives, writes, "For black farmers in the rural South, there has been a 'continuing crisis' for this entire century. Black farmers have faced not only the general decline in the farm economy, but also fraud, neglect, racial discrimination and economic exploitation."[3]

Although the wealthiest black middle class in U.S. history exists in the 1990s, the height of black landownership goes back to near the turn of the century. In 1910, the U.S. Census of Agriculture found that African Americans owned 15 million acres of land. Since that time, black landownership has declined. In 1960, African Americans owned only 6 million acres and, by 1987, that had dropped to 2.4 million acres. By the mid-1990s, African Americans were losing land at a rate of 1,000 acres per day. According to one low calculation, this costs the black community over $262 million a year in the early 1980s.[4] Almost a decade later, the House Committee on Government Operations reported, "The sad truth is that little has changed since the 1982 publication of the U.S. Civil Rights Commission report....[T]he Committee finds that ironically, FmHA [the Farmers Home Administration] has been a catalyst in the decline of minority farming."[5]

As the *Washington Post* reported, "Black farmers wait far longer for loan decisions, and are more likely to be rejected for loans, than their white counterparts....USDA investigators said that white farmers...typically waited 84 days for loan decisions while black farmers had to wait an average 222 days. Investigators also found that 84 percent of the white applicants had their loan applications approved, while only 56 percent of black applicants were granted loans." It went on to state,

> Government studies show that minority farmers are underrepresented on the local committees that make loan decisions, particularly in the South. One internal USDA probe found that local officials were "rude and insensitive to black farmers," that their projected crop yields were calculated differently from those of white farmers and that blacks were sometimes rejected because of "computation errors."

The 1982 U.S. Civil Rights Commission report, ominously predicted that if land loss trends continued, "there will be no more black farmers by the year 2000."[6] From 1982 to 1992, the number of black farmers dropped from 33,250 to 18,816.[7]

Leading the fight to save black land and black farmers, as well as to address farm issues more generally, is the Federation of Southern Cooperatives. It has worked in coalition with a number of other groups, including the Rural Coalition, Indian Tribal Agriculture Council, North Carolina Land Loss Project, Rural Advancement Fund, Arkansas Land and Farm Development Corporation, Rural Development Leadership Network, National Family Farm Coalition, and National Council of La Raza.

It would be unfair, of course, not to acknowledge the progressive movement in the South, which consists of activists of all colors. From progressive elected officials, such as Rep. Cynthia McKinney (D–GA) and Alabama State Senator Hank Sanders, to longtime anti-racist activists, such as Anne Braden and Gwen Patton, the southern progressive movement is alive and strong. In addition to the traditional civil rights groups, such as the NAACP and SCLC, organizations like the Federation of Southern Cooperatives, Institute for Southern Studies, Southern Poverty Law Center, Center for Democratic Renewal, and others have been on the frontline challenging racist and class attacks on working people in the region.

The fact remains, however, that the region continues to be the center of national racial strife. The illusion of a reconstituted South is continually shattered by the reality of inequities, discriminatory public policies, and the predicates of a conservative cultural resurgence. As the century ends, in the South, churches are burning, Confederate flags are still flying, chain gangs are breaking rocks, and the South has reemerged in the imagination of the nation.

Race Governs

On June 27, 1981, out for a good time on a hot summer night, 17-year-old Susie Deer and several friends went joyriding through the small town of Hot Springs. The car full of drunken white teenagers made the fateful decision to go to the black section of town. It was about 4 a.m.

Driving through the neighborhood, the teens threw beer cans and yelled racist epithets at the few folks who were out at the time. Billy Ray Washington and his wife were walking home from a late-night bar and restaurant when someone in the car chucked a beer can at Washington and called him a "motherfucking nigger." In response to these provocations, Washington picked up a slab of concrete and threw it at the car, where it went through a window and smashed Deer in the face.

Bleeding profusely from the mouth and nose, Deer was rushed to the emergency room at Ouachita Memorial Hospital. Since the injury was not considered life-threatening, she was not even brought into the operating room, where the doctors were to perform plastic surgery to repair her teeth, nose, and jaw, until about 9 a.m.

The operation proceeded well for a while, with no apparent concerns. About three hours into it, however, a serious problem arose. The doctors asked the nurse-anesthetist to move the oxygen tubes that were in Deer's nose to her throat, a common procedure known as re-intubation, so that they could perform the nose surgery. At first, no one noticed that the nurse was having trouble moving the tubes and, by the time they did, Deer had stopped breathing. One of the doctors, James Griffin, finally had to do the task. For more than an hour, the doctors worked to get Deer breathing again, with no success. At 1:13 p.m., Deer was pronounced dead.

As it turned out, this particular nurse had a history of problems in the operating room. Records showed that she often read racing forms or filed her fingernails while administering anesthesia to patients. Even more disturbing, at the time of Deer's death, this nurse was being sued for negligence by the family of Laura Lee Slayton, who had died at Ouachita Memorial the year before. In that case, minor elective surgery turned into tragedy when the nurse had trouble getting oxygen to the patient. The case was eventually settled in the family's favor.

Given the circumstances under which Deer died, the case was turned over to the state's medical examiner, Dr. Fahamy Malak. Under Arkansas law, Malak had sole authority for determining how to rule on Deer's official cause of death. The circumstances of the case and the written summations by the doctors involved in the operation would lead one to believe that Malak would conclude that the hospital and nurse bore responsibility for Deer's untimely demise. But this was Arkansas. Malak ruled that Deer had been murdered. Billy Ray Washington was arrested, charged with negligent homicide, and spent several months in jail.

Now this is where our story becomes interesting. Malak had a long history of professional incompetence. He once ruled that a man who had been shot five times in the chest had committed suicide. Pathologists from around the country would routinely come to Arkansas and give counter-testimony to Malak on the witness stand. His rulings were so notorious and frequently wrong that a citizens' group was formed specifically to have him ousted from office. The group was named VOMIT—Victims of Malak's Incompetent Testimony.

Malak had been appointed by Clinton during his first term as governor (1979–1980). The Deer-Washington incident occurred during the two-year period (1981–1982) when Clinton was out of office, but Malak still retained his position as the state's medical examiner. Clinton was returned to office in 1982 and held the position until he ran for president in 1992. For most of the period of his second coming, Clinton refused to fire or punish Malak. In 1991, just three weeks before he announced his presidential candidacy, Clinton fired Malak, but only after Joycelyn Elders had found him a $70,000 position as an official at a state hospital.

The nurse in this drama was Virginia Dwere Kelley, Clinton's mother. No one accused Clinton of aiding either his mother or his appointee Malak. They certaintly couldn't accuse him of helping Washington.

Traveling Down Nigger Road

"Nigger" still has the power to emote. For blacks and whites, the term initiates a strong reaction. As researcher Geraldine Wilson writes, "For black people the word *nigger* symbolizes almost four hundred years of anti-African racism and cultural repression" [emphasis added].[9]

"Nigger" was quite a public term at the turn of the century. It was regularly uttered from the lips of the nation's leaders in public venues. The word also adorned many symbols of popular culture. With in-your-face boldness, numerous products were sold that brazenly used the term "nigger" as a selling and marketing point. Among them were Nigger Head Brand canned fruits and vegetables, Nigger Head stove polish, Nigger Head teas, Nigger Head tobacco, and Nigger Head oysters.[10]

In the aftermath of the civil rights and Black Power movements, few public figures would dare use the term, as it became a sign of political retrogression. Though doubtless used with great abandon in private, to be caught using the term in public now challenges the official story of color blindness and racial progress and is the kiss of political death.

The term saw a public resurgence in the 1980s and 1990s. Employing what cultural theorist Richard Merelman has termed "black cultural projection," rappers and the hip hop generation have attempted to seize the term and construct counter-narratives and a different reading of the word. Merelman defines black cultural projection as "the conscious or unconscious effort by a social group and its allies to place new images of itself before other social groups, and before the general public."[11] Rappers boastfully see themselves as "niggers with attitude," where nigger is a badge of authenticity. It is not only being a nigger that is key, but accepting the term as a definition of one's self. In the hands of rappers, the term also embodies notions of masculinity and male bonding. Women are or can be niggers to the degree that they reflect images of black maleness, images that are more often than not media-created stereotypes of violence-prone, predatory, destructive behavior.

Despite these tortured efforts by black youth (and white youth who called themselves "wiggers"), the term still retains oppressive power. Few African Americans, if any, accept the term in any form from whites—not as a slur, not as a term of endearment, and very suspect even in academic settings. Fighting words.

Though hurled from coast to coast, in the minds of many, it is the sound of nigger with a southern drawl that most symbolically and viscerally evokes racism and days long thought forgotten. Visions of lynchings, beatings, castrations, and brutal death echo in the resonance of southern tones, be they aristocrat or redneck. To hear the word "nigger" in the South generally means the initiation of a chain of events that do not have a happy ending.

Given this context, it remains disturbing and significant that after hundreds of years of struggle, the defense of the word "nigger" by some whites in the South has resurfaced. The *New York Times* reported in November 1996 that in eastern Kentucky a battle has ensued in Magoffin, Rockcastle, Knox, and other counties between local residents and county officials, on the one side, and civil rights groups and the state Human Rights Commission, on the other. As part of the effort to bring these areas out of their social backwardness, a number of changes have been initiated, including putting up road signs where none previously existed. The commission, however, has adamantly refused to use the local popular names for the roads. Local whites there have resisted the removal and changing of road names that are racist and offensive.[12]

In those counties, there are a number of well-traveled roads with names such as Nigger Fork, Little Negro Creek, Negro Town Hill Road, and Negro Creek. Residents have told county officials, who have responded to complaints from the local NAACP and other civil rights groups in the area, that they will continue to use the old names. One resident, Betty McCarty, offered up the folktale that Nigger Fork was named in honor of a deceased black midwife from the area. She added that this midwife was buried in an unmarked grave.

The Fires this Time

I vividly remember the moment, as a child of 10, when I found out that four young girls had been killed in the bombing of a black church in Alabama. On September 15, 1963, only 18 days after Martin Luther King Jr. had delivered his famous "I Have a Dream" speech in the nation's capital, a bomb ripped through the 16th Street Baptist Church in Birmingham on Youth Sunday. I can recall my own fear and confusion, rage and bewilderment as the minister in our church in Detroit told a weeping congregation about the event and then asked everyone to go home and pray. Those four girls—Addie Mae Collins (14), Denise McNair (11), Carole Robertson (14), and Cynthia Wesley (14)—were the victims of an atmosphere of racial hatred, made even more evil and depraved by choosing a site of worship and religious sanctuary for the base act.

In the 1990s, echoes of that incident arose as a spate of church burnings spread across the South. According to the Center for Democratic Renewal, there were 33 church arsons from January 1990 to December 1994. In 1995, there were 41 church arsons; in 1996, that number rose to 288.[13] In every southern state, from Alabama to Virginia, there were arsons, vandalism, and fire bombings. From churches in tiny towns, such as Hatley, Mississippi's St. Paul A.M.E. and Hemingway, South Carolina's Sandhill's Frewill Baptist Church, to places of worship in the big cities, such as Apostolic Faith Assembly in Louisville, Kentucky or Inner City in Knoxville, Tennessee, the fires raged.[14]

Throughout history, the black church has served as the last haven of security for African Americans, the final gathering ground against the storm of racism. To attack the church is to attack the soul of black people. On a daily level, the black church, rural and urban, North and South, carries on programs of assistance to the black poor that cannot be found anywhere else. This includes housing, child care, job training, medical services, and other programs that bond them to large parts of the black community. The black church is also a central point of communication for African Americans as well as a source of information and potential mobilization. It was the black church, of course, that served as a basis for the efforts of Martin Luther King and the civil rights movement, and 20 years later, for the historic presidential campaigns of Rev. Jesse Jackson in 1984 and 1988. As a number of observers have noted, the financial independence of black ministers, in many cases, allows for a freedom of expression and resistance that has historically thrown up black ministers as leaders.

As voices from the black community identified the growth of church attacks, those voices became a movement demanding local and federal investigations of these crimes. History led many to believe that these burnings were not simply spontaneous, but may indeed be part of a larger, coordinated effort. It became hard to know what was more frightening—a conspiracy involving organized racists who were systematically assaulting black churches, or instead, widespread, random hatred that may be even more difficult to stop.

After much protest, the Clinton administration established the National Church Arson Task Force. In its investigation, it found that 331 church arsons, bombings, and attempted bombings had occurred. About 150 suspects had been arrested for their involvement in over 100 cases. More than 30 of these cases resulted in prosecutions. Millions of dollars were raised through federal and volunteer efforts. The Bureau of Alcohol, Tobacco and Firearms received $24 million to continue their investigation, while the Department of Housing and Urban Development received $10 million to assist some of the churches in their rebuilding.[16]

The movement to stop the church attacks served as a vehicle for black church mobilization. Not only did churches in the South come together, but they also found solidarity with black church activists in the North. The National Council of Churches became one of the national leaders in the effort to expose the situation and to push the administration to respond. The movement also embarrassed white church leaders, even including the Christian Coalition, which has been spearheading and promoting conservative policies and politicians across the country. The Christian Coalition offered a $25,000 reward for information on who was attacking the black churches. Many of the black ministers, however, saw this for the hypocrisy that it was. As Rev. Joseph Lowery of the SCLC noted, "We'd be glad to join with any members of the community of faith to fight injustice, to fight poverty. But they're not going to absolve themselves by exploiting these fires."

Long Live the Confederacy

Oh I wish I was in the land of cotton, good times there are not forgotten. Look away, look away, look away, Dixieland.

According to Republican leader Pat Buchanan, the Confederate flag is a symbol of courage and honor. He also stated that singing "Dixie" was the equivalent of African Americans singing "We Shall Overcome." His views have been echoed in a number of incidents in recent years that show that, for some, the Civil War is still being fought. For many white (and black) journalists, academics, and politicians, it is easy to dismiss the Buchanans of the world as dinosaurs whose little brains will eventually lead to their extinction. Why get upset over a few silly symbols and even sillier defenders of those symbols?

At one level, they simply miss the critical point that if the victims of these symbols do not raise a challenge to these politics, then who will? While many whites might feel offense at the Confederate flag, few have bothered to take an activist stand against it. At another level, these symbols are mobilizing forces in the support and perpetuation of racist ideologies. They are not neutral elements devoid of concrete historical and social capital, but instead function as socializing forces in an overarching ideological system of white supremacy and black oppression.

Needless to say, there are those who do vigorously defend the flag. In 1996, a new controversy arose in Maryland when the state issued 78 special license plates emblazoned with the Confederate flag. Protests led the Maryland Motor Vehicle Administration (MVA) to recall the plates, which they had issued on behalf of the 25,000-member Sons of Confederate Veterans (SCV). The group is comprised of people who can prove that they had an ancestor who fought as a Confederate soldier. SCV member Charles Goolsbie claims that blacks participate in their events and "are not bothered by the flag." But at the time, no African Americans came to their defense. MVA spokesperson Ronald Freeland acknowledged, "As a state agency, the MVA must be sensitive to symbols that may be offensive or otherwise objectionable to members of the general public."

In January 1997, clearly in response to the criticisms and controversy from the license plate incident, SCV got its first black member, Anthony Cohen. At the ceremony inducting Cohen, the Confederate flag was raised and the gathering sang "Dixie." Cohen, who is of mixed black and white heritage, stated, "I came to join the Sons of Confederate Veterans to honor my family history and to honor American history."[17] More ironically, Cohen is an historian. He did not say which family history he was honoring. Was it the African American side of his family, who one would presume were slaves and unlikely defenders of that one great southern tradition known as slavery? Or was it the heritage of his white family, which fought to maintain their right to own human beings? The picture of Cohen standing under the Confederate flag and bellowing out "Dixie" with the good ole boys must surely have warmed the hearts of people like David Duke and Mark Furhman.

Cohen claims he is writing a book on the Underground Railroad. It is difficult to see how he can reconcile anything positive about the Underground Railroad—whose goal was to help blacks escape from slavery—with his membership in the SC, whose purpose, in effect, is to honor the slaveholding tradition.

SCV has taken the role of incorporating a black defense of the Confederacy even further. They are promoting the work of Dr. Edward Smith, who they note is a *black* professor and dean of American Studies at American University. In the *Black Confederate Heritage*, Smith notes that "tens of thousands served the Confederacy" and goes on to describe a number of "black" Confederate war heroes (see http://www.scv.org). While acknowledgment of and scholarship on the role of blacks during the Civil War is legitimate and worthy, the SCV operates with a more disturbing agenda, which is to rationalize a conservative analysis of the racial politics of the war and the United States more generally. Academics, such as Smith, naively play into this project, at best, and at worst, collaborate in celebrating racist interpretations of the Civil War and the ongoing effort by conservatives to deny the fallacy of the melting pot thesis.

Meanwhile, in Alabama, the debate over flying the Confederate flag took on an even more bizarre character. Charles Davidson, a white candidate for the state senate, argued that not only was black slavery justified, but that the source of justification was the Bible. In a speech he was to give in an upcoming senate debate over the flag, he wrote, "People who are bitter and hateful about slavery are obviously bitter and hateful against God and his word, because they reject what God says and embrace what mere humans say concerning slavery.... The incidence of abuse, rape, broken homes and murder are 100 times greater today in the housing projects than they ever were on the slave plantations in the old South. The truth is that nowhere on the face of the earth, in all of time, were servants better treated or better loved than they were in the old South by white, black, Hispanic, and Indian slave owners."[18]

Davidson's rationale for defending the flag was extreme, to say the least, but his stated purpose was well within the logic of those who link the flag to the honor of the South. He argued, "The issue is not race. It's southern heritage. I'm on a one-man leadership crusade to get the truth out about what our southern heritage is all about." There is not a single word or intent there that is different from the more "acceptable" Republican leaders, from Buchanan and Reagan to Bob Dole, George Bush, and Gingrich.

The state and national Republican Party tried to create some distance from Davidson. State GOP National Committee member Martha Foy moaned, "I've never heard anything like all this. It's shocking to me." Yet there is no reason to be shocked. The GOP has created and fostered an atmosphere that not only allows, but encourages racism and white supremacist tendencies. Davidson mercifully lost.

"Dixie" is not the only song playing on the southern conservatives' top ten hits. In most states in the South, the official state songs are unsubtle praise for the slave period. In Virginia, the battle over "Carry Me Back to Old Virginny" rages on. The song was written in the 1870s by James Black, a black New York minstrel who had never been a slave himself. Phrases in the song refer lovingly to "old massa" and yearn for a return to the slave fields with lyrics like "Dat's where dis old darkey's heart am long to go." To his credit and as a reality check on his power, L. Douglas Wilder unsuccessfully agitated against the song for most of his public life, beginning back around 1970 through his tenure as governor and to the present. Although the Virginia House of Delegates had voted to kill the song's status as the state's official song (established in 1950), it was not until 1997 that a compromise was reached in which a majority in the Virginia Senate voted to retire the song as emeritus.[19]

Defenders of the Confederacy argue that there is a moral equivalency in the South's role in the Civil War that others miss. They contend that southerners' defense of slavery was rooted in the great American and southern traditions of states' rights, private property protection, and individual freedom. Of course, there is little discussion that the rights that are being defended involved the bartering, brutalizing, and murdering of human beings; that the private property being protected was African Americans in bondage; and individual freedoms stopped at the door of white skin.

"It's the Sound of the Men ..."

Chain gangs have returned to the nation with a vengeance. In 1995, espousing the get-tough-on-criminals line that has come to dominate contemporary approaches to criminal justice, Alabama reinstituted the notorious chain gang system.

On May 3, 1995, under the rule of Republican Governor Fob James and Ron Jones, the commissioner of the Alabama State Department of Corrections, Alabama became the first state to reinstitute the chain gangs after their disappearance more than 30 years ago. Films like *Cool Hand Luke* and recent documentaries on southern chain gangs led to national repulsion at the cruelty and inhumanity of that particular prison custom.

But this is the 1990s, and traditional values are back in favor. Alabama's Limestone Correctional Facility became the test site for the modern day chain gang. Inmates from the prison are chained together in groups of five in leg irons and put out on the state's highways and back roads. They wear uniforms with the words "Chain Gang" stitched in large letters on the backs. Generally, they work 12 hours a day.

Initially, the inmates cleaned up highways, painted fences, and dug ditches. Jones apparently felt that this was coddling and soon the prisoners found themselves breaking rocks into gravel. "The rock breaking programme is our way of finding something meaningful for these inmates to do," Jones stated.

As if busting rocks was not difficult enough, chained inmates also face unique dangers and embarrassments. Truck and car drivers, many distracted by a sight that they had only seen in the movies, zoom by at high speeds, guaranteeing multiple victims if there is an accident of any kind. Given that it is the Alabama countryside, poisonous snakes are also a constant threat, exacerbated by the inability to flee in any useful manner. Inmates also remain chained when they have to relieve themselves into a chamber pot, which is carried with them during their work.

Some prisoners refused to go on the chain gangs, complaining of the dangers and inhumanity of the experience. Instead, they ended up with a visit to the "hitching post," a metal bar where prisoners are handcuffed with their arms above their head and kept for up to 10 hours in the sun and without food.

In his first year in office in 1995, Jones followed the lead of recent federal crime legislation and abolished such inmate "privileges" as television (black and white as well as color) and weight rooms. He went even further, however, than those on Capitol Hill. He took away inmates' access to orange juice and coffee. Jones had other innovative ideas concerning prison reform. According to *The Nation,* Jones also proposed:

- housing prisoners in tents;

- calling black prisoners "niggers";
- an electric fence around one prison for a "lethal shock";
- destroying vegetable plants tended by inmates with AIDS;
- caning inmates; and
- making prisoners who masturbate in front of women wear pink prison suits.[20]

Jones' tenure was cut short when he went one step too far. Happy with his work with male prisoners, he also proposed putting women prisoners on chain gangs. Whether Governor James actually supported the idea or not, the embarrassment to the state forced him to publicly criticize Jones, who was ultimately made to resign.

Despite being a brutal throwback, the chain gangs are popular. As can be imagined, blacks and whites see things differently. A poll taken by the *Mobile Register* and the University of South Alabama found that while 77 percent of whites favored chain gangs, only 43 percent of blacks did. Although the chain gangs are racially mixed, they are disproportionately black and the image that has been popularly conveyed is that of African-American prisoners.

Unfortunately, Jones' views are in vogue in Congress and there are a number of bills that would nationalize these policies. Rep. Dick Zimmer (R–NJ) has proposed H.R. 663—the "No-Frills Prison Act. This bill would restrict federal funds for prison construction only to those states that abolish smoking, weightlifting, and family visits for prisoners. On the Senate side, Alabama Republican Richard Shelby has proposed a bill forcing states to work prisoners a minimum of 48 hours a week plus another 16 hours of mandatory study as requirements for inmates to enjoy the very few privileges they have left. Like the Zimmer bill, federal dollars are to be withheld if states do not comply.

Alabama may have been the first, but it is not the last. Florida and Arizona have also instituted chain gangs. Wisconsin and several other states, at this writing, were debating the issue. The southernization of the nation continues.

Of Louis Farrakhan
and Others

At the turn of the century, Booker T. Washington was the most influential black leader of his time, or perhaps even in U.S. history. From 1895, when he delivered his infamous "Atlanta Compromise" speech, to his death in 1915, he single-handedly wielded influence over vast areas of black life, including presidential appointments, jobs in business and education, and funding from foundations and philanthropists. In that speech, Washington stated that African Americans are "the most patient, faithful, law-abiding, and unresentful people that the world has seen....In all things that are purely social we can be as separate as the fingers, yet one as the hand in all things essential to mutual progress....The wisest among my race understand that the agitation of questions of social equality is the extremist folly."[1] In his words, he essentially declared that he would lead the muting of black resistance to racism and side with the racists who were aggressively instituting official American apartheid. Under his leadership, he would implore African Americans to make no political demands on the government, separate themselves from the mainstreams of social life and power, and ignore the increasing racism of the period.

Thus, when W.E.B. Du Bois chose in 1903 in his book *The Souls of Black Folk* to challenge Washington's position as the preeminent black leader of his era, Du Bois' entire career, livelihood, and standing in the black community were on the line.[2] Yet his integrity and sense of principles would not keep him silent and he courageously took on the Washington machine. The historic burden of moving the black community forward fell on the shoulders of Du Bois and the radical activists around him. Their critique of the conservative and race-limited views of Washington, and later Marcus Garvey, would usher in a new era of black radical thought and practice.

Du Bois' sense of urgency was driven by important changes in the racial climate of the period: the persistence of lynchings and other forms of racial violence, decreasing access to the ballot, a virtual end to black elected officials at the federal and local levels, and the codification of segregation in nearly every institution of public life.[3] Du Bois believed that neither black conservatives nor black nationalists could provide the leadership so desperately needed by the black community in the face of the advancing technology, rising racist violence, expanding global relations, and emerging capitalist social vision that had all come into being early in the century. Even though he was sharply critical of the racism and white reaction of the times, he nevertheless argued that a radical united front between African Americans and others was not only possible, but necessary. This view conflicted sharply with that of Washington and his white supporters.

In the 1990s, a new world order and a rapidly approaching future requires that black leadership move beyond the limits of the conservatism, nationalism, and liberalism ideologies. Of the four political trends that have historically existed in black politics—conservatism, liberalism, nationalism, and radicalism—the latter holds the most promise for advancing the cause of black liberation. Black radicalism stands at a unique juncture on the scale of black political agency. On the one hand, only the radicals and liberals, in general, see the necessity and benefit of multiracial organizing and solidarity. On the other hand, only the radicals and the nationalists, in general, see the necessity of systemic transformation. In other words, in terms of arguing for a multiracial assault on capital and racism, and the social destruction they have wrought, black radicals stand alone.

In this last decade of the 20th century, Minister Louis Farrakhan, leader of the Nation of Islam (NOI), has risen to the top of the black leadership totem pole. Leading up to and following the success of the Million Man March (MMM), his popularity and renown within the black community seem boundless. Many of those in the black community who had written him off as too extremist, anti-white, anti-Semitic, homophobic, a defender of patriarchy, and theologically suspect were clamoring to be on his stage on October 16, 1995 when he stood before over one million black men (and women) with tens of millions more watching around the nation and the world. Unlike

Washington, Farrakhan is loathed by many whites and, until the post-march period, was persona non grata in mainstream white political circles. Yet he appears ubiquitous in the white media and news programs. He has appeared solo on *Donahue, Nightline,* and *Meet the Press,* among other shows, and he has been the subject of numerous debates on these programs and others. The NOI has also been the subject of debate in Congress, having the distinction of being the *only* group in the history of the United States to be rebuked by a congressional resolution for a speech deemed racist by one of its members, Khalid Muhammad. The obsession by the white media and political elite with Farrakhan and the NOI is premised on the belief that his leadership in the black community, whether desired by the mainstream black political class or not, is significant enough to require a consistent monitoring of his words and deeds.

Farrakhan and the NOI are also international in their reach and popularity. Distinct from most African-American leader, Farrakhan is a global figure. Before and after the march, the NOI has spread its organizational wings with affiliations and influence among blacks throughout the diaspora. The NOI has chapters in Jamaica, Canada, and England, as well as supporters in many nations on the African continent. In 1990, it opened a mission in Accra, Ghana.[4] From October 5 to 9, 1994, the NOI held International Savior's Day in Ghana, an event that was opened by Ghanian President Jerry Rawlings and drew about 30,000, including 2,000 African Americans.[5] Farrakhan's 20-nation "World Friendship Tour," following the MMM, also gave him a global stage on which to build his popularity and spread his gospel. Nationally and internationally, Farrakhan's time has come.

To offer a harsh critique of Farrakhan's politics, framed by the nexus of black nationalism, patriarchy, and conservatism, which this chapter tries to do, is no idle undertaking and is presented with the utmost seriousness and calculation. It is also humbly understood that a single examination, no matter how sincere or well-argued, will have minimum impact on an individual and institution of Farrakhan's stature, power, and reach. Criticism of Farrakhan and the NOI, in particular, has resulted in accusations of being a race traitor, to put it mildly. Journalist Salim Muwakkil notes, "Many of those with serious criticisms of the Nation of Islam's authoritarian methods are reluctant to speak on the record."[6] More generally, one's position on Farrakhan has become, as political scientist Adolph Reed explains, a litmus test for whites and blacks.[7] A black leader's entrance to or continual residence in the mainstream is contingent upon a public rejection of Farrakhan. This racist criteria has been visited upon Rev. Jesse Jackson, Rev. Al Sharpton, NAACP chief Kweisi Mfume, and other contemporary black leaders. In the black community, often in response to the racism of the white predisposition to determine black leadership, "the more he is attacked, the greater his authenticity and the more emphatically he must be defended."[8] For blacks, as has often been the case in the past, criticisms of black leaders, even from a Left perspective, are seen as an attack on the whole black community and frequently dismissed out-of-hand. Yet, from my vantage, there is no more urgent task in black politics than a rigorous, principled, and unyielding self-critique of the state of black leadership as we edge into the next millennium, and that means that Farrakhan as well as other contemporary black leaders must be fairly, but sharply assessed.

For many, with the success of the MMM, Farrakhan has achieved the Holy Grail of black nationalist objectives: the mobilization of millions of African Americans along the lines of race-based unity. That such an effort was constructed on the basis of a conservative and antifeminist program underscores the criticality of an analysis that attempts to negotiate the seemingly conflictual politics of a militant, even radical rhetoric and a moderate, even reactionary agenda. It is with this nationalist agenda, with its complex history and multiple varieties and expressions, that we begin our interrogation.

Calling our BLUF

Black nationalism, as social perspective and praxis, is as old as the black presence in the United States. Theoretically, black nationalism is less an ideology than a framework through which views along the political spectrum are expressed. In other words, conservative and radical perspectives have been acted out on the stage of black nationalism, which comes in many modes, including religious, cultural, political, territorial, and economic expressions.

At the core of black nationalist thought is the notion that a single—that is, mobilizable—black interest exists among African

Americans, an interest that can be operationalized through the unity of black leaders. That paradigm, which I call the Black Leadership Unity Fallacy (BLUF), has resulted in both progress for African Americans in their struggle against white supremacy and racism, and immense limitations as it has obscured real differences and conflicting interests that arise from the diversity of the black community.

The BLUF argues that, first, despite ideological, political, class, and gender differences among African Americans, a basis for a united front against racism exists. Indeed, these other identities, regardless of their saliency, intensity, and intersectionality, are flattened and subsumed under the category of race. The black united front against racism, the organizational expression of the BLUF, takes the form of a coalition of black leadership in which all parties should have an equal voice. Efforts to build such a front have occurred throughout black history, including, *inter alia,* the National Negro Convention Movement, National Negro Congress, Congress of African People, National Black Political Assembly, National Black United Front, National Black Independent Political Party, National Black United Front, and National African American Leadership Summit. Black nationalism essentializes blackness, that is, the experience of being black is read as a bonding character for all African Americans in spite of other identities, experiences, or worldviews. That other identities mitigate, inform, and filter the race dynamic is theoretically avoided and politically disallowed.

Black nationalists have also sought different objectives. While some have advocated a separate territory for African Americans within the boundaries of the United States, others have longed and organized for a mass return to Africa.[9] Many nationalists seek cultural separation, generally asserted through some form of claiming an African identity, theology, cosmology, ethos, or system of values. This often results in the selection of an African name, the wearing of African garb, eschewing relations with whites as much as possible, and a worldview bordering on eugenics. Viewing these identifications as more than just symbolic, black cultural nationalism, in the form of Pan-Africanism or Afrocentrism, seeks a rupture with the African-American present by embracing a (mythologized) African past.

The Rise of the Nation of Islam

The NOI, however, emerges out of a different nationalist tradition. While advocating racial separation, it dispenses with African cultural manifestations. Instead it locates its place in the dual and intersecting historiographies of African Americans and Islam. According to researcher Allan Austin, African Muslims were found in the New World prior to Columbus.[10] Estevanico, a black Muslim, was the first non-Indian to enter the lands that would become New Mexico and Arizona and is said to have planted the first wheat crop in the Americas. Most of the African Muslims who ended up in the United States were slaves, perhaps as much as 10 percent of the slave population.[11] By the time the NOI emerged in the 1930s as the creation of the mysterious Wallace D. Fard, who is viewed in NOI lore as the messenger of Allah (God), and his most loyal disciple Elijah Poole (later Elijah Muhammad), it stood on a long history of Islamic faith in the black community. The narrative constructed by Elijah Muhammad broke significantly from the traditions of Islam and created a black supremacist vision for black America in which whites were "blue-eyed" devils created by a mad scientist, Yacub, and were doomed to perish.[12] Throughout the 1940s and 1950s, advocating black self-help, moral rectitude, economic development, and an avoidance of political participation, the Honorable Elijah Muhammad, as he became known, built the NOI—on the hard work of inner-city, working-class blacks and prison recruits—from a small sect to the most visible black organization in most northern cities.

The politics of the NOI, despite its anti-white theology, were extremely conservative and much attention was given to what could be considered European values, dress, and standards of behavior. Men and women were trained in proper etiquette and dress, for instance, that evoked Victorian morality more than African or African-American norms. Women, in particular, were given very distinct and generally subservient roles in NOI theology and practice. Economically, the NOI advocated the building of black-owned small businesses in the black community. These businesses, it was argued, would lead to a form of black economic independence, a crucial element in the liberation model constructed by the NOI theology. While not specifically calling this endeavor black capitalism, the economic logic and practical applications of the effort were consistent with the general exploitation and limited development of small businesses under capitalism. Workers in NOI businesses, similar to workers in small businesses everywhere, were underpaid, overworked, had few real benefits, such as health care and retirement, and minimum opportunity for growth. From this economic program, the NOI found success and grew substantially.

During this period, the NOI gained two crucial recruits: Malcolm Little in New York, later known as Malcolm X, and Louis Eugene Walcott in Boston, later to become Louis Farrakhan Muhammad. Born on May 11, 1933, Farrakhan was born in the Bronx to a Jamaican father, Percival Clark, and his mother, Mae Clark, from St. Kitt. Farrakhan's father, whom he barely knew and who died when he was young, was extremely light-skinned and perhaps of Portuguese heritage. Indeed, Farrakhan has even speculated that his father's ancestors may have been "members of the Jewish community," a critical point given the antagonistic relationship that Farrakhan has had with Jews.[13]

A talented child who played the violin and sang, Farrakhan was one of the first blacks to appear on national television when he won on *Ted Mack Original Amateur Hour*.[14] Although he had a potentially successful career awaiting him as a singer and nightclub performer, he joined the NOI in 1955 in New York. His oratory and political skills quickly made him valuable and he became Malcolm X's assistant at Mosque Number 7 in Harlem. He was later sent to Boston, where he soon became the minister of that mosque. In 1964, after Malcolm X split from the NOI, Farrakhan returned to New York to take Malcolm's place as head minister at Mosque Number 7, later participating in the NOI campaign to silence and rebuke Malcolm X. At one point, Farrakhan wrote in *Muhammad Speaks,* "Such a man as Malcolm is worthy of death."[15] Despite the animosity that many in Harlem and elsewhere felt toward the NOI after Malcolm's February 1965 assassination, Farrakhan and the mosque managed to survive and eventually thrive. Farrakhan's success would lead to him being appointed the national spokesperson for the NOI under the leadership of the Honorable Elijah Muhammad. Fortunes would change, however.

In 1975, on the February 25th death of Elijah Muhammad, the NOI was taken over by his seventh son, Wallace, who quickly began to make profound changes in the theology and operation of the NOI. White-skinned people were no longer seen as the devil and were allowed to join the NOI. More important, the group began to move closer to traditional Islamic teachings and to downplay the NOI's nationalistic rhetoric and teachings. Given his position under Elijah Muhammad, Farrakhan was viewed as a potential threat and was removed from the center of the organization. He was transferred to the West side of Chicago, which at the time was a backwater for the NOI. His speeches were monitored and, in general, he was pushed to the political periphery. In November 1976, the group's name was changed from the NOI to the World Community of al Islam in the West (WCIW) and, in April 1978, it would change again to the American Muslim Mission (AMM). The Fruit of Islam, the NOI's security force, was dissolved.

In should be noted that the U.S. government had a vested interest in who would succeed Elijah Muhammad. This was in keeping with the long history of infiltration and covert operations against the group by the FBI and local police forces. As early 1969, the FBI concluded that Wallace Muhammad was the only one who "could give proper guidance to the organization."[16] It wrote, "The NOI appears to be the personal fiefdom of Elijah Muhammad. When he dies a power struggle can be expected and the NOI could change direction. We should be prepared for this eventuality. We should plan how to change the philosophy of the NOI....The alternative to changing the philosophy of the NOI is the destruction of the organization. This might be accomplished through generating factionalism among the contenders for Elijah Muhammad's leadership or through legal action in probate court on his death."[17] Wallace Muhammad, as far as the FBI was concerned, was "the only son of Elijah Muhammad who would have the necessary qualities to guide the NOI in such a manner as would eliminate racist teachings."[18]

Farrakhan and the Revival of the NOI

Farrakhan (and others) grew more and more disenchanted with these new directions, and on November 8, 1977, he announced that he was leaving the WCIW and reestablishing the old Nation of Islam "on the platform of the Honorable Elijah Muhammad."[19] While holding onto much of the theology, ideas, and structure of the old NOI, such as reinstituting the Fruit of Islam and closing membership to whites, the NOI under Farrakhan's leadership made some significant adjustments. Its decision to become involved in Jackson's campaign and even run candidates for office was a critical break from the nonpolitical involvement that the earlier NOI preached and that frustrated Malcolm X. The NOI under Farrakhan also became more aggressive in seeking a seat at the table of black leadership. In a number of black coalition efforts, the NOI was involved, or created a controversy by its noninvolvement generally in situations where liberal black leaders sought to also involve leaders and organizations from the Jewish community.

For much of the late 1970s and early 1980s, Farrakhan and the NOI remained obscure to those outside the black community—except for the Jewish community, which had long identified Farrakhan as the nation's leading black anti-Semite—and was viewed as somewhat fringe by many black activists. Just as the AMM would begin to seek a more middle-class membership, so too would the new NOI. Although the NOI was still rooted in black working-class communities, black professionals were increasingly recruited and given visible positions in the group. Farrakhan's projection on the national mainstream political stage, however, would not be through the work of the NOI, but the racial dynamics of presidential politics. In 1984, Farrakhan's relative obscurity would change dramatically as a result of his involvement in the Jackson campaign for the Democratic nomination. As numerous scholars and journalists have documented, Farrakhan's threatening rhetoric toward the black *Washington Post* reporter, Milton Coleman, who exposed Jackson's anti-Semitic, off-the-cuff remarks brought him to the attention of the major media, black political leaders, and the nation as a whole.[20] Jackson's forced disavowal of Farrakhan raised the latter's profile even higher.

Farrakhan's support for Jackson highlights the inherent problems of the BLUF, exacerbated by the fact that the NOI's incursion into the electoral arena took place on the terrain of mainstream politics. The NOI backed Jackson despite basic and unresolvable contradictions in political line, style, and objectives between the two. While Jackson sought for himself a placemat at the table of the Democratic Party, which views racial politics in soley integrationist terms, and a more generous welfare state for his rainbow constituency, this profoundly contradicted the NOI's advocacy of self-help separatism, policy of no coalition with whites, and attitude that the Democratic Party was irredeemably racist. Yet accommodation could be found due to the belief that race rules and, perhaps, naïveté that Jackson would side with blacks when the inevitable and predictable racial controversy arose.

Since that time, Farrakhan has never been far from the news and was cautiously, but begrudgingly brought into the family of black leaders. The embrace of Farrakhan was so sensitive that the Congressional Black Caucus held secret meetings with him, clearly aware of the spark that could be ignited if it became known that they were gathering with him, let alone actually working with him and the NOI. The perceived political impotence of the caucus and other black leaders is also the groundwork on which the NOI rebuilt itself during the Reagan era. As civil rights leaders and black elected officials engaged in racial bargaining and polite compromise, Farrakhan slowly built a constituency outside of NOI adherents among working-class and middle-class blacks who had grown doubly frustrated by the social and economic attacks of the period and the absence of even a strong rhetorical response.

The NOI has been attractive to many African Americans for the work that the organization does in communities around issues such as drug trafficking, AIDS, youth gangs, and security at inner-city housing projects. While other black organizations have little visible presence at the street level in the black community, the highly visible NOI—with its distinct persona of clean-shaven, bow-tie wearing, and pressed dress suit-sporting men—is ubiquitous as it provides security services, operates small businesses, and sells its newspaper, *The Final Call*. The complete abandonment by the state of any responsibility for the wretched and oppressive life that poor African Americans struggle with on a daily basis is further reason for the often positive reception that the NOI receives from the black community. The religiosity of the black community is also a basis for acceptance in that it is believed, whether one embraces Islam or not, that a spiritual force is driving the work of the NOI, and their membership in an African-American ecumenical alliance—a subplot of the BLUF—is wanted and necessary.

Beyond their community work, in many circles in the black community and most outside, the NOI is viewed as a radical organization whose goal is nothing short of the overthrow of white power in the United States. The apocalyptic rhetoric of Farrakhan and spokespersons for the NOI have helped flame the fires of a racial divide that the NOI did not create, but has been able to exploit. They have threatened and predicted all types of calamities and devastation that will be visited on the United States for its treatment of African Americans and other people of color. This militancy has led many young African Americans, the so-called hip hop generation, to believe that Farrakhan is the only national black leader offering a consistent and even revolutionary challenge to racism. The NOI's outreach to black youth, particularly young black men and rappers, distinguishes the efforts of the NOI from most black organizations.

Conservatism and the NOI

These efforts, notwithstanding their positive aspects, obscure the broader conservative agenda and program that the NOI brings to black politics. Its small capitalism economic plan, its willful alliance with political conservatives and reactionaries, and its conservative cultural agenda, in which regressive gender politics is central, are much more significant for understanding the political role of Farrakhan and the NOI in black politics than the media-driven debates over his anti-Semitism. Underlying the thrust of the NOI's politics, and black nationalism in general, is the politics of patriarchy. As a number of black feminist scholars have argued, patriarchy and anti-feminism are organically theorized in black nationalism, creating an intraracial conflict that, in this period, is most embodied in the public posture of Farrakhan.

The essence of Farrakhan's politics can be seen in how he problematizes the crisis facing the most desperate sectors of black America. As he envisions it, the most fundamental issue facing African Americans, particularly poor blacks, is not economic exploitation, political disempowerment, or an anti-black social agenda. While he does not deny these factors, often incorporating them into his speeches, they remain secondary and peripheral to the philosophy, politics, and practices of the NOI. For Farrakhan, it is the mind-set, behavior, and cultural praxis of African Americans that must be corrected. It is this perspective that brings Farrakhan into the sphere of conservative politics occupied by Newt Gingrich, Pat Buchanan, Pat Moynihan, and Charles Murray.

In this sense, the politics of the NOI harken back to the ideological mode of Booker T. Washington. While Farrakhan does not indulge in "darkie" jokes or promote a "turn-the-other-cheek" response to attacks on the black community, as Washington did, Farrakhan does engage in chastising African Americans for the ills they suffer. It is the inadequacies of African Americans that animates Farrakhan's efforts, economic and political. He also melds with Washington on the issue of racial separatism. Although it could be argued that he has serious doubts that African Americans and whites can be "one as the hand in all things essential to mutual progress," at the same time, he would find little disagreement that "in all things that are purely social, we can be as separate as the fingers."

NOI's Black Capitalism Project

The NOI under Farrakhan, similar to the old NOI, preaches the gospel of bootstrap capitalism. The ideology of economic self-help has meant, at one level, a focus on small business creation by the group. NOI enterprises include the Salaam Restaurant chain, Shabazz Bakeries, Fashahnn Islamic Clothings, food markets, NOI Security Agency, *The Final Call* newspaper, Clean 'N Fresh skin and hair care products, and Abundant Life clinics, as well as involvement in real estate, fish markets, farmland, and book and tape production and distribution.[21] While it is impossible to know how profitable these businesses are, media reports, public tax records, and statements from the NOI itself indicate the struggles that have occurred to keep the business side afloat. In early 1995, the NOI proudly announced the opening of the $5 million Salaam Restaurant in Chicago. About six months later, the restaurant was in receivership. Reports in the *Detroit Free Press*, *Chicago Tribune, New York Times*, and *Washington Post* detail the management and administrative problems that the NOI has encountered in operating the sprawl of businesses that it has built.

The problem is not the failure of the NOI's business agenda; small businesses fail at alarming rates in the United States. What is problematic here is the lack of candor on the part of the NOI about the apparently serious rate of nonsuccess and severe indebtedness that NOI's businesses have suffered. The black community is repeatedly asked to support these enterprises with little accountability in return. This adherence to an economic model that is fundamentally flawed is pernicious in two ways. First, it diverts energy and attention from the economic issues that affect large numbers of African Americans, such as access to job training, health care benefits, retirement plans, and other concerns. Second, the bootstrap model facilitates the illusion that business in the United States is a private matter rather than the dynamic interrelationship between public policy and capitalist economic development. The only thing that is private about the so-called private economy is the news that it is not.

A very disturbing hypocrisy on the part of the NOI also exists regarding the ideology of self-help. A central theme of the organization is the need for the black community to practice self-help and stop demanding a handout from the government. At one level, the arrogance of the statement ignores a long, long history of nothing but self-help on the part of the black community. But what makes this view really disingenuous is that, according to their own documentation, the NOI has grossed millions of dollars in government contracts since the late 1980s. Through their security services at public housing sites, which initially began as volunteer activities, the NOI has secured Department of Housing contracts that may be as much as $10 million. These contracts have inspired vicious and racist attacks on the NOI from the reactionary Representative Peter King (R-NY), who in 1996 forced congressional hearings on the matter. King's racist agenda notwithstanding, the NOI has little right to demand of others what it clearly is not practicing itself. It appears that the growth in the number of middle-class members turned the NOI toward more sophisticated skills needed to reappropriate, via federal and local grants, tax dollars.

Face the Nation: The NOI's Right-Wing Alliance

"He sounds like us." [22]— Armstrong Williams

The link between the NOI and conservatives has come under increasing criticism from black progressives. In March 1997, a debate flared up among Republicans after Farrakhan attended and spoke at the 13th annual gathering of Republican Party executives and investors held by conservative economist Jude Wanniski in Boca Raton, Florida. According to conservative columnist Robert Novak, this was only the third time in Farrakhan's long career that he spoke to an all-white audience.[23] Novak, who has attempted to bring Farrakhan closer to the Republican Party fold before, noted that the speech was a cross between "the Christian Coalition and libertarianism" and that "Farrakhan's stress on self-help and moral values evoked the longest sustained applause I have seen from the rich, sophisticated listeners—several of them Jewish."[24] In Novak's estimation, "Farrakhan…is knocking on the door of the Republican Party—the first modern black popular leader to do so," and that is not only significant for the party, but for the nation as a whole because "Republican aspirations to be a true majority would be enhanced by a foothold among African-Americans. More significantly, the racial animosity in this country could be diminished."[25]

While the immediate reaction among Republicans and the white media was outrage bordering on hysteria, only a few observers in the black community appeared concerned with this budding alliance. According to scholar Manning Marable, "The cordial relationship between Minister Farrakhan and white conservatives like Jude Wanniski also illustrated that black nationalism could be just as conservative as Reagan Republicanism. Newt Gingrich and Farrakhan both agree on conservative patriarchal family values, racial self-help, supply-side economics, and both oppose lesbian and gay rights."[26] There is little hope that a full-blown collaboration politically will occur between the Republican Party and the NOI, in spite of their ideological affinity. Neither the base of the Republican Party nor of the

NOI can be won over to going beyond the racial rhetoric that serves both sides and yet limits them from addressing the more fundamental ideological interest they share.

Farrakhan's conservatism has gone further than just his tentative relations with the Republican Party. Increasingly, the NOI has aligned with one of the most notorious fascists in the country, Lyndon LaRouche. An extremist by any definition, LaRouche has a long, thoroughly documented history of promoting, defending, and expressing racist and fascist views. In the past, LaRouche's organizations have attempted to destroy, manipulate, and corrupt, for their own purposes, black organizations and black churches. Even though LaRouche has formed close working relationships with neo-Nazis, Ku Klux Klan leaders, and other racists, he has also aggressively tried to infiltrate black southern churches using various front groups and by seducing elder civil rights activists with promises of political support. In the 1970s, one of LaRouche's front groups physically assaulted a number of black organizations.

In a variety of public forums since the early 1980s, LaRouche's followers have spoken in solidarity with members of the NOI. The two groups have mutually praised each other and freely quote from each other's publications. One of LaRouche's obsessions has been the Federal Reserve. He has developed all kinds of crackpot theories about the illicit power of the Reserve and the secret cartels that control it. These views have wound up in *The Final Call* and in the public presentations of NOI representatives.

This alliance is stranger still because, in 1985, LaRouche's newspaper, *New Solidarity,* attacked Farrakhan and the NOI. It wrote, "Rev. Louis Farrakhan is building a Nazi-communist terrorist movement closely linked to the Greens and their backers in the United States."[27] Yet, by the end of the decade, members of both organizations were meeting together around a variety of issues. The Center for Democratic Renewal, the black-run, Atlanta-based research center that has played a leading role in exposing the growth of racist and fascist organizations in the United States, wrote that by 1990, representatives of the NOI were singing LaRouche's praises. The center reported that NOI spokesperson Dr. Abdul Alim Muhammad had stated at one LaRouche gathering, "To Mr. Lyndon LaRouche and his wife, and to those members of his organization, especially those who are the teachers and writers who put out the *New Federalist* newspaper and the *Executive Intelligence Review,* I want to say on behalf of Minister Louis Farrakhan and the entire Nation of Islam, how much we admire you and respect you for the great work that you are doing."[28]

LaRouche is also linked to the NOI through Rev. James Bevel, who played an increasingly visible role around the MMM and its subsequent activities. Bevel was a close associate of Martin Luther King during the early days of the civil rights period. Bevel fell out with the movement, accusing it of being taken over by the FBI, and spent a number of years out of the limelight on a farm in Maryland. He resurfaced in the 1980s associated with right-wing religious forces such as Rev. Sun Moon. In 1992, Bevel emerged as LaRouche's vice presidential running mate.

The role of Benjamin Chavis Muhammad, former NAACP executive director and presently director of the National African American Leadership Summit (NAALS), in all of this is perhaps most egregious because he cannot claim ignorance of LaRouche's reactionary and racist politics. In 1986, he wrote an article in the *New York Voice,* titled, "LaRouche Invades the Black Community." In the article, Chavis Muhammad dwells on how important it is for African Americans to not allow LaRouche and his supporters to gain a foothold into the black community because "the LaRouche organization is clearly racist, works closely with the Klan, and is a supporter of the South African government as well."[29] Yet, a decade later, Chavis Muhammad shares podium after podium with LaRouche's surrogate, Bevel, and in at least one known instance (described below), with the man himself. In early 1997, Chavis Muhammad, who was one of the leaders of the MMM, announced that he had joined the NOI.

While Chavis Muhammad can perhaps be considered just an opportunist, Farrakhan's politics fit snugly into LaRouche's niche. As Marable wrote on another occasion, "Similarly, Farrakhan's conservative social and economic agenda finds parallels with LaRouche's fascist program."[30] The politics of the NOI are similar to LaRouche's in more ways than one. Just as LaRouche did not hesitate to try intimidation tactics on his perceived enemies, an atmosphere of intolerance for opposing views emerged regarding those in the black community who voiced criticism of the march. The charge of racial traitor awaited anyone, no matter what their politics, who dared criticize Farrakhan, the NOI, or the politics of the MMM. Racial authenticity was measured by how strong one supported or did not support the march.

March leaders had promised to hold a national black political conference after the MMM that would be the equivalent of the historic 1972 National Black Political Assembly. After months and months of delay and loss of support from key activists, such as political activist Ron Daniels and political scientist Ron Walters, a gathering was held in St. Louis in September 1996 sponsored by the remnants of the march leadership and NAALS. It was most notable for who was not there and what was not accomplished. Unlike the march, no celebrities, prominent elected officials, or nationally known activists showed up. Beyond the well-known, also missing were labor groups, civil rights groups, and of course, black feminist groups. Noted Harvard University scholar Cornel West spoke at the event, continuing his association with the march leadership and representing a token Left presence.

One person who did show up was Lyndon LaRouche. Although Chavis Muhammad and Bevel were apparently going to allow him to speak, protests from those in the crowd who recognized him and from others who simply could not figure out why a white man was going to speak at a black nationalist event prevented that embarrassment from happening. The fact that there was even a debate over LaRouche's presence, however, reveals the depths to which the link between nationalism and conservatism can sink. Even the harshest critics of the MMM's leadership would not have predicted that such an overt concession to reactionism could occur. At least one activist who attended the gathering believes that LaRouche and his organization played a key role in financing the event.

Farrakhan's consorting with reactionaries has not been limited to the borders of the United States. In March 1996, Farrakhan went on a World Friendship Tour, or what some called a "World Dictatorship Tour," of 20 nations in Africa and the Middle East. Without exception, he chose to visit and honor dictators and repressive regimes in

Nigeria, Zaire, Iran, Libya, the Sudan, and elsewhere. In Nigeria, the brutal Abacha regime has killed peaceful dissenters and jailed hundreds unjustly. Farrakhan's response to charges regarding the regime's execution of world-renowned Nigerian writer Ken Saro-Wiwa was, "They said that you hanged one man. So what? Ask them, too, 'How many did you hang?'"[31] His reported remarks led Randall Robinson, president of the black lobbist group TransAfrica, to comment, "His statements and the things that were said appear to make Minister Farrakhan an apologist for an authoritarian, corrupt, and repressive regime."[32] In the Sudan, despite denials by the Sundanese government, slavery and the slave trade continue in the country, as demonstrated by *Baltimore Sun* reporters Gregory Kane and Gilbert Lewthwaite in their investigative report from the Sudan following Farrakhan's trip.[33]

His defense of these visits boiled down to his declaration that he could go wherever he chose—a right never questioned by anyone in the black community, as far as I can tell. In some instances, he acknowledged that some of these regimes were far from democracies, but they could be excused, he argued, because they were relatively new nations and the United States, with its long history of slavery and imperialism, had little moral authority to criticize another nation. While the latter is true, it has little relevance to his unwarranted defense of murderers and slave traders. And it is doubtful that the masses of people suffering under these regimes cared little about Farrakhan's right to travel or the historic and contemporary human violations carried out by the United States.

Conclusion

Farrakhan has long been accused of sprouting reactionary views on everything from gender to homosexuality to Jews. His general response has been that much of what he has said has been taken out of context or are simply attacks on his leadership from racist whites or sell-out blacks. However, despite the truth of his assertion that he is under attack and that some of his words have been distorted, there is plenty of documentation of Farrakhan's statements, in *The Final Call* no less, and those statements have been the reason many black progressives have kept their distance. A black conservative agenda, albeit dressed in black nationalist clothing, will not free black America. Whether it comes from Clarence Thomas or Louis Farrakhan, it merely perpetuates the crisis that already exists for at least of a third of all African Americans and half of all black children.

Beyond Patriarchy and Conservative Nationalism

The plethora of statistics and data chronicling the spiraling and multiple crises affecting large parts of the black community is more than an accumulation of depressing social analysis. Collectively, this information captures the tragic and growing collapse of African-American civil society (AACS). The space in which the black community reproduces itself, its culture, social relations, language, and even imagination of itself has been undergoing a dual process of external aggression and self-destruction. The array of social issues contributing to the havoc and despair raging through the black community, particularly but not exclusively in the inner cities, should not be an excuse, however, to romantically harken back to the Jim Crow segregation era.

It has become popular in some parts of the black community to nostalgically look back on the segregation period through rose-colored glasses. Although African Americans were legally suffering brutal dehumanization under separate and unequal circumstances, some academics and most black leaders maintained and popularized the view that a cross-class, cross-gender harmonious unity existed that generated an environment that collectively raised children, saw limited drug abuse, had minimal crime, and promoted communal de-classed relationships.[1] This "back-when-we-were-colored" perspective dangerously erases the negative socially debilitating impact of segregation, the accompanying (and state-supported) racist violence of the period, the very real and sharp class divisions that have always existed in the black community, and the particularly vulnerable position that African-American women faced. Unsurprisingly, this mythology arises from the class-privileged sector of the black community. As writer Adolph Reed, Jr., notes, "Only middle-class children who were protected from its social and institutional realities—or those who didn't live it at all—could remember the segregated world so fondly, as a naïve, communitarian metaphor."[2]

The progressive impulse behind the thirst for this imagined community is the attempt to rescue a picture of daily life in which relations of cooperation overwhelm relations of exploitation. It was this need that was touched upon and exploited by the Million Man March movement and event. It affected who came out to the march, what they viewed as solutions to the problems facing the black community, and the subsequent follow-up issues that emerged in the march's wake. Yet the conservative politics of the march eliminated the possibility that it would be the tool to hammer into place a rebuilt AACS. The struggle to reconstruct AACS must be contextualized within the framework of the cultural logic of postindustrial capitalism: for African Americans, the commodification and commercialization of social relations, occurring in an era of labor downsizing and job elimination, profoundly transforms the arenas of contestation and struggle. Increasingly, for African Americans, the physical and virtual manifestations of black community life take place at a multitude of sites, including work, leisure, family, public spaces, political enclaves, prison, and habitats of the welfare state, such as unemployment or welfare offices, all of which are themselves undergoing dramatic restructuring.

This chapter not only identifies the problems inherent in using the MMM as a vehicle for the reconstruction of AACS, but looks beyond the march to a reconceptualization of what African Americans will confront in the years ahead and what societal transformations must happen if there is to be progress and development. In one sense, this is an ideological and political struggle over the definition of the black community. The perspective that there is a heterogeneous black community fosters narrow and flawed strategies that are unable to address the diversity of black interests that collectively can be seen as a "community." It can be argued that there are, in fact, several black communities, shaped and oriented through the prisms of ideology, politics, class, gender, and regional location—communities that have distinct and often even competing interests. Yet, within the nationalist context that framed the MMM, there was a concerted effort on the part of the march's leadership to mute and suppress these differences. That effort undermined the internal discourses and struggles necessary to forge the broadest possible progressive political movement inside the black community, while it also surrendered critical political ground to external anti-black forces.

Nationalism and the Million Man March

Historically, in periods of massive white backlash, such as the present era, black nationalism grows and challenges the ideological dominance of liberal integrationism within black politics. In this sense, black nationalism is not only an oppositional discourse to racism, but also to the dominant ideological strategy within black politics. Yet, in each period, black nationalism emerges in new forms and with new political directions and purposes defined by the leadership of the time, the historic options available, and the capabilities of other political forces to contend for hegemony. Thus, as scholar E. Frances White notes about Afrocentricity, it can be said that black nationalism as a "site of counterdiscourse is itself contested terrain."[3] While some contemporary expressions echo many of the traditional themes and politics of past nationalisms, other variations bear little more than symbolic resemblance to their predecessors. In the last period of strong nationalist sentiment three decades ago, progressive nationalists who called for a radical program of systemic economic and political transformation vastly overwhelmed their more politically conservative counterparts, who desired to focus mainly on cultural or social issues within the black community. This was true on both a domestic and global scale, where nationalist movements led to the overthrow of colonial regimes in Africa, Asia, and Latin America. In contemporary black politics, a conservatism that is barely distinct from right-wing Republicanism is the dominant manifestation of black nationalist expression. Conservative black nationalism reduces and imprisons the categories of gender, nation, class, and culture to the realm of race, thus obscuring other modes of interactive struggle that can and must take place.

In a time when a growing, rapacious corporate authority is creating more of a basis for African Americans to unite with broad sectors of society, a vocal core of black nationalists call for more isolation.

This is not to minimize the resistance by whites and even other people of color to such a unity. The point here is that the objective basis for unity has grown as a result of economic and social changes, even as the subjective character of race has worsened. It is within this paradox that the possibilities of cross-racial unity and alliance, if it is to happen at all, rests. The politics of black nationalism eviscerates that possibility completely. In a period of global transnational corporate development and concentrated economic power, some nationalists advocate a romanticized and doomed black capitalism. In an era when institutional and systemic power is consolidated around racist and anti-working-class public policies, a core of black nationalists are arguing that individual morality and lack of personal responsibility are the chief causes of mass suffering. At a time when the exploitation of women's labor and a concomitant attack on women's rights are expanding, black nationalist patriarchy advocates a diminished leadership role for black women and condemns their issues to the back burner of black and national politics. In the 1990s, in the internal ideological battle within black nationalist politics, progressive black nationalists have had little public voice or political agency.

This culmination of contemporary, conservative black nationalism is nowhere more visible than in the movement around and the incidence of the MMM. Without question, the October 16, 1995 event was the largest mobilization of African Americans in U.S. history. It was championed not only by black nationalists, but by black elected officials, black conservatives, and a wide range of civil rights leaders. More important, it received support from millions of men and women in the black community. Despite the fact that the event was conceived and organized by Minister Louis Farrakhan and Reverend Ben Chavis (now Ben Chavis Muhammad), both of whom have been controversial within and without the black community, many well-known progressives participated in, promoted, and defended the march. From Rev. Jesse Jackson and scholars Cornel West and Michael Eric Dyson to civil rights leader Dorothy Height and poet Maya Angelou to millions of black men and women from around the nation, involvement was strong and overwhelming.

In the aftermath of the event, many black publications became vehicles for the continuing celebration of the success of the day. *The*

Black Scholar, Emerge, and other black journals and magazines devoted numerous pages to essentially uncritical, celebratory pieces that rarely interrogated the core politics of the MMM and tended to focus on the *potential* benefits of black men feeling good about themselves and possibly taking on the family and community responsibilities that they had abandoned before the march occurred. And there were credible stories of grassroots organizing, increased black child adoptions, growth in memberships of black organizations, increased black male voter registration and turnout, and many more offshoots that were directly attributed to the consequences of the MMM. The MMM was so successful that even for those who have quietly expressed a wide array of criticisms of the event, its leaders, its politics, and the problems of follow-up, there has been a reluctance to speak out in public against the march. As journalist Salim Muwakkil notes, "Many of Farrakhan's would-be critics prefer to downplay their disagreements for the sake of African American unity." Subsequent events have led some earlier supporters of the MMM to publicly criticize Farrakhan and Chavis, though not necessarily to repudiate the march itself. This includes well-known scholars and activists, such as activist Ron Daniels, political scientist Ron Walters, historian Manning Marable, and nationalist Ron Karenga.

What still remains to be done, however, is to pursue a critical dialogue among black progressives that is not simply focused on the political foibles of Farrakhan and Chavis, but addresses the logic of the conservatism and gender politics of contemporary black nationalism . This means taking seriously the criticisms and analysis offered by scholars and activists critical of the MMM, such as Barbara Ransby, Nikol G. Alexander, Robin D.G. Kelley, Adolph Reed, Jr., James Steele, Julianne Malveaux, Mary Frances Berry, Angela Davis, and many others whose progressive voices were drowned out in the wave of exhilaration flowing from the march. This discourse was absent at the time of the march and has had very little exploration since. It means that scholars and activists must soberly assess the role of the MMM as a historic moment in black politics and the long-term implications of its legacy. Rather than an uncritical reading of the event or a knee-jerk rejection of its simply because of the controversial character of its leadership, a more rigorous interrogation needs to occur that raises the level of debate on the MMM and similar political events emanating out of the complexities of contemporary black politics. For black progressives, in particular, it is necessary to continue to project an alternative vision and strategy to the current political trends of conservatism, nationalism, and liberal integrationism that confronts state and corporate power and reconstructs AACS.

The MMM has become a marker in black politics and black life. It has become a point of reference for this generation and is unlikely to be paralleled in the lives of most participants and observers. It is critical, however, that an iconization of the gathering and its accoutrements be nullified and that it not become a symbol beyond reproach and analysis. Like all great events, the MMM is a site of contestation over meaning, significance, relevance, and purpose. For progressives who have been hesitant to criticize the widely heralded gathering, the broad based support for the MMM requires even more that a critical discernment and inquiry into its role in black politics be done.

In my view, at one level, the MMM was a conservative, patriarchal call for black male mobilization—based on the faulty and gendered thesis of black male endangerment and rampant African-American cultural pathology—whose meaning was code-switched by many, if not most, of those who attended the event to an alternative interpretation that dismissed Farrakhan's central role, saw the need and value for spiritual bonding among black men, and advocated more personal commitment to black advancement. The political and gender meanings underlying the themes of black male endangerment and African American cultural pathology have been most sharply analyzed by political scientist Nikol Alexander.[4] Underneath this framework, a more important ideological operation was occurring: the popularization and canonization of right-wing views and propositions that politically united conservative Republicans, new Democrats, civil rights leaders, nationalists, some black male progressives (ostensibly with feminist sensibilities), and a cross-section of black women eager for epiphanic transformations at the personal, community, and racial levels. That this mosaic of interests could be forged around an agenda that effectively surrendered the mantle of resistance that has defined black struggle historically, identifies the depth and force of the rupture of radical politics from African-American life.

Surveying the Marchers and their Views

If we are to extract the long-term meaning and impact of the march, it is necessary to investigate exactly who was and who was not mobilized. For the purposes of social analysis, it can not and should not be assumed that an undifferentiated black mass came to Washington that day. It is important to know, as much as possible, exactly what demographic cohort(s) came to the march, why they came, and what they believed on a range of political and social issues relative to the black community. The march was promoted as a vehicle to allow black men to bond in their effort to reclaim responsibility for their community. Who were the men that came to the event? What did they think? What were their politics?

There were two major surveys done of those who attended the October 16th march. One was a joint operation between some faculty and students of Howard University's Political Science Department and the New Jersey-based Wellington Group, a black marketing firm.[5] The other study was done by black researcher and pollster Ron Lester for the *Washington Post*. The two surveys, in important ways, reinforced the findings of each other on a number of demographic and research variables.

In the Howard survey, 1,070 marchers were interviewed, all male, at the event. The study found that the marchers were overwhelmingly middle-class in terms of income and level of education. A large number of the participants (41 percent) had household incomes above $50,000 a year. Another 20 percent had incomes between $35,000 and $49,000. In terms of educational level, 78 percent had some college or above. The average age of the marchers was 36. Most of the marchers, 79 percent, were employed full-time. Overall, the attendees were solidly middle-class and middle-aged, and did not represent descriptively that strata in the black community—the lower-income poor (often mistakenly referred to as "the underclass")—that was much of the focus of the issues that the march sought to address. There was, in other words, a critical disjuncture between those who attended the march and the target of what has popularly been seen as the "endangered black male." Given the broad outreach that occurred in the black community in building the march, the absence of the lower-income strata appears to be caused either by a lack of resources to attend or conscious disengagement. A survey of those who did not attend, which did not happen, would have been extremely interesting.

Politically, a majority of the marchers identified themselves as either liberal (31 percent) or moderate (22 percent). About 13 percent said they were conservative while another 10 percent called themselves nationalist, meaning that despite the nationalist leadership of the march, 90 percent of the attendees did not identify themselves as such. This probably indicates both the limited number of African Americans who actually do identify themselves as nationalists, assuming nearly every nationalist in the country made an attempt to be at the event, and at the same time, the saliency of nationalist ideas (albeit through conservative and progressive filters) in the black community, particularly for middle-class African Americans, where coming together as blacks is viewed as important and a source of authentication. In terms of party preference, 62 percent declared themselves as Democrats, 20 percent as independents, and 3 percent as Republican. These numbers were fairly consistent with poll numbers, which in general show the black community to be political. What was politically different, however ,was the number of attendees who stated that they were registered to vote: 86 percent. This number may have been inflated, given that nationally there are about eight million unregistered African Americans and that large numbers of black males are unable to vote due to being disenfranchised because of their criminal record. It is likely that at the MMM, it was simply unpopular to state one's nonregistered status.

Given his role in organizing the event, it was not surprising that a large number of the marchers (44 percent) viewed Farrakhan as one of the most important leader in the black community. He was followed by Johnnie Cochran (36 percent), Coretta Scott King (34 percent), Maxine Waters (33 percent), Ben Chavis Muhammad (32 percent), Colin Powell (30 percent), Jesse Jackson (29 percent), Mary Frances Berry (21 percent), Al Sharpton (18 percent), and Clarence Thomas (8 percent). It is important to note that respondents were given a list of names rather than asked to volunteer their own choices. To some degree, the list of suggested leaders reflected popularity and it was difficult to know, for example, how respondents defined leadership, what issues they used to measure leadership capabilities, and how even these particular leaders were viewed as affecting their lives and communities. These responses should be seen as snapshots of the popularity and exposure of these particular black leaders at the moment of the march. Cochran, for example, was virtually unknown outside of the Los Angeles area before the O.J. Simpson trial, and Simpson's acquittal in his criminal trial happened only a few days before the march.

Although the march won support from millions, including an untold number outside the black community, it was the cohort identified above that most represented the base of support for the themes and symbols of the event. This group signified a complicated array of liberal and conservative ideas that are in contestation in the black community over which way forward and under what political and ideological banner.

The Politics of the March

Analysis and criticism of the MMM falls into several categories: the overall politics and themes of the MMM; the issue of gender exclusion; the reactionary politics of key leaders of the march; and the response by those around the march to those who detracted from it. These arenas of criticism do not stand apart from each other. Gender exclusion, for instance, was consistent with the theme of black male endangerment and the solutions proffered by the march's leaders, and their response to criticisms surrounding how they handled the concerns of black women about the politics of the event.

The politics of the march were conservative, moralistic, and patriarchal. They were conservative in that the fundamental causes of the problems driving the crisis for so many in the African-American community were seen as black behavior and attitude issues. In this way, the original call could be seen as a black version of the Republican "Contract with America." The focus on personal responsibility, atonement, and reconciliation fit snugly into similar conservative themes that obviate real questions about power and the role of the government, policymakers, and transnational corporations in determining the conditions of black life. Placing the burden for the perpetuation of problems confronting the black community on African

Americans themselves also becomes the framework for the solution to those dilemmas. Thus, by overrepresenting the concern about the lack of personal responsibility and self-help strategies on the part of African Americans, the march became a vehicle for protesting the black community and its "pathologies." This then becomes the real politics of the march and not the controversy over Farrakhan, Chavis, or other figures associated with the event. The perverted genius of the march, its magical essence, was that many African Americans who sincerely sought to both support the march and distance themselves from Farrakhan, the NOI's conservatism, and patriarchy missed the critical and decisive point that whether Farrakhan and his central role were present or not, the politics that he advocated were. Many of those attending the march were vocal in declaring their opposition to Farrakhan and stated that their attendance was not a sign of support for Farrakhan or his politics. The fact that so many felt obligated to make it known that they did not agree with the NOI's views was itself a sign of the pivotal role that the NOI and Farrakhan had over the march. While most of those in attendance may disagree with much of what Farrakhan had to say, it was Farrakhan who held the stage and determined who else was on it. Even if many of his destractors were not clear what at least in part the MMM was about, Farrakhan surely was: the projection and elevation of his leadership in national black politics.

This point apparently confused a number of intellectuals. Harvard Political Scientist Martin Kilson presented one of the most bizarre reasons for supporting the march. It was apparently his fear and disagreement with the "extremism" of the NOI that compelled him to endorse the event and attempt from the inside to defeat the forces of Farrakhan. He wrote, "We who endorsed the march—challenged in this sometimes by our intellectual and political allies among some Jewish intellectuals—must now make sure that the goal of taming and purging xenophobic and extremist patterns among groups like Farrakhan's Nation of Islam organization does in fact take place."[6]

The call of the march was for a "Holy Day of Atonement and Reconciliation" on the part of African-American men. The view behind this call was that the irresponsibility of black men was primarily responsible for the myriad of problems facing black people. According to the march's organizers, Farrakhan in particular, decades of family abandonment and disregard for community had reduced black men to less than what they could or should be. As the mission statement noted, "Some of the most acute problems facing the black community within are those posed by black males who have not stood up."[7] While there was occasional mention of the oppressive role of outside forces on the black community, generally under the broad sweep of racism and white supremacy, the focus was overwhelmingly on the need for self-actualization and personal responsibility. This agenda does not call for an explicit political and public policy challenge, and even more, strongly mirrors the conservative ideas of Gingrich, Reagan, and other Republican rightwingers. It substitutes moral righteousness and a theocratic stance for a democratic assault on the institutions and systems of political power that dominate black life. It should be noted that a number of activists close to the march, such as New York's Ron Daniels, fought for a more politically explicit agenda, but were rebuffed for the most part.

The reactionary views of Farrakhan dominated the politics of the movement that built the march and the march itself. As radical political scientist Adolph Reed wrote, "Farrakhan embraces a deeply conservative, politically quietest agenda for black people. Like Marcus Garvey, Farrakhan has wed an anti-democratic, conformist and morally repressive program to a superficial race militancy that gives it the feel of populist radicalism. This is the kernel of fascism, and Farrakhan's view of the world is truly fascist. His vision for organization of black American life is racist, authoritarian, sexist, homophobic, and theocratic."[8] Reed's critique is harsh, but not inaccurate. Those politics logically lead to support from and strategic alliances with political forces that represent some of the most reactionary and racist views in the country.

In fact, a large number of conservatives enthusiastically embraced the politics of the march even as they denounced Farrakhan. Rejection of Farrakhan, in the past, was mostly limited to his anti-Semitic remarks more than anything else. Former Republican presidential candidate Jack Kemp called the NOI's self-help program "wonderful."

In the main, the march failed to make any demands on the state, a state that is profoundly responsible for the conditions facing millions of African Americans and working people across the country. This squandered opportunity is made even more tragic by the relentless attacks emanating from Congress on a daily basis, attacks that are racially coded and driven, but for the most part remain unaddressed by the march's leadership. Even as the marchers stood a million strong on the steps of the Capitol, inside conservative policymakers were attacking, through racial coding, welfare, affirmative action, education grants, funding for drug treatment, minority set-asides, and other programs that disproportionately benefit the black community.

Gender Exclusion

"When African American men are exhorted to 'be a man' and 'take control,' what does that mean for African American women?"[9] —Julianne Malveaux

As a gendered worldview that gives priority to racial unity above all else, black nationalism has found no common ground with feminism. Viewed as a white women's ideology, feminism has not only been rejected by black male nationalists, but also by many black women, nationalist and otherwise. While black feminist discourses have gained some territory within academia in recent years, they still remain abused stepchildren within black politics. This schism would surface in the context of the MMM.

Scholar Pauline Terrelonge argues that there are five reasons why feminist consciousness has had limited reception by so many black women:

- The view that feminist consciousness is a wedge that potentially generates conflict between black women and black men.

- A hesitation by black women to bond with white women given the ideology of racism that often appears alongside of feminism as expressed by white women.

- A perception that liberation of the black man is more critical than that of the black woman.

- The notion that black men must combat the development of black matriarchy, where feminism is seen as feeding and breeding.
- The role of the black church and a theology that supports gender inequality.[10]

Much of the opposition and outrage concerning the march in the black community had to do with the principle in the original call and in the buildup for the event regarding the exclusion of black women. Although women did much of the work of organizing the march—as has been the case historically in black politics—the march explicitly privileged the plight of the most serious issue facing African Americans, and women were asked to stay at home that day and educate the children. After months of unrelenting criticism, the march organizers changed their initial posture and let it be known that if women showed up they would not be harassed or asked to leave, and they allowed some women to speak at the event, including the late educator (and Malcolm X's widow) Dr. Betty Shabazz, Cora Masters Barry (wife of D.C. Mayor Marion Barry), civil rights legend Rosa Parks, and author Maya Angelou. Though successful and exemplary in their own right, none of these women could be viewed as strong feminists or threats to publicly challenge the sexism of the event.

The problem, however, was not just the proposed physical exclusion of women from the Mall, a position that could not realistically or legally be defended in any case. The problem, in a larger sense, was the political exclusion of black women's issues and concerns. While it makes little sense to oppose a single gender event on principle, in the context of the MMM, gender exclusion was not a progressive stance. The politics of the march's leaders essentially said that only issues facing black men were issues for the whole black community, while issues facing black women were not. The march was boldly stated as being about the reassertion of black men as leaders of the black community. This view was fallacious on several points. First, black women have always had to fight for leadership roles in every area of black politics and community life. The presumption that black men are not the dominant leadership force in black community politics and social life flies in the face of history and contemporary circumstances. Second, the issues facing black men confront black women as well because they are issues that affect the black family and its stability. Arguably, black women may be even more harmed by destabilized black communities given the multiple roles they play as domestic and workforce labor. Third, in many, many ways, black women are doing worse than black men. Black women earn less money, are going to prison at a greater rate, and must fight triple racial, class, and gender oppressions. Black women are also victims of rape and spousal abuse at alarming rates, issues that rarely reach a level of community outcry except in rare instances of interraciality.

Black women have been demonized more than any other group in U.S. society. In addition to being stereotyped along with all African Americans as disproportionately criminal, shiftless, and stupid, black women are attacked by white politicians, academics, and journalists as welfare queens, promiscuous vamps, and demented bitches, Saffires, Jemimas, and Jezebels. One only need note the recent portrayals of the controversies surrounding Sistah Souljah, Anita Hill, Lani Guinier, Joycelyn Elders, and other black women in the media as opposed to the men that were involved in those incidents. And, as witnessed by the vicious attacks on the mostly black female jury that found O.J. Simpson not guilty in his criminal trial, white feminists also have little hesitation in making broad sweeping stereotypical and racist statements about black women.

Add to this the voices of gangsta rappers who gleefully and incessantly call black women "hos", bitches, skeezers, cunts, teasers, and other derogatory and dehumanizing terms. Black women have to endure the black male view that they are emasculating, money grubbing, and domineering, and that much of the attacks on black (male) leaders come from the "traitorous" behavior of black women—views routinely echoed in NOI doctrine and rhetoric. Rather than criticize Supreme Court Justice Clarence Thomas, D.C. Mayor Marion Barry, former Congressperson Mel Reynolds, or boxer Michael Tyson for not taking responsibility for their personal behavior in scandals that they have been involved in. Farrakhan and others have accused the women in these incidents of bringing or attempting to bring down these men.

The MMM did little to challenge any of these views and, indeed, may have reinforced them. In patronizing and absurd fashion, Farrakhan and others offered the disingenuous notion that they had asked and received permission from black women to hold the march. Farrakhan stated, "We have asked our women if they would permit us as their men to finally take the point and make a stand for our women and children on behalf of our suffering communities in the name of our ancestors for justice."[11] The use of "our" is not inarticulate; it buttresses the underlying view that the black community and everyone in it is owned by black men. Barbara Arnwine, executive director of the National Lawyers' Committee for Civil Rights under Law, had an appropriate response. She said, "It's a throwback. The role African-American women are given in this march is to tend the bake sale, raise the money or stay at home and take care of the children. I think that it is awful." [12]

After spending a year declaring that this would be a men-only march, similar to the men-only meetings that Farrakhan had been holding, in an effort to beat back the criticism while denying that such criticism had any legitimacy or even existed, a new line developed that said, "Of course there is a role for black women regarding the march." That role, as it turned out, was to be the laborers where possible. At the same time, a number of black professional women were prominently displayed and given positions to logistically move the march forward. They had no role whatsoever in determining the political and ideological thrust of the event except to agree with it. Many of these women accepted the view that to raise gender issues was divisive and that, indeed, it was time for black men to stand up and take responsibility for leading the black community. That black women's concerns were erased was rationalized as a necessary sacrifice given the "endangered" status of black men.

One reason the patriarchal black nationalist view has gained a wider forum is due to the general absence of a popular black male feminist expression. Black male progressives who have viewed themselves as feminists and supportive of gender equality, for the most part, have failed to defend the hidden and not-so-hidden injuries of race-gender oppression and the attacks on black women or, as described below, have been equivocal as they have attempted to reconcile their feminism with black nationalism. From misogynist music lyrics to attacks by white politicians, black women have often been left alone to fend off those attacks. And, in some instances, when black men have joined the defense, it has been from a vantage point that is patronizing and sexist, or what writer bell hooks calls "benevolent patriarchy." A genuine cross-gender movement against sexism and for gender equity in the black community and the broader society has yet to come together. Until that happens, gender-divisive movements like the MMM will continue.

Not all black nationalists, it is important to note, support the march or its sexist overtones. One activist and writer that came out against the march, who has generally been viewed as a nationalist, was Kalamu Ya Salaam, best known as the former editor of *The Black Collegiate*. Although he had numerous disagreements with the politics of the march, he mainly focused on the way in which women were dismissed and disrespected. He wrote, "I didn't go mainly because I disagree with the exclusion (& diminishing) of women both explicit and inherent in the call....Black women who did openly criticize and/or oppose the march were an obvious and ostracized minority."[13] Salaam also stated, "I am unwilling to pretend that there is even one iota of salvation in this genuflecting to a patriarchal, genetically based struggle."[14]

The response by the black gay and lesbian community was generally to not endorse the march because of what many viewed as "its sexist and patriarchal tone and the homophobic comments made by some march organizers."[15] Some black gay and lesbian activists did advocate participation, however. The National Black Gay and Lesbian Leadership Forum (NBGALF), for example, refused to formally endorse the march but encouraged "all black gay and lesbian people, and particularly men, to participate openly and visibly in the March," stating that "We will no longer allow outsiders to dictate who is welcome at the black family table or to divide African Americans by sexual orientation or by gender."[16] According to NBGALF, "We believe the March provides a unique opportunity to empower black gay men and lesbians and black gay youth. Because black gay people are part of the black community, we will see positive images of open, courageous, proud, and diverse black gay people. Hundreds of black gay people participating openly in such an event will send a powerful message, one that will enable many black gays to abandon their masks of invisibility and assume or maintain their rightful place as citizens, mentors, and leaders of their communities."[17]

Black Progressive Responses

Many well-known black progressives capitulated to the march. Most notable were scholars and popular authors Dr. Rev. Cornel West and Dr. Rev. Michael Dyson, both of whom have written extensively against sexism and patriarchy. Although both voiced hesitation at supporting a gathering that (initially) formally asked women not to attend, focused exclusively on the issues facing black men, offered a conservative solution to the problems facing African Americans, and was led by someone that West and Dyson have both criticized as undemocratic, homophobic, anti-Semitic, and patriarchal, they endorsed and supported the march, even making appearances with Farrakhan on national television.

The march's call for atonement and reconciliation for the behavior of black men segued nicely into West's well-known motif of black "nihilism."[18] That Farrakhan's atonement and West's nihilism serve the interest of the conservative movement in constructing a view of the black community that blame it for the problems that the black community faces went generally unacknowledged. Scholar Peniel Joseph, however, did see the link between the two. He wrote, "Even as racism continues to provide the theoretical underpinnings for conservative and anti-black public policy the state has made blacks the racists and black men have accepted Farrakhan's public articulation of Cornel West's misguided notion of 'nihilism' rather than systems of domination, oppression, and racism as *the* reason behind continued black underdevelopment."[19] In a similar way, writer Stephen Steinberg asserts that "West's problem…is not that he discusses crime, violence, drugs, and the other notorious ills of ghetto life. Rather the problem is that he presents social breakdown and cultural disintegration as a problem sui generis, with an existence and momentum independent of the forces that gave rise to it in the first place."[20]

Dyson also found himself in a compromising position. He wrote that he "sympathizes with the many Jews, gays, women, lesbians, whites and blacks who were troubled by the March."[21] He noted, correctly, that "crucial elements of the language of responsibility, in which the moral aims of the march were couched, remain deeply problematic for women and for sexual minorities." [22] Again, on the theme of sexism, Dyson wrote, "It must be admitted…that the march did not entirely repudiate distorted notions of masculinity."[23] In spite of these reservations, Dyson decided to endorse the event. Needless to say, West and Dyson were not alone among black male progressive academics, activists, and journalists who decided to support the march. Was it the genius of Farrakhan or the misguided and confused politics of some black male progressives that could elicit harsh criticisms of the politics and gender issues of the march and yet provide their ringing and active endorsements?

There were a significant number of progressives, women and men, who did not support the march. Historian and longtime activist Barbara Ransby was one. She wrote, "Many of those who will be attending the march have good and noble motives. But I still cannot support this march. I have fundamental criticisms of the politics behind the march, and the leadership at the helm. The most obvious problem is the sexist and inexcusable exclusion of women. Women have worked behind the scenes, and a few will be allowed on the podium as speakers, but the majority of us—more than half the race—have been told to stay home, take care of the children, and leave the business of political leadership to the men."[24]

Progressive economist Julianne Malveaux, who was afraid that the march would end up as a "feel-good mistake," argued against the idea that women had taken over the lead from men in black political life.[25] She wrote, "The justification for this gender bifurcation was that women had shouldered the burden to date and now it was 'men's turn'….If the history of leadership of our nation's civil rights organizations were examined in even a cursory way, one would have to say it wasn't so."[26] Malveaux contended that not only have men led, but that it has been at the expense of black women's agency and participation: "From where I sit, it is disingenuous for people to ask that men have a turn when, in terms of visibility and leadership, it has always been men's turn—often to the detriment of women."[27]

Mary Frances Berry, chairperson of the U.S. Commission on Civil Rights, stated her repulsion at the leadership of Farrakhan and Chavis. She wrote in the *Washington Post,* "I have not endorsed the march because I do not support the leadership of Mr. Farrakhan and Benjamin Chavis. Mr. Farrakhan routinely expresses the most despicable, anti-Semitic, racist, sexist and homophobic attitudes imaginable. Mr. Chavis' role in practically destroying the NAACP makes any enterprise in which he is engaged suspect as far as I am concerned. African Americans as a community are in deep trouble at this hour. However, let me make it unmistakably clear: I do not trust Louis Farrakhan or Benjamin Chavis to lead us to the Promised Land."[28]

New York University historian and progressive scholar Robin D.G. Kelley also came out against the march. He was critical of both the conservative and patriarchal politics of the march's call and linked it to the popular conservative intonation about "family values." Kelley wrote, "In many ways, Farrakhan's call was not only a historical, but also a step backward, akin in some respects to the words of conservative 'family values' advocates who insist the root of black people's problems is lack of male-headed households....I think that the assumptions and rhetoric that drove the march were fundamentally sexist and conservative. For this reason alone, I could not attend the march."[29]

Most black Congressmembers, in the end, either supported the march or opposed it quietly. Both Representatives Kweisi Mfume and Donald Payne, respectively chairpersons of the Congressional Black Caucus for the 103rd and 104th Congresses, were present on stage and gave remarks. One black Congressmember who was vocally critical of the event was Representative Major Owens. He wrote, "I refuse to participate in Farrakhan's march because the agenda is purposefully shrouded in contradiction and conflicting messages. March leaders consistently have been autocratic, reckless, and divisive. As a leader and elected member of Congress, I can not support a group whose isolationist posture and separatist strategy pose a long-term threat to the survival of the African American community."[30]

While many criticisms of the march came from individuals, there was at least one effort to collectively come together. In New York, Agenda 2000 was formed, a group of black women and men who sought not just to focus on criticizing the march, but to use the opportunity to construct a progressive dialogue in the black community on gender relations. At a press conference held by the group, a number of the women shared their views on the march. Scholar and well-known activist Angela Davis read from the groups' statement, "Justice cannot be served by countering a distorted racist view of black manhood with a narrowly sexist vision of men standing 'a degree above women.'"[31] Davis was referring to statements that had appeared in the NOI's newspaper declaring that men were a degree above women. Another Agenda 2000 member, historian Paula Giddings, stated that the politics of Farrakhan and the march represent "19th-century solutions to 21st-century problems."[32]

The Post-March Movement

Events since the march have bore out many of the criticisms raised about the trustworthiness of Farrakhan, Chavis, and Bevel's leadership. On October 16, 1996, the one-year anniversary of the march, a rally was held outside the United Nations in New York City. Crowd estimates were about 50,000, according to a number of sources. Farrakhan, Chavis, and Bevel all spoke in addition to local black leaders such as Rev. Al Sharpton. In a bizarre episode, Winnie Mandela was flown in from South Africa to speak. When it came time for her to talk, Chavis told the crowd that the U.S. State Department would not allow her to give a presentation so her remarks had to be given through someone else. The State Department and the South African government both later denied that they had placed any such restrictions on her.

Farrakhan's speech was basically apocalyptic. In his remarks, he stated that we live in a time of "darkness and doom," and no political leaders could do anything to "avert the war of Armageddon."[33] The solution, of course, was to follow the spiritual leadership of Farrakhan and the NOI.

In early 1997, Chavis announced that he had joined the NOI and changed his name to Benjamin Chavis Muhammad. He stated that he had been contemplating joining for some time and had been studying the Koran for at least five years. Many suspected that he was giving into the reality that he had nowhere else to go or that he was attempting to position himself to inherit the leadership of the NOI after Farrakhan. For his part, Chavis Muhammad stated that his conversion was religious-based and that he now viewed his life's mission to convert African-American Christians to Islam. Within a very short time after his joining, resentment and criticism from within toward Chavis Muhammad began to emerge, indicating that his tenure within the group may be unpleasant and short-lived.[34]

By the end of 1996, many had jumped on the bandwagon of condemnation of the march leaders. The lack of follow-up, Farrakhan's "Grand Dictator" tour to Africa and the Middle East, the black convention fiasco in St. Louis, Chavis Muhammad's megalomaniac and inept leadership of NAALS, and the suffocating dominance of the NOI were all charges made in the pages of *Emerge, Jet,* and black newspaper columns. Some saw the source of the problems in the egos and individualism of Farrakhan and Chavis Muhammad. Activist Ron Daniels, who had been involved in the leadership of the march at various stages, attributes the decline of the movement around the MMM and NAALS to the failure of Farrakhan and Chavis to operate in a collective and consultative manner. [35]

While all of these reasons are accurate, they tend to avoid a more disturbing, but perhaps truer conclusion: that the politics of Farrakhan and Chavis have been consistent and that their behavior has been the logical outcome of those politics. Farrakhan's global tour was not a mistake or a consequence of his not talking to black foreign policy experts. He was absolutely clear on why he went where he did, even if some of his supporters were not. His soft critics were also naive if they thought that after years of struggling to obtain the position of leadership afforded him by the march, he was about to decentralize his authority, particularly since the NOI was providing the foot soldiers and critical funding for the movement. His alliance with LaRouche, just as the NOI of Elijah Muhammad had formed tentative alliances with the Ku Klux Klan and the American Nazi movement, was also not a mistake or casual encounter. It was an ideologically driven choice that has every basis to grow and continue.

Within black politics, the dialogue concerning gender equality remains combative. While the march could have been an opportunity to highlight the issues facing both black men and women, the failure to do so allowed the atmosphere that demonizes black women to go unchallenged. Less than a year after the march, Congress passed and

Clinton signed welfare reform legislation; the long-term impact will be devastating to the black community, black families and children in particular. The opportunity to raise at least one million black voices—very likely a once-in-a-lifetime chance—in defense of needed social programs came and went. Given who led the march, however, even if the issue of welfare had been addressed, it is doubtful that the views expressed would have been that different from those of Gingrich and Clinton.

It is understandable why many in the black community so strongly supported the march. There is a desperate yearning for leadership, mobilization, and unity. And the issues facing black men are real (as are those faced by women, who are the majority of the black community). These sentiments and circumstances were exploited by Farrakhan and Chavis. While these issues are larger than Farrakhan, the march and the movement around and subsequent to it all have the permanent imprimatur of Farrakhan. The urgency with which people deny Farrakhan's role only highlights it. More important, it is Farrakhan's politics that are present even when he is not.

A black conservative agenda, albeit dressed in black nationalist clothing, will not free black America. Whether it comes from Clarence Thomas or Louis Farrakhan, it merely perpetuates the crisis that already exists for at least of a third of all African Americans and half of all black children. It is a moralistic and capitalistic vision, reinforced, in Farrakhan's case, by an authoritarianism that seeks to crush all voices of dissent.

Finally, in relationship to (re)building AACS, the MMM failed in several respects. Its call for African Americans to join black organizations, while not a problem in itself, is consistent with the moderate ideology of self-help that obscures the relationship between civil society, the state, and the market economy. This view also misses the point that the growing needs of millions, exacerbated by a job-destroying globalized economy and a shrinking welfare state, far outstrip the capacities of volunteer organizations. Massive public policy intervention, eschewed by the march's leadership, is required if even a modicum of possibility of advancement is to happen.

A Call for Insurgency

"However deeply American Negroes are caught in the struggle to be at last at home in our homeland of the United States, we cannot ignore the larger world house in which we are also dwellers. Equality with whites will not solve the problems of either whites or Negroes if it means equality in a world society stricken by poverty and in a universe doomed to extinction by war. All inhabitants of the globe are now neighbors. This world-wide neighborhood has been brought into being largely as a result of the modern scientific and technological revolutions."[36] —Martin Luther King, Jr.

In this era, with its world-changing, globalized economies and communities, an insurgent and bold Black leadership is needed now more than ever. This is a leadership that must not be captive to any of the major political parties which have made it clear that racial equality is, at best, a rhetorical device to buffer black resistance, and at worst, no longer a social or political objective. This is a leadership that must address the problems and intractability of race, gender, class, age, and nation without being mired in the limits of those identities. This is a leadership that challenges the power of the state and the economic elite, targeting their pivotal role in the destabilizing of poor black communities, while avoiding diatribes that blame the victims of these assaults. This is a leadership that must struggle with the difficult transitions in racial forms in the United States and beyond that are reconfiguring the black-white dynamic that has driven much of the racial heritage of the nation. This is a leadership that must fight to reconstruct AACS from within and without against the odds and against forces with significantly more ideological and material resources. If African Americans are to advance in the 21st century, this is a leadership that must come into existence.

There has never been a time when the consolidation of black leadership into one single individual has ever benefited African Americans. Whether it was the white-anointed reign of Booker T. Washington or the black groundswell that bolstered Jesse Jackson, a diverse and wide-ranging leadership has been necessary. This will become even more true in the coming years, as the arenas of struggle expand and new venues of cultural, social, and political expressions, some created by innovative and revolutionary technologies, emerge.

In the current and coming period, black activists of all types have an important role to play. Most important will be the creation of popular vehicles that foster and allow for the generation, expression, and validation of grassroots leadership on a broad scale. Too often, the black poor have been "represented" by civil rights leaders, nationalists, and even conservatives, rather than allowed to be their own voice and the creator of their own machines of resistance. The resources, skills, talents, insights, and experiences possessed by activists should be converged with similar and complementary attributes from the people whose interests are ostensibly being advocated. The power of the civil rights and Black Power eras was not in the national leaders and national organizations that gained fame for their heroic deeds, but the rising up of millions of ordinary, everyday people who created and joined groups that fought for inclusion and equality throughout AACS. What has characterized the post-1960s period has been the disappearance of massive organic involvement by African Americans of all classes and strata in structures of struggle.

This activism should not be seen as missionary work, where the community is rescued and saved by outsiders with the correct word and vision. Nor is it a call to romanticize the black community as a progressive stronghold that just needs a spark to ignite it. A complex and competing array of perspectives exist in the black community that, at any given time, can forge extremely conservative or harshly radical discourses and battlefronts. Black intellectuals, both inside and outside of academia, can play a critical role in the reconstruction of AACS. As intellectuals, those who are committed to sorting through the way in which ideas manifest and shape society, the creation of accessible and relevant intellectual work, *inter alia*, in the areas of economics, culture, politics, and sociology would link needed scholarship with social activism. On the one hand, such an effort would combat the anti-intellectualism that reigns not only in the black community, but in U.S. society at large. On the other hand, the highly correct black criticism of the uselessness of much of what is produced by black intellectuals could be abated. Perhaps it is most critical that black intellectuals do not view themselves as separate from the black community, but as one wing of it with specific responsibilities and skills to contribute.

African Americans and the Global Civil Society

Many of the issues and concerns being confronted by African Americans in the United States are also being struggled with by other communities around the globe. Job displacement, cuts in social programs, a shrunken and disappearing welfare state, and racial and ethnic assaults are endemic to this period. Although in the past the black community did not have the luxury to ignore its connection with the rest of the world, it is with even greater peril today that an isolationist view must be avoided. As argued throughout this book, the option to act locally has vanished and every decision, in today's world, is a step into the international arena.

African Americans have a long history of solidarity with the global community and with peoples who have struggled for justice and fairness. African Americans supported Cuba in its independence struggle, fought in the Spanish Civil War, actively opposed Apartheid in South Africa, gave support to the Palestinians, marched against the Vietnam War, and, in general, have been engaged in global struggles for centuries. The forging of the black community itself was an expression of the internationalization of commerce, politics, and ideology that launched the slave trade, slavery, and racism. Black leaders, from Ida B. Wells and W.E.B. Du Bois to Malcolm X, Angela Davis, and Martin L. King Jr. to Louis Farrakhan, Colin Powell, Jesse Jackson, and Dorothy Height, not only advocated but practiced international politics at the highest level. From conservative to progressive interventions, black leaders have seen the necessity to comment and participate in the global issues that defined their era. In essence, the black community has always been an active member of the global civil society.

In the period ahead, new opportunities and challenges to global participation abound. Technologies have made access to the global community relatively easy, fast, and efficient. Never before in history has it been so convenient to obtain information and data on the issues confronting people from Africa and Asia to Europe and the Caribbean. In every area of life, from the social and political to the economic and cultural, the world can be touched with a few keystrokes or a phone call. Global reach is not just available to the world's elite. Millions of people can now bypass governments, parties, and other intermediaries in order to directly connect with their counterparts and people of similar views and interests. This ease and efficiency of linkage opens up numerous possibilities for constructing a world community that can collectively address the issues of this age and facilitate the global civil society project.

This reach also carries dangers. Much of the ultimate control of the new technologies is in the hands of unaccountable, unregulated, and uncaring transnational corporations whose efforts at economic and technical domination are helped by policymakers, who, in vain attempt to maintain the nation-state, are willing to make unholy concessions. Many, if not most, of these elected officials, the world over, have been purchased by these transnational corporations and have long surrendered any pretense of acting in the interests of the majority of the people they were elected to represent. With this power also comes efforts at ideological dominance. Racist ideology, mainly though not exclusively from the American perspective, is increasingly finding wider and wider audiences as it is broadcast and otherwise distributed to the global community via films, cable television, music videos, the Internet, and other medium. In a similar way, issues of gender, class, and nation are narratives being told from the point of view of a global elite.

The resolution of the tension between opportunity for solidarity among the global masses, and expanded economic and ideological hegemony for the transnational corporations will determine the stability and strength of global civil society. The contributions that can be made to this project by African Americans are immense. Positioned in the center of where much of the key economic, political, and even technology battles have and will unfold—from NAFTA and GATT to the Internet—African Americans are uniquely situated to expose, confront, and otherwise disrupt the process of power that threatens the future of those in the United States and beyond. In unison with others engaged in similar struggles internationally, African Americans can be part of the global work crew that builds King's "world house."

Imaging an Alternative Black Future

> "Racism is no mere American phenomena. Its vicious grasp knows no geographical boundaries. In fact, racism and its perennial ally—economic exploitation—provide the key to understanding most of the international complications of this generation." [37] —Martin Luther King, Jr.

King's dream was a global one. Contrary to reductive efforts to limit King's hopes to notions of racial friendship and harmony, he projected a radical vision that demanded a fundamental restructuring of society and the global community. He did not just want an end to segregation, but called for an end to racism. He did not just want to help the poor, but called for an end to poverty. He did not just seek to question U.S. involvement in Vietnam, but called for an end to all wars and the exploitation that generates them.

In spite of his visionary insights, King was a product of his times. He did not place gender equity at the center of his political vision, although it is implied in his work more consistently than other black leaders of the period. Neither did he speak at great length about, and perhaps was not able to see, the changing racial structure of the United States with the growth of the Asian and Hispanic communities. Nor could King, or anyone else at the time, predict the fall of global communism and the end of the Cold War that had determined international politics, economics, and culture for more than six decades. King was born into and died during the Cold War era. Finally, he could not appreciate in full how new technologies and globalization would (and continue to) restructure the world and daily life in both progressive and deadly ways. Amazingly, King did see the impact of technologies on the workforce even back then when he wrote of his distress "at thousands of working people displaced from their jobs with reduced incomes as a result of automation while the profits of the employers remain intact."[38] That millions of people would be displaced and that this phenomena would become the dominant character in modern economic life was, of course, unforeseen.

Learning from those historically shaped limits, King's world house is still on the agenda. African Americans have a vested interest in thinking globally and acting globally even as we address the immediate local and national issues that confront us. It is critical that we appreciate the historic transformations that are occurring right before our eyes in our neighborhoods, our cities, in the nation, and around the world. Working-class black communities around the globe, from Soweto to Brixton to Rio to Toronto, are hurting and disproportionately suffering from unemployment, economic downsizing, a retreating welfare state, drug trafficking, lack of educational opportunities, and inadequate housing. At the same time, tremendous struggles are being waged to fight those problems that manifest locally but are part of a global system. Racism, in conjunction with sex, class, and national dynamics, are driving these conditions as well as shaping the fight back. For African Americans, it is timely and appropriate to unite and join other struggles and ours. The world house, however, is larger than just the African disapora. Communities of the poor and working class are engaged in struggles that are also of meaning and importance to the black community. Winning battles against corporate power, to save a ravaged environment, and for cultural diversity also require a global vision that is inclusive.

Central to the unfolding vision necessary to move forward is the issue of gender equity and inclusion. The black community will not and can not advance as long as patriarchal ideas shape its thinking and practice. In this period, the black community must resist wholeheartedly the dominant ideology, shared by many black male leaders, that preaches that the problems facing African Americans are centered around the breakdown of the traditional family and the absence of a male presence in the home. On virtually every indices, black women are doing worse than black men, and increasingly so. This is also true for women on a global scale, where women "do two-thirds of the world's work, earn ten percent of the world's income, and own less than one percent of the world's property."[39]

King's world house is still under construction. It is being built by children in Harare who are logging onto the Internet and communicating with children in Harlem. It is being built by the Zapatistas in Mexico who are resisting the outrages of NAFTA, thereby fighting in the interests of communities in Mexico, the United States, and Canada. It is being built by women farmhands in Indonesia who sit on panels with women farmhands from Jamaica at a conference in England fighting globalization. It is being built by students in China, Brazil, and South Africa who are computer linked and exchanging ideas on any number of subjects. It is being built by African Americans in South Central Los Angeles who take Spanish lessons so they can better work with their neighbors. The global civil society that will inhabit King's world house must include the black community. This is the task indeed the mission that we must embrace in the days ahead.

Notes

1. Globalization's Impact on Race Relations

1. Quoted in Kevin Danaher, ed., *Corporations Are Gonna Get Your Mama: Globalization and Downsizing of the American Dream* (Monroe, ME: Common Courage Press, 1996), 204.

2. Medea Benjamin, "Nike's Exploited Workers," in *Corporations Are Gonna Get Your Mama,* 86. Also, see J.B. Strasser and Laurie Becklund, *Swoosh: The Unauthorized Story of Nike and the Men Who Played There* (New York: HarperBusiness, 1993). Michael Jordan's role as the highest-paid black athlete hawking sports products may be superseded by golf phenomenon Tiger Woods. In 1996–97, Woods signed endorsement contracts of $40 million with Nike, $20 million with Titleist, $20 million with American Express, and at least another $8 million for books and other products. See Tim Lacey, "Tiger, 21, Signs for Millions," *Washington Afro-American,* 24 May 1997, 1.

3. James Rinehart, "The Ideology of Competitiveness: Pitting Worker Against Worker," *Corporations Are Gonna Get Your Mama,* 90.

4. Benjamin, "Nike's Exploited Workers," 86.

5. John Hoberman, *Darwin's Athletes: How Sport Has Damaged Black America and Preserved the Myth of Race* (Boston: Houghton Mifflin Co., 1997), 34.

6. Patricia J. Williams, "Disorder in the House: The New World Order and the Socioeconomic Status of Women," in *Theorizing Black Feminisms: The Visionary Pragmatism of Black Women,* eds. Stanlie M. James and Abena A. Busia (New York: Routledge, 1993), 118.

7. Jerry Mander, "The Dark Side of Globalization," *The Nation,* 15-22 July 1996, 9.

8. Anthony Giddens, *The Consequences of Modernity* (Stanford, CA: Stanford University Press, 1990), 64.

9. Robert Burnett, *Global Jukebox: The International Music Industry* (New York: Routledge, 1996), 12.

10. Lester C. Thurow, *The Future of Capitalism: How Today's Economic Forces Shape Tomorrow's World* (New York: William Morrow and Co., 1996), 114.

11. See Richard Barnet and John Cavanagh, *Global Dreams: Imperial Corporations and the New World Order* (New York: Simon & Schuster, 1994); Jerry Mander and Edward Goldsmith, eds., *The Case Against Globalization: And for a Turn toward the Local* (San Francisco: Sierra Club Books, 1996); Benjamin R. Barber, *Jihad vs. McWorld: How the Planet is Both Falling Apart and Coming Together, and What This Means for Democracy* (Toronto: Times Books, 1995); Bennett Harrison, *Lean and Mean: The Changing Landscape of Corporate Power in the Age of Flexibility* (New York: Basic Books, 1994); William Greider, *One World,*

Ready or Not: The Manic Logic of Global Capitalism (New York: Simon & Schuster, 1997); David C. Korten, *When Corporations Rule the World* (West Hartford, CT: Kumarian Press, 1995); and Robert B. Reich, *The Work of Nations: Preparing Ourselves for 21st Century Capitalism* (New York: Vintage Books, 1992).

12. Jeremy Rifkin, *The End of Work: The Decline of the Global Labor Force and the Dawn of the Post-Market Era* (New York: Putnam Books, 1995), 68.

13. Ibid., 71.

14. Sidney Wilhelm, *Who Needs the Negro?* (Cambridge, MA: Schenkman, 1970), 163.

15. Ibid., 156–7.

16. Holly Sklar, "Persistent Impoverishment," *Ecologist*, July/August 1996, 188.

17. Jeremy Brecher and Tim Costello, *Global Village or Global Pillage?: Economic Reconstruction from the Bottom Up* (Boston: South End Press, 1994), 27.

18. Ibid., 28.

19. United Nations Development Program, *Human Development Report 1992* (New York: United Nations, 1992), 6.

20. "A Divided World," *North–South,* November 1995, 9.

21. See "Employment in the World, 1996/1997," International Labor Organization, United Nations, 1997.

22. Barnet and Cavanagh, *Global Dreams*, 286.

23. Nicholas Hildyard, Colin Hines, and Tim Lang, "Who Competes?: Changing Landscapes of Corporate Control," *Ecologist*, July/August 1996, 128.

24. Lori S. Robinson, "Canada's Justice," *Emerge,* April 1996, 16.

25. Ian Grant and Rafik Benale, "May Day Marchers Protest Racism and Unemployment in France," http://www.tbwt.com/views /feat/feat69.htm.

26. Lori S. Robinson, "Black Latin America," *Emerge,* April 1995, 14.

27. Thomas D. Boston, *Race, Class and Conservatism* (Cambridge, MA: Unwin Hyman, 1988), 48.

28. Rachel Kamel, *The Global Factory: Analysis and Action for a New Economic Era* (Philadelphia: American Friends Service Committee, 1990), 20.

29. Barnet and Cavanagh, *Global Dreams*, 275–6.

30. Ibid., 292.

31. Nicholas Hildyard, Colin Hines, and Tim Lang, "Who Competes?" 127.

32. Kamel, *The Global Factory*, 15.

33. Barnet and Cavanagh, *Global Dreams*, 293.

34. William Julius Wilson, *When Work Disappears: The World of the New Urban Poor* (New York: Alfred A. Knopf, 1996), 29.

35. Rochelle Sharpe, "In Last Recession, Only Blacks Suffered Net Employment Loss," *Wall Street Journal,* 4 September 1993.

36. Ibid.

37. "Displacement Rate, Unemployment Spells, and Reemployment Wages by Race," General Accounting Office, Washington, D.C., September 1994, 3

38. David C. Korten, "The Limits of the Earth," *The Nation,* 15-22 July 1996, 18.

39. Thurow, *The Future of Capitalism*, 26.

40. "Why Today's Big Profits Mean Big Trouble," *Too Much,* Fall 1995, 1.

41. Holly Sklar, "Scapegoating and Slander," *Ecologist*, July/August 1996, 185.

42. Ibid.

43. See *Too Much,* Fall 1995, 3.

44. Wilson, *When Work Disappears*, 29-30

45. Lester Henry, *NAFTA and GATT: World Trade Policy Impacts on African Americans* (New York: Du Bois Bunche Center for Public Policy, 1995), 11.

46. Robert C. Smith, *Racism in the Post-Civil Rights Era: Now You See It, Now You Don't* (Albany, NY: State University of New York, 1995), 134.

47. Henry, 28-29. See Julie Graham, "Multinational Corporations and the Internationalization of Production: An Industry Perspective," in *Creating a New World Economy,* eds. G. Epstein, J. Graham, and J. Newbhard (Philadelphia: Temple University Press), 221–41.

48. Barnet and Cavanagh, *Global Dreams*, 313.

49. Reich, *The Work of Nations*, 213.

50. Ibid., 212.

51. Barnet and Cavanagh, *Global Dreams*, 311.

52. Sklar, "Scapegoating and Slander," 190.

53. Ibid.

54. Ibid., 189–90.

55. Martin Carnoy, *Faded Dreams: The Politics and Economics of Race in America* (New York: University of Cambridge Press, 1994), 236–7.

56. Thea M. Lee, "The Likely Impact of NAFTA on Women and Minorities," testimony before the Employment, Housing and Aviation Subcommittee of the U.S. House Committee on Government Operations, U.S. House of Representatives, 10 November 1993, 1.

57. William Lucy, "The Price of NAFTA: Guaranteed Short-Term Pain With No Guaranteed Long-Term Benefits," *Third World Viewpoint*, Spring 1994, 16.

58. *Congressional Record,* 17 November 1993, H9957.

59. Reich, *The Work of Nations*, 225-40.

60. Donald L. Barlett and James B. Steele, *America: Who Stole the Dream* (Kansas City, MO: Andrews and McNeel, 1996), 140–1.

61. Ibid., 133.

62. Alfred Edmond, "Coming on Strong," *Black Enterprise*, June 1994, 78.

63. Lorrie Grant, "GATT Gains Ground for Minority-Owned Firms," *Emerge,* February 1995, 25.

64. U.S. Bureau of the Census, "New York Metro Area Leads List for Black-Owned Firms, Los Angeles Tops in Women-Owned Businesses, Census Bureau Reports," press release, 16 March 1996.

65. U.S. Bureau of the Census, "Black-Owned Businesses Up 46 Percent Over Five Years, Census Bureau Survey Shows," press release, 12 December 1995, and "Number of Minority-Owned Businesses and Revenues Increase Substantially between 1987 and 1992," press release, 18 November 1996.

66. Ibid.

67. Barnet and Cavanagh, *Global Dreams*, 302.

68. Marian Wright Edelman, "A Portrait of Inequality in America," *Washington Afro-American,* 26 April 1997, A5.

69. Ibid.

70. Ibid.

71. Robin Wright, "UNICEF Report Cites U.S. as Leader in Child Poverty," *San Jose Mercury News,* 12 June 1996.

72. Ibid.

73. Samuel I. Rosenman, *The Public Papers and Addresses of Franklin D. Roosevelt* (New York: Harper & Row, 1950), 41.

74. Ibid.

75. Ron Dellums, "Seven More Members of the House Join Original 16 Cosponsors of H.R. 1050, 'A Living Wage, Jobs For All Act,'" *News & Views From Ron Dellums of California*, 8 February 1996.

76. H.R. 1050.

77. Dellums, *News and Views*.

78. See *Corporate Power and the American Dream* (New York: Labor Institute, 1994), 119.

2. If I Were a Rich Man

1. Martin Luther King, Jr., "Where Do We Go From Here: Chaos or Community?" in *A Testament of Hope: The Essential Writings and Speeches of Martin Luther King, Jr.,* ed. James M. Washington (New York: HarperCollins, 1986), 617. 37. Ibid., 621.

2. See Michael Harrington, *The New American Poverty* (New York: Penguin, 1985).

3. Mack H. Jones, "The Political Thought of the New Black Conservatives: An Analysis, Explanation and Interpretation," in *Readings in Political Issues,* eds. Franklin Jones and Michael Adams, (Dubuque, IA: Kendall/Hunt Publishing Co., 1987).

4. Adam Fifield, "Corporate Caseworkers," *In These Times,* 16 June 1997,14.

5. Ibid.

6. Ibid., 15-16.

7. Data on the characteristics of welfare recipients, unless otherwise noted, is taken from the 1994 House Ways and Means Committee's *Green Book* on federal

entitlement programs. This data is available on CD-ROM from the Government Printing Office.

8. Ibid.

9. Ibid.

10. Ibid.

11. Ibid.

12. Ibid.

13. Ibid.

14. The Twentieth Century Fund, *Medical Reform: A Twentieth Century Fund Guide to the Issues,* (New York: Twentieth Century Fund Press, 1995).

15. Ibid.

16. Ibid.

17. Ibid.

18. Ibid.

19. Ibid.

20. Ibid.

21. Ibid.

22. Ibid.

23. Ibid.

24. 1994 House Ways and Means Committee *Green Book.*

25. Ibid.

26. Children's Defense Fund, *Welfare Reform Briefing Book* (Washington, DC: CDF, January 1995), 4.

27. 1994 House Ways and Means Committee *Green Book.*

28. Ibid.

29. Ibid., Children's Defense Fund, 4.

30. Julianne Malveaux, *Sex, Lies, and Stereotypes: Perspectives of a Mad Economist* (Los Angeles: Pines One Publishing, 1994), 36.

31. Bill Clinton and Al Gore, *Putting People First: How We Can All Change America* (New York: Times Books, 1992), 164.

32. Ibid., 165.

33. Ibid., 12.

34. Ibid., 11.

35. "Survey Finds Corporate Welfare Spending Exceeds Social Welfare: Nader Criticizes Clinton's Welfare 'Reform' for Ignoring Corporate Entitlements," press release, (Washington, DC: Essential Information).

36. James P. Donahue, "The Fact Cat Freeloaders: When American Big Business Bellys Up to the Trough," *The Washington Post,* 6 March 1994.

37. Ibid.

38. Mark Zepezauer and Arthur Naiman, *Take the Rich Off Welfare* (Tucson, AZ: Odonian Press, 1996), 6.

39. Janice C. Shields, "Strange Bedfellows," *In These Times,* 12 May 1997, 28-9, 36.

40. Ibid. See *Wealthfare Reform Organizing Kit, (*Boston: Share the Wealth).

41. Activists have created sites on the World Wide Web that provide insight and data regarding corporate welfare. See, for example, the Share the Wealth Project (http://www.stw.org/); Cato Institute's reports, "Ending Corporate Welfare as We KnowIt"and"How Corporate WelfareWon" (http://www.cato.org/pubs/pas/pa~254es.html); Essential Information (http://www.essential.org); Rachel's Corporate Welfare Information Center (http://ww.environlink.org/issues/corporate/welfare/index.html); and *Utne Reader*'s Corporate Welfare Resources (http://www.utnereader.com:80/archive/lens01/exchange/1naderres.html).

42. "Survey Finds Corporate Welfare Spending Exceeds Social Welfare."

43. Joseph G. Conti and Brad Stetson, "Are You Really a Racist?: A Common-Sense Quiz," in *Black and Right: The Bold New Voice of Black Conservatives in America,* eds. Stan Faryna, Brad Stetson, and Joseph G. Conti (Westport, CT: Praeger, 1997), 71.

44. Brian W. Jones, "Two Visions of Black Leadership," in *Black and Right,* 41

45. Telly Lovelace, "No Need for a Government Handout," in *Black and Right,* 47.

46. Louis Farrakhan, "The Sickness of Envy," speech delivered at Muhammad University, Chicago, 7 March 1990, cited in Mattiass Gardell, *In the Name of Elijah Muhammad: Louis Farrakhan and the Nation of Islam* (Durham, NC: Duke University Press, 1996), 319.

47. Wahneema Lubiano, "Black Ladies, Welfare Queens, and State Minstrels: Ideological War by Narrative Means," in *Race-ing Justice, En-Gendering Power* ed. Toni Morrison (New York: Random House, 1992), 339.

48. Barbara Ransby and Tracye Matthews, "Black Popular Culture and Transcendence of Patriarchal Illusions," in *Words of Fire: An Anthology of African-American Feminist Thought*, Beverly Guy-Sheftall (New York: The New Press, 1995), 526.

49. Lubiano, "Black Ladies," 332.

50. Children's Defense Fund, "Strategies to Protect the Safety Net for Children, Families, and Average Americans," (Washington, DC: CDF), 1.

51. Ibid., 38.

52. "Making Welfare Work: An Outline for Constructive Welfare Reform," (Washington, DC: Joint Center for Political and Economic Studies, 1995), 1.

53. The WGNANT recommendations were: (1) Job stimulus based on private-sector inducements for job creation for both poor men and women, supplemented where necessary by public-sector investments; (2) Education and job training—especially on-the-job training, two of the most important factors proven to help people move from welfare to work; (3) Adequate rewards for work—for example, expanding the Earned Income Tax Credit and raising the minimum wage in order

to make work pay; (4) Time limits that take differences among welfare recipients into consideration—for instance, shorter limits for those job-ready and longer ones for those who are not; (5) Labor law reforms—for example, expanding the unemployment insurance program to include contingency workers, and encouragement of collective bargaining in the low-wage sector; (6) Family-friendly policies—including eliminating disincentives in AFDC for two-parent families, increasing asset limits, raising earning disregards, increasing standards of need to fill the gap, budgeting, encouraging extended and step-parent families, strengthening voluntary paternity establishment procedures, providing nourishing homes for teen parents—including voluntary enrollment in group homes where necessary, providing support for single parents to combine work and family, and establishing required parenting classes for all adolescents in public schools; (7) Children-friendly reforms—for example, promoting early childhood development through more quality child care institutions, child support assurance for all children, building public-private partnerships to provide additional or alternative role models for children in single-parent families, providing the same range and quality of reproductive services for the poor that affluent people enjoy, and building a public campaign not only against unwed motherhood, but also toward valuing all children, regardless of the marital status of their parents, and; (8) Equal opportunity and anti-discrimination provisions to govern all aspects of welfare reform and level the playing field—including full civil liberties, civil rights, minimum wage protections, equal pay for equal work, and rights to earn seniority in jobs.

54. For a critique of Clinton's role in the welfare debacle, see Peter Edelman, "The Worst Thing Bill Clinton Has Done," *Atlantic Monthly,* April 1997.

55. Robin D. G. Kelley, "The Black Poor and the Politics of Oppression in a New South City, 1929-1970," in *The Underclass Debate: Views from History,* ed. Michael B. Katz (Princeton, NJ: Princeton University Press, 1993), 294.

56. Marcia Bok, *Civil Rights and the Social Programs of the 1960s* (Westport, CT: Prager, 1992), 150.

57. See Mimi Abramovitz, *Under Attack, Fighting Back: Women and Welfare in the United States* (New York: Monthly Review Press, 1996).

58. James Jennings also writes about several advocacy groups, including the Massachusetts Human Services Coalition, the Coalition for Basic Human Needs, Up and Out of Poverty Now (Detroit), and Congress for a Working America (Milwaukee). See James Jennings, *Understanding the Nature of Poverty in Urban America* (Westport, CT: London, 1994), 143.

3. California Scheming

1. John Wildermuth, "Immigrants Boost State Population to 31.3 Million," *San Francisco Chronicle,* 16 February 1993.

2. Elaine Woo, "Prison Spending Hurts Schools and Black Students, Report Says; Government: Study Says State Has Shifted Its Priority from Education to Incarceration. Spokesman for Governor Calls Conclusions 'Mindless Drivel,'" *Los Angeles Times,* 23 October 1996.

3. Ibid.

4. Mary Ellen Leary, "California Runs out of Jail Space as Voters Worry More about Schools than Crime," *Pacific News,* 11 December 1996.

5. Chris McGinn, "NAFTA Index: Three Years of NAFTA Facts," *Public Citizen,* Washington, D.C., 14 January 1997, 1.

6. Ibid., 3.

7. Brad Edmondson, "Life without Illegal Immigrants," *American Demographics,* May 1996.

8. Ibid.

9. Alejandro Ramos, "The Use and Abuse of Statistics: The Case of Proposition 187," http://www.aad.berkeley.edu/95journal/alejandroramos.html.

10. Ibid.

11. Alejandro Alonso, University of Southern California, http://www-bcf.use.edu/%7eaalonso/academic/187.html.

12. Haya El Nasser and Gale Holland, "'187 Awakes 'A Sleeping Giant': Opponents Promise to Be 'A Force,'" *USA Today,* 10 November 1994.

13. Deeann Glamser, "California's Ballot Vote Now Spreading Fear 'Far and Wide,'" *USA Today,* 16 November 1994.

14. Brenda Payton, "Black Vote for 187 No Surprise," *Oakland Tribune,* 11 November 1994.

15. Jan Adams, "Pro 187—What's to Be Learned?" *Racefile,* January-February 1995, 20.

16. Martin Luther King, Jr., *Where Do We Go From Here:Chaos or Community?* (Boston, MA: Beacon Press, 1968).

17. Pamela Burdman, "Minority Applications Slip for 2nd Year at UC," *San Francisco Chronicle,* 5 February 1997.

18. George Skelton, "After 209, What's Next for Connerly?" *Los Angeles Times,* 18 November 1996.

19. California Senate Office of Research, "Taking a Look at Affirmative Action," 19 January 1995, 5.

20. Richard Morin, "Affirming Affirmative Action Hires," *Washington Post,* 12 January 1997.

21. See http://www.igc.apc.org/cfg/whoiscfj.html.

22. Bettina Boxall, "California Elections/Proposition 209; Opponents Go Their Separate Ways; Two Women's Groups and Civil Rights Organizations Leave Coalition. Some Call It a Rift, Others Say It Is a Division of Labor," *Los Angeles Times,* 11 October 1996.

23. "Elections '96; State Propositions: A Snapshot of Voters," *Los Angeles Times,* 7 November 1996.

24. Ibid.

25. Mortimer B. Zuckerman, "Black America's Mirror Image," *U.S. News and World Report*, 6 May 1996, 76.

26. Malik Miah, "Why the Leadership Vacuum?" *Against the Current*, July/August 1996, 13.

27. Farai Chideya, "Affirmative Action—Beyond Black and White: Equality? I'm Still Waiting," *New York Times*, 11 March 1995.

28. See http://www.qsanfrancisco.com/qsf/95fall/aff-action.html.

29. David G. Savage, "White House Joins Attack on Prop 209," *Los Angeles Times*, 21 December 1996.

4. To Be or Not to Be

1. James Baldwin, "If Black English Isn't a Language, Then Tell Me What Is?" *The Price of a Ticket: Collected Nonfiction, 1948-1985* (New York: St. Martin's/Marek, 1985), 652.

2. William L. Van Deburg, *New Day in Babylon: The Black Power Movement and American Culture, 1965-1975* (Chicago: University of Chicago Press, 1993), 222.

3. Some critical works on BEV that came out of the period were: J. L. Dillard, *Black English: Its History and Usage in the United States* (New York: Vintage, 1973); William Labov, *Language in the Inner City: Studies in the Black English Vernacular* (Philadelphia: University of Pennsylvania Press, 1972); Paul Stoller, ed., *Black American English: Its Background and Its Usage in the Schools and Literature* (New York: Dell, 1975); and Robert L. Williams, ed., *Ebonics: The True Language of Black Folks* (St. Louis: Institute of Black Studies, 1975).

4. Many linguists argue that BEV has its own syntax structure, pronunciations, and slang. For example, there is often no "s" at the end of third, person-singular verbs; the "k" at the end of words is translated to "x" ("ask" = "ax"); the "r" on the end of certain words is dropped ("for"="fo"), and many words ending in "th" are changed to end in "f" ("with"="wif").

5. See Robert L. Williams, *Ebonics: The True Language of Black Folks* (St. Louis: Institute of Black Studies, 1975).

6. Steve Holmes, "Black English Debate: No Standard Assumptions," *New York Times*, December 30, 1996.

7. "Who Said What about Ebonics, " *University Faculty Voice*, February 1997, 6.

8. Ibid.

9. "Jackson Assails Recognition of Black English," *Washington Post*, 23 December 1996.

10. Ros Davidson, "Jackson Shifts Stance on Black English Effort," *Washington Post*, 31 December 1996.

11. "Ebonics: Q & A," *Jax Fax*, 2 January 1997.

12. *JaxFax*, 23 January 1997.

13. *Sacramento Bee*, 23 December 1996.

14. Linguistic Society Resolution on "Ebonics," http://www.lsa.umich.edu:80/ling/jlawler/ebonics.html.

15. Lori Olszewski and Rick DelVecchio, "Ebonics Plan Toned Down in Oakland," *San Francisco Chronicle,* 13 January 1997.

16. Ibid.

17. Ibid.

18. Karen DeWitt, "Not So Separate: Ebonics, Language of Richard Nixon," *New York Times,* 29 December 1996.

19. Baldwin, *The Price of a Ticket,* 650.

5. O.J. and the Symbolic Uses of Racial Exceptions

1. Jonathan T. Lovitt, "Poll: More Now Believe O.J. is Guilty," *USA Today,* 4 October 1996.

2. Ibid.

3. Howard Goldberg, "Poll: Black-White O.J. Gap Narrows," *Associated Press,* 22 January 1997.

4. See Harry Edwards, *The Revolt of the Black Athlete* (New York: The Free Press, 1969); and David K. Wiggins, "Critical Events Affecting Racism in Athletics," in *Racism in College Athletics: The African American Athlete's Experience* eds. Dana Brooks and Ronald Althouse (Morgantown, WV: Fitness Information Technology, Inc., 1993), 23-49.

5. Edwards, *The Revolt of the Black Athlete,* 76.

6. Betsy Peoples, "Graduation Blitz," *Emerge,* November 1995, 56.

7. See Anne DuCille, *Skin Trade* (Cambridge: Harvard University Press, 1996). Also see, John Hoberman, *Darwin's Athletes: How Sport Has Damaged Black America and Preserved the Myth of Race* (Boston: Houghton Mifflin Company, 1997).

8. Leola Johnson and David Roediger, "'Hertz, Don't It?': Becoming Colorless and Staying Black in the Crossover of O.J. Simpson," in *Birth of a Nation 'hood,* eds. Toni Morrison and Claudia Brodsky Lacour (New York: Pantheon, 1997), 202.

9. Ibid.

10. Edward Helmore, "Making a Mint out of Murder," *The Independent,* 18 June 1995.

11. Garth Alexander, "America turns Simpson trial into big bucks," *Sunday Times,* 30 April 1995.

12. Ibid.

13. Ibid.

14. Ibid.

15. Helmore, "Making a Mint."

16. Alexander, "America turns Simpson."

17. Helmore, "Making a Mint."

18. Alexander, "America turns Simpson."

19. Helmore, "Making a Mint."

20. DuCille, *Skin Trade*, 161.

21. Alexander, "America turns Simpson."

22. A. Leon Higginbotham, Jr., Aderson Bellegarde Francois, and Linda Y. Yuch, "The O.J. Simpson Trial: Who Was Improperly 'Playing the Race Card?'" in *Birth of a Nation 'hood,* eds. Toni Morrison and Claudia Brodsky Lacour (New York: Pantheon, 1997), 40.

23. Ibid., 53.

24. Nikol G. Alexander and Drucilla Cornell, "Dismissed or Banished? A Testament to the Reasonableness of the Simpson Jury" in *Birth of a Nation 'hood: Gaze, Script and Spectacle in the O.J. Simpson Case* eds. Toni Morrison and Claudia Brodsky Lacour (New York: Pantheon, 1997), 57-96.

25. "Simpson Trials by the Numbers," Associated Press, January 18, 1997.

26. See Beverly Guy-Sheftall, ed., *Words of Fire: An Anthology of African-American Feminist Thought* (New York: The New Press, 1995).

6. Thug Life

1. "Life Goes On," *All Eyes on Me* (Death Row Records, 1995).

2. Others on this list include Mike Tyson and Michael Jackson. While some political figures, such as Rev. Jesse Jackson and Min. Louis Farrakhan, also enjoy international fame, global American blackness is reified in athletes and entertainers.

3. Luther Campbell and John R. Miller, *As Nasty As They Wanna Be: The Uncensored Story of Luther Campbell of 2 Live Crew* (Fort Lee, NJ: Barricade Books, 1992), 151-61.

4. Mark Naison, "Outlaw Culture," *Reconstruction*, Vol. 1. No . 4, 128.

5. Cornel West, *Race Matters* (Boston, MA: Beacon Press, 1993), 15.

6. Robert Burnett, *Global Jukebox: The International Music Industry* (New York: Routledge, 1996), 3.

7. Ibid., 8.

8. MTV is owned by media mogul Sumner Redstone, who also owns Viacom, VH-1, Lifetime, Showtime, The Movie Channel, and Nickelodeon, and has controlling interest in Paramount. He also has five television stations and 12 radio stations.

9. Naison, *Outlaw Culture*, 129-30.

10. See Charles Jones, ed., *The Black Panther Party Reconsidered* (Baltimore: Black Classic Press, 1997).

11. "I Wonder if Heaven's gota Ghetto," *2 Pac* (Death Row Records, 1994).

12. "Correctional Populations in the United States, 1994," *Bureau of Justice Statistics Executive Summary,* U.S. Department of Justice, Office of Justice Programs, 1.

13. Connie Bruck, "The Takedown of Tupac," *The New Yorker*, 7 July 1997, 46.

14. Chuck Phillips and Alan Abrahadson, "Government Probing Whether Rap Label is a Criminal Enterprise," *Washington Post*, 31 December 1996.

15. "Outlaw," *2 Pac* (Death Row Records, 1993).

7. Globalizing the Media

1. Lawrence Grossman, *The Electronic Republic* (New York: Viking, 1995), 173-74.

2. Polly E. McLean, "Mass Communications, Popular Culture, and Racism," in *Racism and Anti-Racism in World Perspectve,* ed. Benjamin Bower (Thousand Oaks, CA: Sage Publications, 1995), 84.

3. Devin Walker, "The Media Lords: The Great Deceivers of the Earth," *The Kermit Report*, August-September 1991, 2.

4. "The National Entertainment State," *The Nation*, 3 June 1996.

5. See http://www.thenation.com/extra/publish/map1.html.

6. Herbert Schiller, "On that Chart," *The Nation,* 3 June 1996, 16.

7. Ernest Holsendolph, "Who Owns What," *Emerge,* May 1995, 21.

8. Robert W. McChesney, "The Global Struggle for Democratic Communication," *Monthly Review,* July-August 1996, 2.

9. Barnet and Cavanagh, *Global Dreams*, 156.

10. Gracian Mack, "How to Spot Hot Entertainment Stocks," *Black Enterprise*, June 1994, 269.

11. Mark Lowery and Nadirah Z. Sabir, "The Making of 'Hollyhood,'" *Black Enterprise*, December 1994, 112.

12. I.R., "African Americans' Viewing Habits on the Rise," *TV Guide*, 26 March 1994, 36.

13. Barnet and Cavanagh, *Global Dreams*, 156.

14. David Lieberman, "Time Warner Picks Parsons as President," *USA Today*, 1 November 1994; Gary Hoover, Alta Campbell, and Patrick J. Spain, eds., *Hoover's Handbook of American Business, 1994* (Austin, TX: The Reference Press, 1993), 1036.

15. Matthew S. Scott and Tariq K. Muhammad, "The Top 50 Black Power Brokers in Entertainment," *Black Enterprise*, December 1994, 59-80.

16. Carolyn M. Brown, "Fighting for Air Time," *Black Enterprise*, December 1994, 96.

17. Ibid. 96-7.

18. Paul Farhi, "Johnson's Dream of a Team," *Washington Post*, 22 August 1994.

19. Ibid.

20. Ibid.

21. Mike Mills, "Going Shopping for a Black Audience," *Washington Post*, 20 July 1994.

22. Ibid., 16.

23. Barnet and Cavanagh, *Global Dreams*, 157.

24. Christopher Vaughn, "Simmons' Rush for Profits," *Black Enterprise*, December 1992, 67.

25. Ibid.

26. Ibid.

27. Paul Farhi, "Is Murdock Getting the Most for His Money," *Washington Post,* 1 September 1996.

28. McChesney, "The Global Struggle," 3.

29. Ibid.

30. The "edu" and "gov" signatures denote educational and governmental sites.

31. Paul Taylor, "Internet Users 'Likely to Reach 500m By 2000,'" *Financial Times,* 13 May 1996, 4.

32. Peter Golding, "World Wide Wedge: Division and Contradiction in the Global Information Infrastructure," *Monthly Review,* July-August 1996, 76.

33. McChesney, "The Global Struggle," 6.

34. Golding, "World Wide Wedge," 85.

35. Sarah Anderson and John Cavanagh, *The Top 200: The Rise of Global Corporate Power,* Institute for Policy Studies, 25 September 1996, 1.

36. Ibid.

37. Ibid.

38. Michael Dawson and John Bellamy Foster, "Virtual Capitalism: The Political Economy of the Information Highway," *Monthly Review,* July-August 1996, 43.

39. Ninety-one percent of the world does not have telephones according to the United Nations Development Program, *Human Development Report, 1996,* 167.

40. Golding, "World Wide Wedge," 82.

41. Ibid.

42. Ibid., 83.

43. Ibid.

44. Ibid.

45. McChesney, "The Global Struggle," 17.

46. Bill Gates, *The Road Ahead* (New York: Viking, 1995), 171.

8. How Cracked is the CIA-Contra Drug Connection?

1. See Patricia McRae and David J. Ackerman, "The Illegal Narcotics Trade (INT) as a TNC: Implications for the TNC/Government Interface," unpublished paper.

2. John F. Kerry, "Organized Crime Goes Global While the U.S. Stays Home," *Washington Post,* 11 May 1997, C4.

3. Juanita Darling, "Nicaragua's Coastal Epidemic: A Deadly Habit is Devastating Miskito Communities on Nation's Remote Eastern Shores," *Los Angeles Times*, 8 February 1997.

4. See articles by Gary Webb, *San Jose Mercury News*, 18-20 August 1996, at http://www.sjmercury.com/drugs.

5. "CIA Official Sees No Evidence of Crack Role," *New York Times*, 24 October 1994.

6. Bush was a former CIA director and under his watch a whole range of similar CIA drug-trafficking operations occurred. See Jonathan Marshall, *Drug Wars: Corruption, Counterinsurgency, and Covert Operations in the Third World* (Forestville, CA: Cohen and Cohen Publishers, 1991), 41, 46.

7. See Geri Smith, "Mexico's Drug Problems are also NAFTA's," *Business Week,* 10 March 1997.

8. Gary Webb, "America's 'Crack' Plague Has Roots in Nicaragua War," *San Jose Mercury News,* 18 August 1996.

9. Blandon sold automatic weapons and sophisticated communications equipment to Ross and his partner. He even tried to sell them a grenade launcher. See Gary Webb, "Testimony Links U.S. to Drugs-Guns Trade," *San Jose Mercury News*, 19 August 1996.

10. Webb, "America's 'Crack' Plague."

11. Douglas Farah, "Drug Dealer Depicted as Contra Fund-Raiser," *Washington Post*, 6 October 1996.

12. Ibid.

13. Doyle McManus, "Examining Charges of CIA Role in Crack Sales," *Los Angeles Times*, 12 October 1996.

14. Gary Webb, "Shadowy Origins of 'Crack' Epidemic," *San Jose Mercury News,* 19 August 1996.

15. Ibid.

16. Ibid.

17. McManus, "CIA Role in Crack Sales."

18. Brian Freemantle, *The Fix* (New York: Tom Doherty Associates, 1985), 32.

19. Henrik Kruger, *The Great Heroin Coup* (Boston: South End Press, 1980), 14, 31.

20. Alfred W. McCoy, *The Politics of Heroin: CIA Complicity in the Global Drug Trade* (New York: Lawrence Hill and Co., 1991), 18.

21. Kruger, *The Great Heroin Coup*, 89.

22. McCoy, *The Politics of Heroin*, 25.

23. Ibid., 19.

24. Ibid.

25. Ibid., 437.

26. Ibid., 438.

27. Ibid., 439.

28. Ibid., 478.

29. Jonathan Marshall, "Drugs and U.S. Foreign Policy," *Dealing With Drugs,* (Pacific Research Institute, 1987) , 166.

30. McCoy, *The Politics of Heroin*, 483.

31. U.S. Senate Subcommittee on Terrorism, Narcotics, and International Operations of the Committee on Foreign Relations, , *Drugs, Law Enforcement, and Foreign Policy,* December 1988, 36.

32. Ibid.

33. Ibid.

34. David E. Early, "MN Series Stirs National Debate," *San Jose Mercury News,* 6 October 1995.

35. Ibid.

36. Michael Tonry, "Race and the War on Drugs," *University of Chicago Legal Forum,* (1994): 144.

37. Omnibus Anti-Drug Abuse Act of 1988, Public Law No. 100-690.

38. Bureau of Justice Statistics, Department of Justice, "Drugs, Crime, and the Justice System," national report, December 1992, 24.

39. U.S. Sentencing Commission, monitoring data files, 1 April-1 July 1992. This was a representative sampling of all drug cases for FY 1992.

40. See "C.I.A., Crack, the Media," *The Nation,* 2 June 1997.

41. Jesse Katz, "Deposed King of Crack; Now Free after 5 Years in Prison, This Master Marketer was Key to the Drug's Spread in L.A.," *Los Angeles Times,* 20 December 1994.

42. Ibid.

43. Walter Pincus, "A Long History of Drug Allegations," *Washington Post,* 4 October 1996.

44. Geneva Overholser, "The CIA, Drugs, and the Press," *Washington Post,* 10 November 1996

45. See Michael A. Fletcher, "Conspiracy Theories Can Often Ring True," *Washington Post,* 4 October 1996.

46. Letter from Representative Maxine Waters to Attorney General Janet Reno, 30 August 1996.

47. See letter from Senator Barbara Boxer to CIA Director John Deutch, 29 August 1996, and letter from Senator Dianne Feinstein to Attorney General Janet Reno, 30 August 1996.

48. Peter Kornbluh, "CIA, Contras, and Crack," *JaxFax,* 10 October 1996.

49. Natalie Hopkinson, "Law Students Protest CIA-Crack Scandal," *The Hilltop,* 4 October 1996, 1.

50. Early, "MN Series Stirs Debate."

51. Ibid.

52. "CIA Official Sees No Evidence of Crack Role," *New York Times,* 24 October 1994.

53. Jerry Ceppos, "To readers of our 'Dark Alliance' series," *San Jose Mercury News,* 11 May 1997.

54. Ibid.

55. Ibid.

56. Ibid.

57. See Georg Hodel, "Hung Out to Dry: 'Dark Alliance' Series Dies," http://www.delve.com/confl.html.

9. The Souls of White Folk

1. Kimberlé Williams Crenshaw, "Color-blind Dreams and Racial Nightmares: Reconfiguring Racism in the Post-Civil Rights Era," in *Birth of a Nation 'hood,* eds. Toni Morrison and Claudia Brodsky Lacour (New York: Pantheon, 1997), 110.

2. See Richard J. Herrnstein and Charles Murray, *The Bell Curve: Intelligence and Class Structure in American Life* (New York: The Free Press, 1994); Dinesh D'Souza, *The End of Racism* (New York: The Free Press, 1995).

3. Richard Morin, "A Distorted Image of Minorities: Poll Suggests That What Whites Think They See May Affect Beliefs," *Washington Post,* 8 October 1995.

4. Ibid.

5. Haya El Nasser, "Poll: Whites Increasingly Accept Blacks," *USA Today,* 11 June 1997.

6. Ibid.

7. "Resources on Eugenics and Racist IQ Theories," *RaceFile,* May-June 1996, 34. See *Wall Street Journal,* 13 December 1996, for a long list of scholars who advocate racist theories regarding intelligence and genetics.

8. Ibid.

9. Patricia J. Williams, "Apologia Qua Amnesia," *The Nation,* 14 July 1997, 10.

10. See Martin Luther King, Jr., "Letter from a Birmingham Jail," in *A Testament of Hope,* 289-302.

11. Ibid.

12. See President Bill Clinton, University of California at San Diego commencement speech, 14 June 1997.

13. Crenshaw, "Color-blind Dreams," 105

14. Clinton, UC-San Diego commencement speech.

15. Randall Kennedy, "Where Do We Go from Here?" *Washington Post,* 15 June 1997.

16. Clinton, UC San Diego commencement speech.

17. Senator Bill Bradley speech in Los Angeles, "Race Relations in America, 11 January 1996.

18. Ibid.

19. Ibid.

20. Ibid.

10. Old Stories from the New South

1. Anne Eckman, "AFDC on the Block," *Southern Exposure,* Fall 1996, 8.

2. Sarah Anderson and Karen Harris, "After NAFTA," *Southern Exposure,* Fall 1996, 13.

3. John Zippert, "Not One More Acre," *Christian Social Action,* October 1994, 36.

4. Ibid.

5. Ibid. 37.

6. Ibid.

7. Michael A. Fletcher, "Black Farmers Allege Racism at USDA," *Washington Post,* 11 December 1996.

8. See Mark Hosenball, "Arkansas Gothic," *The New Republic,* 3 August 1992, 14-6; and James Risen and Edwin Chen, "Clinton's Ties to Controversial Medical Examiner Questioned," *Los Angeles Times,* 19 May 1992.

9. Geraldine Wilson, "Sticks and Stones and Racial Slurs Do Hurt: The Word Nigger is What's Not Allowed," in *Children, Race and Racism* (New York: Racism and Sexism Resource Center for Education, 1980), 16.

10. Marilyn Kern-Foxworth, *Aunt Jemima, Uncle Ben, and Rastus: Blacks in Advertising, Yesterday, Today, and Tomorrow* (Westport, CT: Praeger Publishers, 1994), 30.

11. Richard Merelman, *Representing Black Culture: Racial Conflict and Cultural Politics in the United States* (New York: Routledge, 1995), 3.

12. "Kentucky Faces Tradition of Offensive Road Names," *New York Times,* 11 November 1996.

13. "Church Fires Still Worry Task Force," *USA Today,* 17 January 1997.

14. See Center for Democratic Renewal "Black Church Burnings, Fire Bombings, Vandalism: January 1990–April 1996."

15. "Church Fires Still Worry Task Force," *USA Today,* 17 January 1997.

16. "Evangelicals Urged to Speak against Burning of Churches," *San Francisco Chronicle,* 18 June 1996.

17. "Confederate Group Inducts First Black," *Washington Post,* 20 January 1997.

18. Phillip Rawls, "Alabama Candidate Argues Slavery is Justified," *Buffalo News,* 10 May 1996.

19. "Retiring Old Virginny," *Washington Post,* 1 February 1997.

20. "In Fact…," *The Nation,* 27 May 1996, 7.

11. Of Louis Farrakhan and Others

1. Louis R. Harlan, *Booker T. Washington: The Making of a Black Leader, 1856-1901* (New York: Oxford University Press, 1972), 218.

2. See W.E.B Du Bois, *The Souls of Black Folk* (New York: Penguin, 1989).

3. See John Hope Franklin, *From Slavery to Freedom: A History of Negro Americans* (New York: Alfred Knopf, 1974).

4. Mattias Gardell, *In the Name of Elijah Muhammad: Louis Farrakhan and the Nation of Islam* (Durham, NC: Duke University Press, 1996), 142.

5. Ibid., 143.

6. Salim Muwakkil, "Why Did the Force of the Million Man March Stall."

7. Adolph Reed, Jr., "The Rise of Louis Farrakhan," *The Nation,* 21 January 1991, 56.

8. Ibid., 56.

9. See Wilson Jeremiah Moses, *The Golden Age of Black Nationalism, 1850-1925* (New York: Oxford University Press, 1978); and Raymond L. Hall, *Black Separatism in the United States* (Hanover, NH: University Press of New England, 1978).

10. See Allan Austin, *African Muslims in Antebellum America* (New York: Garland Publishing), 1997.

11. Ibid.

12. See C. Eric Lincoln, *The Black Muslims in America* (Trenton, NJ: Africa World Press), 1994.

13. Henry Louis Gates, "The Charmer," *The New Yorker,* 29 April and 6 May 1996, 125.

14. Michael Eric Dyson, *Race Rules: Navigating the Color Line* (Reading, MA: Addison-Wesley, 1996), 165.

15. Gardell, *In the Name of Elijah,* 82.

16. Ibid., 369.

17. Ibid., 100.

18. Ibid., 101.

19. Ibid., 123.

20. Ellen Hume, "Race Rhetoric Puts Farrakhan in Spotlight in Jesse Jackson Camp," *The Wall Street Journal,* 26 April 1984.

21. Gardell, *In the Name of Elijah,* 318.

22. Armstrong is a black conservative who made this comment about Louis Farrakhan's self-help message. Robert Novak, "Standing Behind Words on Farrakhan," *Buffalo News,* 27 March 1997.

23. Robert Novak, "Farrakhan is Knocking on GOP's Door," *Buffalo News,* 7 March 1997.

24. Ibid.

25. Ibid.

26. Manning Marable, "Toward a New Dialogue about Race,", http://www.tbwt.com /views/manning/default.htm.

27. "Day of Resistance against Neo-Nazis," *New Solidarity,* 5 March 1985.

28. "LaRouchians Feint to the 'Left,'" *The Monitor,* March 1991, 14.

29. Benjamin F. Chavis, "LaRouche Invades Black Community," *New York Voice,* 2 August 1986, 1.

30. Manning Marable, "The Million Man March: One Year Later, Part Two," http://www.columbia.edu/cu/iraas/million2.html.

31. Steven A. Holmes, "Farrakhan's Angry World Tour Brings Harsh Criticism at Home," *New York Times,* 22 February 1996.

32. Ibid.

33. Gregory Kane and Gilbert Lewthwaite, "Horror in Village Haunted by Slavery," *Baltimore Sun,* 17 June 1996; and Gregory Kane and Gibert Lewthwaithe, "Brothers Down Here...Are in Darkness," *Baltimore Sun,* 17 June 1996.

12. Beyond Patriachy and Conservative Nationalism

1. See Henry Louis Gates, *Colored People: A Memoir* (New York: Knopf, 1994), and Clifton L. Taubert, *Once Upon a Time When We Were Colored* (Tulsa, OK: Council Oak Books, 1989).

2. Adolph Reed, Jr., "Dangerous Dreams: Black Boomers Wax Nostalgic for the Days of Jim Crow," *Village Voice,* 16 April 1996, 27.

3. E. Frances White, "Africa on My Mind: Gender, Counterdiscourse, and African American Nationalism," in *Words of Fire: An Anthology of African-American Feminist Thought,* ed. Beverly Guy-Sheftall.(New York: New Press, 1995), 511.

4. See Nikol G. Alexander, "Selling Black: Black Public Intellectuals and the Commercialization of Black and Black Feminist Studies (Or, Race, Class, and Gender Go to Market) unpublished paper; and Nikol G. Alexander, "A World Without Feminism?: Reading Gender In(to) Nationalist Politics, " unpublished paper.

5. The Wellington Group, at one point, had worked in partnership with the Nation of Islam in POWER, one of the NOI's businesses. This author was one of the coordinators of the Howard/Wellington survey.

6. Martin Kilson, "The Interaction of the Black Mainstream Leadership and the Farrakhan Extremists," in *MultiAmerica: Essays on Cultural Wars and Cultural Peace,* ed. Ishmael Reed (New York: Viking Press, 1997), 245.

7. Maulana Karenga, "The Million Man March/Day of Absence Mission Statement," *The Black Scholar,* Fall 1995, 3.

8. Adolph Reed, Jr, "Whatever the March May Mean, Farrakhan is Not the Answer," *Ledger-Enquirer,* 29 October 1995.

9. Julianne Malveaux, "Not a 'He Thing' But a 'We Thing,'" *CommonQuest,* Spring 1996, 30.

10. Pauline Terrelonge, "Feminist Consciousness and Black Women," in *Words of Fire,* ed. Beverly Guy-Sheftall (New York: New Press, 1995), 496–8 .

11. Donald Muhammad, "The Role of the Black Woman in the Million Man March," *News Dimension,* 11 August 1995, 7.

12. Michel Marriott, "Black Women are Split over All-Male March on Washington," *New York Times,* 14 October 1995.

13. Kalamu Ya Salaam, "A Million is Just a Beginning," in *Million Man March/Day of Atonement: A Commemorative Anthology: Speeches, Commentary, Photography, Poetry, Illustrations, Documents,* ed. Haki Madhubuti and Maulana Karenga (Chicago: Third World Press, 1995), 110.

14. Ibid.

15. Keith Boykin, Dennis Holmes, and Steve Walker, "The Million Man March: What about Us?," position statement, National Black Gay and Lesbian Leadershi-Forum, 24 September 1995.

16. Ibid.

17. Ibid.

18. See Cornel West, *Race Matters* (Boston: Beacon Press, 1994); and Cornel West, "Nihilism in Black America," *Dissent,* Spring 1991.

19. Peniel E. Joseph, "'Black' Reconstructed: White Supremacy in Post-Civil Rights America, *The Black Scholar,* Fall 1995, 55.

20. Stephen Steinberg, *Turning Back: The Retreat from Racial Justice in American Thought and Policy* (Boston: Beacon Press, 1995), 130.

21 Michael Eric Dyson, "Redeeming Black Manhood," *CommonQuest,* Spring 1996, 30.

22. Ibid.

23. Ibid., 31.

24. Barbara Ransby, "Sexism in the March," *The Miami Herald,* 12 October 1995.

25. Malveaux, "Not a 'He Thing' but a 'We Thing,'" 30.

26. Ibid., 29

27. Ibid., 29.

28. Mary Frances Berry, "I Have Not Endorsed the March," *Washington Post,* 10 October 1995.

29. Robin D.G. Kelley, "The Million Man March: Beyond Self-help," *WeSpeak!,* Winter 1995, 12.

30. Major R. Owens, "Statement of Congressman Major R. Owens on the October 16th Million Man March," press statement, 16 October 1995, 1–2.

31. Marriott, "Black Women are Split."

32. Ibid.

33. Herb Boyd, "Farrakhan: 'This is Time of Doom,'" *Amsterdam News,* 19 October 1996, 1.

34. See Jehron Hunter, "Ben Chavis Fumbles First Interview as Muslim Minister," *News Dimension,* 21 February 1997, 4.

35. See Ron Daniels, "Vantage Point: Million Man March, NAALS Fail to Fulfill Expectations," http://www.tbwt.com/view/rd/index.html.

36. Martin Luther King, Jr., "Where Do We Go From Here: Chaos or Community?" in *A Testament of Hope: The Essential Writings and Speeches of Martin Luther King, Jr.,* ed. James M. Washington (New York: HarperCollins, 1986), 617. 37. Ibid., 621.

38. Ibid., 630.

39. Anne McClintock, "The Angel of Progress: Pitfalls of the Term 'Post-Colonialism,'" *Social Text,* No. 31-2 (1992), 91–2.

Selected Bibliography

Alexander, Nikol G., "Selling Black: Black Public Intellectuals and the Commercialization of Black and Black Feminist Studies (Or, Race, Class, and Gender Go to Market)," unpublished paper.

_____, "A World Without Feminism?: Reading Gender In(to) Nationalist Politics," unpublished paper.

Anderson, Sarah and John Cavanagh, *The Top 200: The Rise of Global Corporate Power,* Institute for Policy Studies paper, September 25, 1996.

Asante, Molefi, *The Afrocentric Idea* (Philadelphia: Temple University Press, 1987).

Austin, Allan, *African Muslims in Antebellum America* (New York: Garland Publishing, 1997).

Baldwin, James, "If Black English Isn't A Language, Then Tell Me What Is?," in James Baldwin, *The Price of the Ticket: Collected Nonfiction, 1948-1985* (New York: St. Martin's/Marek, 1985).

Barber, Benjamin R., *Jihad vs. McWorld: How the Planet is Both Falling Apart and Coming Together and What This Means for Democracy* (Toronto: Times Books, 1995).

Barlett, Donald L. and James B. Steele, *America: Who Stole the Dream* (Kansas City, MO: Andrews and McNeel, 1996).

Barnet, Richard and John Cavanagh, *Global Dreams: Imperial Corporations and the New World Order* (New York: Simon & Schuster, 1994).

Brecher, Jeremy and Tim Costello, *Global Village or Global Pillage?: Economic Reconstruction from the Bottom Up* (Boston: South End Press, 1994).

Burnett, Robert, *Global Jukebox: The International Music Industry* (New York: Routledge, 1996).

California Senate Office of Research, "Taking a Look at Affirmative Action," report, January 19, 1995.

Carnoy, Martin, *Faded Dreams: The Politics and Economics of Race in America* (New York: University of Cambridge Press, 1994).

Crenshaw, Kimberlé Williams, "Color-blind Dreams and Racial Nightmares: Reconfiguring Racism in the Post-Civil Rights Era," in Toni Morrison and Claudia Brodsky Lacour, eds., *Birth of a Nation 'hood* (New York: Pantheon, 1997).

Danaher, Kevin, ed., *Corporations Are Gonna Get Your Mama: Globalization and Downsizing of the American Dream* (Monroe, ME: Common Courage Press, 1996).

Dillard, J.L., *Black English: Its History and Usage in the United States* (New York: Vintage, 1973).

D'Souza, Dinesh, *The End of Racism* (New York: The Free Press, 1995).

Du Bois, W.E.B., *The Souls of Black Folk* (New York: Penguin, 1989).

DuCille, Anne, *Skin Trade* (Cambridge: Harvard University Press, 1996).

Dyson, Michael Eric, *Race Rules: Navigating the Color Line* (Reading, MA: Addison-Wesley Publishers, 1996).

Edwards, Harry, *The Revolt of the Black Athlete* (New York: Free Press, 1969).

Freemantle, Brian, *The Fix* (New York: Tom Doherty Associates, 1985).

Gardell, Mattias, *In the Name of Elijah Muhammad: Louis Farrakhan and the Nation of Islam* (Durham, NC: Duke University Press, 1996).

Gates, Bill, *The Road Ahead* (New York: Viking, 1995).

Gates, Henry Louis, *Colored People: A Memoir* (New York: Knopf, 1994).

General Accounting Office, "Displacement Rate, Unemployment Spells, and Reemployment Wages by Race," Washington, D.C., September 1994.

Giddens, Anthony, *The Consequences of Modernity* (Stanford: Stanford University Press, 1990).

Graham, Julie, "Multinational Corporations and the Internationalization of Production: An Industry Perspective," in G. Epstein, J. Graham, and J. Newbhard, eds., *Creating a New World Economy* (Philadelphia: Temple University Press).

Greider, William, *One World, Ready or Not: The Manic Logic of Global Capitalism* (New York: Simon & Schuster, 1997).

Grossman, Lawrence, *The Electronic Republic* (New York: Viking, 1995).

Guy-Sheftall, Beverly, ed., *Words of Fire: An Anthology of African-American Feminist Thought* (New York: The New Press, 1995).

Harlan, Louis R., *Booker T. Washington: The Making of a Black Leader, 1856-1901* (New York: Oxford University Press, 1972).

Harrison, Bennett, *Lean and Mean: The Changing Landscape of Corporate Power in the Age of Flexibility* (New York: Basic Books, 1994).

Henry, Lester, *NAFTA and GATT: World Trade Policy Impacts on African Americans* (New York: Du Bois Bunche Center for Public Policy, 1995).

Herrnstein, Richard J. and Charles Murray, *The Bell Curve: Intelligence and Class Structure in American Life* (New York: The Free Press, 1994).

Higginbotham, A. Leon, Jr., Aderson Bellegarde Francois, and Linda Y. Yuch, "The O.J. Simpson Trial: Who Was Improperly 'Playing the Race Card'?" in Toni Morrison and Claudia Brodsky Lacour, eds., *Birth of a Nation 'hood* (New York: Pantheon, 1997).

Hoberman, John, *Darwin's Athletes: How Sport Has Damaged Black America and Preserved the Myth of Race* (Boston: Houghton Mifflin Company, 1997).

Hoover, Gary, Alta Campbell, and Patrick J. Spain, eds., *Hoover's Handbook of American Business, 1994* (Austin, TX: The Reference Press, 1993).

International Labor Organization, "Employment in the World, 1996/1997," report, United Nations, 1997.

Johnson, Leola and David Roediger, "'Hertz, Don't It?': Becoming Colorless and Staying Black in the Crossover of O.J. Simpson," in Toni Morrison and Claudia Brodsky Lacour, eds., *Birth of a Nation 'hood* (New York: Pantheon, 1997).

Jones, Charles, ed., *The Black Panther Party Reconsidered* (Baltimore: Black Classic Press, 1997).

Kamel, Rachel, *The Global Factory: Analysis and Action for a New Economic Era* (Philadelphia: American Friends Service Committee, 1990).

Kern-Foxworth, Marilyn, *Aunt Jemima, Uncle Ben, and Rastus: Blacks in Advertising, Yesterday, Today, and Tomorrow* (Westport, CT: Praeger Publishers, 1994).

King, Martin Luther, Jr. in James M. Washington, ed., *A Testament of Hope: The Essential Writings of Martin Luther King, Jr.* (New York: HarperCollins, 1986).

Korten, David C., *When Corporations Rule the World* (West Hartford, CT: Kumarian Press, 1995).

Kruger, Henrik, *The Great Heroin Coup* (Boston: South End Press, 1980).

The Labor Institute, *Corporate Power and the American Dream* (New York: The Labor Institute, 1994).

Labov, William, *Language in the Inner City: Studies in the Black English Vernacular* (Philadelphia: University of Pennsylvania Press, 1972).

Lee, Thea M. "The Likely Impact of NAFTA on Women and Minorities," testimony before the Employment, Housing and Aviation Subcommittee of the U.S. House Committee on Government Operations, U.S. House of Representatives, November 10, 1993.

Lemelle, Sidney and Robin D.G. Kelley, *Imagining Home: Class, Culture, and Nationalism in the African Diaspora* (New York: Verso, 1994).

Lincoln, C. Eric, *The Black Muslims in America* (Trenton, NJ: Africa World Press, 1994.).

Mander, Jerry and Edward Goldsmith, eds., *The Case Against Globalization: And for a Turn Toward the Local* (San Francisco: Sierra Club Books, 1996).

Marshall, Jonathan, "Drugs & U.S. Foreign Policy," *Dealing With Drugs,* Pacific Research Institute, 1987.

_____, *Drug Wars: Corruption, Counterinsurgency and Covert Operations in the Third World* (Forestville, CA: Cohan and Cohen Publishers, 1991).

McCoy, Alfred W., *The Politics of Heroin: CIA Complicity in the Global Drug Trade* (New York: Lawrence Hill and Co., 1991).

McLean, Polly E., "Mass Communications, Popular Culture, and Racism," in Benjamin P. Bowser, ed., *Racism and Anti-Racism in World Perspectve* (Thousand Oaks, CA: Sage Publications, 1995).

McRae, Patricia and David J. Ackerman, "The Illegal Narcotics Trade (INT) as a TNC: Implications for the TNC/Government Interface," paper presented at the 1993 American Political Science Association, Washington, D.C.

Merelman, Richard, *Representing Black Culture: Racial Conflict and Cultural Politics in the United States* (New York: Routledge, 1995).

Owens, Major R., "Statement of Congressman Major R. Owens on the October 16th Million Man March," press statement, October 16, 1995.

Reich, Robert B., *The Work of Nations: Preparing Ourselves for 21st Century Capitalism* (New York: Vintage Books, 1992).

Rifkin, Jeremy, *The End of Work: The Decline of the Global Labor Force and the Dawn of the Post-Market Era* (New York: Putnam Books, 1995).

Rosenman, Samuel I., *The Public Papers and Addresses of Franklin D. Roosevelt* (New York: Harper & Row, 1950).

Smith, Robert C., *Racism in the Post-Civil Rights Era: Now You See It, Now You Don't* (Albany, NY: State University of New York, 1995).

Stoller, Paul, ed., *Black American English: Its Background and Its Usage in the Schools and Literature* (New York: Dell, 1975).

Strasser, J.B. and Laurie Becklund, *Swoosh: The Unauthorized Story of Nike and the Men Who Played There* (New York: HarperBusiness, 1993).

Taulbert, Clifton, *Once Upon a Time When We Were Colored* (Tulsa, OK: Council Oak Books, 1989).

Terrelonge, Pauline, "Feminist Consciousness and Black Women," in Beverly Guy-Sheftall, ed., *Words of Fire: An Anthology of African-American Feminist Thought* (New York: The New Press, 1995).

Thurow, Lester C., *The Future of Capitalism: How Today's Economic Forces Shape Tomorrow's World* (New York: William Morrow and Company, 1996).

U.S. Census Bureau, "Black-Owned Businesses Up 46 Percent Over Five Years, Census Bureau Survey Shows," press release, December 12, 1995.

_____, "New York Metro Area Leads List for Black-Owned Firms, Los Angeles Tops in Women-Owned Businesses, Census Bureau Reports," press release, March 16, 1996.

_____, "Number of Minority-Owned Businesses and Revenues Increase Substantially Between 1987 and 1992, Census Bureau Reports, press release, November 18, 1996.

U.S. Department of Justice, Office of Justice Programs,"Correctional Populations in the United States, 1994," *Bureau of Justice Statistics Executive Summary.*

U.S. Senate Subcommittee on Terrorism, Narcotics, and International Operations of the Committee on Foreign Relations, "Drugs, Law Enforcement, and Foreign Policy," December 1988.

United Nations Development Program, *Human Development Report 1992* (New York: United Nations, 1992).

Van Deburg, William L., *New Day in Babylon: The Black Power Movement and American Culture, 1965-1975* (Chicago: University of Chicago Press, 1993).

West, Cornel, *Race Matters* (Boston, MA: Beacon Press, 1993).

Wiggins, David K., "Critical Events Affecting Racism in Athletics," in Dana Brooks and Ronald Althouse, eds., *Racism in College Athletics: The African American Athlete's Experience* (Morgantown, WV: Fitness Information Technology, Inc., 1993).

Wilhelm, Sidney, *Who Needs the Negro?* (Cambridge, MA: Schenkman, 1970).

Williams, Patricia J., "Disorder in the House: The New World Order and the Socioeconomic Status of Women," in Stanlie M. James and Abena P.A. Busia, eds., *Theorizing Black Feminisms: The Visionary Pragmatism of Black Women* (New York: Routledge, 1993).

Williams, Robert L., ed., *Ebonics: The True Language of Black Folks* (St. Louis: Institute of Black Studies, 1975).

Wilson, Geraldine, "Sticks and Stones and Racial Slurs Do Hurt: The Word Nigger Is What's Not Allowed," in *Children, Race and Racism* (New York: Racism and Sexism Resource Center for Education, 1980).

Wilson, William Julius, *When Work Disappears: The World of the New Urban Poor* (New York: Alfred A. Knopf, 1996).

Index

About South End Press

South End Press is a nonprofit, collectively run book publisher with over 200 titles in print. Since our founding in 1977, we have tried to meet the needs of readers who are exploring, or are already committed to, the politics of radical social change. Our goal is to publish books that encourage critical thinking and constructive action on the key political, cultural, social, economic, and ecological issues shaping life in the United States and in the world. In this way, we hope to give expression to a wide diversity of democratic social movements and to provide an alternative to the products of corporate publishing.

Through the Institute for Social and Cultural Change, South End Press works with other political media projects—*Z Magazine*; Speakout, a speakers' bureau; Alternative Radio; and the Publishers Support Project—to expand access to information and critical analysis. If you would like a free catalog of South End Press books, please write to us at: South End Press, 116 Saint Botolph Street, Boston, MA 02115. Visit our website at http://www.lbbs.org.

Related Titles

African Americans at the Crossroads
By Clarence Lusane

Pipe Dream Blues
By Clarence Lusane

Chaos or Community
By Holly Sklar

Black Liberation in Conservative America
By Manning Marable